"This book is an opportunity for us to wea[...] the tapestry of our psychedelic world."

—**Amanda Feilding, founder and director of the Beckley Foundation**

"You had me at 'Heroines of Mescaline!' I love everything about this book. Psychedelic pioneers deserve praise. Celebrate these women, learn their history, and teach your children."

—**Julie Holland, MD, author of** *Good Chemistry:*
The Science of Connection, from Soul to Psychedelics

"An incredible homage and historical account: *Women and Psychedelics* is a staunch reminder that women throughout time, especially Indigenous women, built the robust mycelium and mycorrhizal networks that the psychedelic industry flourishes on today. We owe the celebrated women herein our acknowledgment and gratitude for their dedication, perseverance, and nurturing."

—**Jennifer Chesak, author of** *The Psilocybin Handbook for Women:*
How Magic Mushrooms, Psychedelic Therapy, and Microdosing
Can Benefit Your Mental, Physical, and Spiritual Health

"The stories in this collection introduce us to women of power and significance who have largely remained unseen in the glare of current psychedelic enthusiasm. The distinctive perspectives, cosmologies, social roles, and sacred (and often secret) practices that are represented here catalog a remarkable geographic, linguistic, cultural, and temporal range of feminine knowledge and influence." —**Maria Mangini, PhD, FNP**

"*Women and Psychedelics* gives us a comprehensive overview of women's unique insight into the potential of psychedelics and expanded states of consciousness. We meet women from different cultures, different times in history, and different traditions, each one offering a personal perspective on the use of psychedelics. The women's stories are inspirational and visionary for everyone interested in how psychedelics can inform our current times. I hope someday we don't need a book like this that highlights women's contributions throughout the history of psychedelic medicines. But at this point in time, we very much need exactly this book, *Uncovering Invisible Voices.*"

—**Rachel Harris, PhD, author of** *Listening to Ayahuasca:*
New Hope for Depression, Addiction, PTSD, and Anxiety **and**
Swimming in the Sacred: Wisdom from the Psychedelic Underground

"The psychedelic experience is, like life itself, necessarily challenging. And just like life, one needs to be led, to be guided, be held, contained, and encouraged to grow, in order for one to meet one's true potential. The role of women in psychedelic research and clinical care is paramount to the culture, and it has always been thus. Gone are the old stereotypes of 'sensitivity', 'gentleness', and 'emotional support'. Instead we see how psychedelic therapies and experiences require strength, leadership, powerful containment, and the ability to provide reciprocal and creative imagination—all such qualities that women provide. This wonderful book keeps, rather than puts, women at the center of this subject. Highly recommended reading for anyone involved in this fascinating field!"

—Ben Sessa, MBBS (MD) BSc MRCPsych, psychiatrist, psychedelic researcher, and author of *The Psychedelic Renaissance: Reassessing the Role of Psychedelic Drugs in 21st Century Psychiatry and Society*

"*Women and Psychedelics* is a compelling collection of essays that casts a long-overdue spotlight on the remarkable, yet often overlooked, contributions of women to the world of psychedelic exploration and healing. . . . In a world that has, for too long, prioritized a legacy of paternalism and disconnection, this book is a beacon of hope and understanding. It beckons us to recognize the value of intuitive, embodied, and relational wisdom that women have carried through the ages. It's a reminder that true healing and balance, both within ourselves and as a collective, can only be achieved by embracing the holistic, interconnected perspectives offered by women. . . . *Women and Psychedelics* is a pivotal work that challenges the prevailing narrative . . . an essential read."

—Devon Christie, MD, CCFP, RTC (Relational Somatic Therapy)

"Attentive to Indigenous histories and colonial legacies, these vivid re-livings render the multifarious powers of the women who shaped psychedelic cultures from Saskatchewan to the Andes in a plurality of dimensions. We are knowledge makers, gatherers, hosts, acolytes, and bearers of meaning. This archive carries forward the complex lived realities of the lively exchanges between women and the entheogens. As an archive of women's freedom, agency, and bodily and psychic autonomy, this treasure trove of intimate portraits is a resoundingly delicious read."

—Nancy D. Campbell, author of *Using Women: Gender, Drug Policy and Social Justice*

"This book is a feast for the feminist psychedelic nerd and pretty much anyone interested in (finally!) having a more complete view of the cultural origin story of psychedelics. It reads as a treasure trove of information about more and less known (and even totally unknown) female characters whose stories have been hidden, till now, in the folds of male-centered narratives. The result of incredibly meticulous research, this anthology brings together a truly impressive variety of both agreeable and questionable characters: lab assistants, psychic readers, drug dealers, writers, Christian therapists, curanderas, and many more . . . unveiling the full kaleidoscopic extent of the psychedelic world, with its lights and shadows. Written in an accessible yet engaging style, this book is a must-have for all who wish to move beyond the limitations of a patriarchal, colonial worldview while keeping a refreshingly sober and 'non-fundamentalist' feminist approach."

—**Chiara Baldini, coeditor of** *Psychedelic Mysteries of*
the Feminine: Creativity, Ecstasy, and Healing

"Highly recommended! In a field dominated by men, this anthology honors the history of women who have moved the psychedelic space forward."

—**Adele Getty, director of Limina Foundation**

"This remarkable volume presents material sorely needed in the field of psychedelics on the often unsung but multifaceted contributions of women to the field of psychedelics. The broad selection of offerings on influences from women from the Americas is a story that is resoundingly told in this textbook. The women highlighted in the chapters are universally inspiring and compelling, as are the scholars who have skillfully written these chapters. These scholars are leaders in the current field of psychedelics in their own right, and we are fortunate to hear their voices and points of view. This compilation is highly recommended and will undoubtedly be cited frequently by numerous scholars who are dedicated to telling the deeper narrative of psychedelic women leaders' practices, values, and wisdom."

—**Janis Phelps, director of the Center for Psychedelic Therapies and Research,**
California Institute of Integral Studies

"I hold my heart in honor and awe at the completion of this marvelous collection. All too often sidelined in their own narratives, Psychedelic Women are moved to the center in this book, not as mere contributors but as the creators. Vibrant in color and birthing new worlds, this book is a radical act of the rematriation of psychedelic medicine, high-lighting that our ignorance of these women reinforces a finite history in an infinite field. *Women and Psychedelics: Uncovering Invisible Voices* highlights that it is in the way women move—intuitively, ancestrally, relationally, and with deep attunement to nourishment and care—that we have the essential brilliance of the history of psychedelics."

—**Danielle M. Herrera, psychedelic psychotherapist**

"No doubt our psychedelic grandmothers are rejoicing! This collection is a beautiful and necessary resource to shine a light on the incredible contributions of women past and present. *Women and Psychedelics* paves the way for our voices to be heard more clearly now and in the future, creating much needed balance to support the evolution of this work. Praise for *Women and Psychedelics* and its dedicated authors."

—**Adele Lafrance, coauthor of** *Emotion-Focused Family Therapy: A Transdiagnostic Model for Caregiver-Focused Interventions*

"When I looked at the table of contents of *Women and Psychedelics*, I time traveled back some 25 years to the first all-women's panel held at a psychedelics conference, where my copanelists, Kat Harrison, Nina Graboi, and Mountain Girl (all contributors to this book) spoke to an audience of fewer than a dozen. It is immensely gratifying to see this wide-ranging anthology of women's interactions with mind-altering plants and the synthetic drugs derived from them. So much more has been transmitted as personal experiences, historic discoveries, and critical studies by and about women, and will continue to be. The multicultural approach gives this book the dimension the subject deserves."

—**Cynthia Palmer, coeditor of** *Shaman Women, Mainline Lady: Women's Writings on the Drug Experience; Sisters of the Extreme: Women Writing on the Drug Experience;* **and** *Moksha: Aldous Huxley's Classic Writings on Psychedelics and the Visionary Experience*

WOMEN AND PSYCHEDELICS

WOMEN AND PSYCHEDELICS

Uncovering Invisible Voices

EDITED BY
ERIKA DYCK, PATRICK FARRELL,
BEATRIZ C. LABATE, CLANCY CAVNAR,
IBRAHIM GABRIELL, AND
GLAUBER LOURES DE ASSIS

FOREWORD BY
KATHLEEN HARRISON

SYNERGETIC PRESS
SANTA FE • LONDON

Published by Synergetic Press
1 Blue Bird Court, Santa Fe, New Mexico 87508
& 24 Old Gloucester St., London, WCIN 3AL, England

Library of Congress Control Number: 2023945449

ISBN 9781957869124 (paperback)
ISBN 9781957869131 (ebook)

Cover design by Lindsey Cleworth
Cover image: Luana Lourenço/Freepik
Interior design by Howie Severson
Typesetting by Jonathan Hahn
Managing Editor: Noelle Armstrong
Production Editor: Allison Felus

Contents

Foreword by Kathleen Harrison   xv

Introduction   xix

SECTION 1: PIONEERS

Susi's Tram Ride: Recognizing the First Woman to Take LSD   3
     Erika Dyck and Maria Mangini

*Esther Jean Langdon: Half a Century of Research
About Shamanism and Ayahuasca*   7
     Isabel Santana de Rose

Mescaline Scribe   13
     Patrick Farrell

Heroines of Mescaline   19
     Ivo Gurschler

Mrs. Amada Cardenas: Keeper of the Peyote Gardens   25
     Stacy B. Schaefer

*Another Aspect of Reality: Maria Nys Huxley's
Influence on Psychedelic History*   31
     Andrea Ens

*"Please Write Up Your Work!": Laura Archera
Huxley as a Psychedelic Pioneer*   35
     Andrea Ens

Nina Graboi, a Forgotten Woman in Psychedelic Lore   41
     Chris Elcock

Wilma Mahua Campos, Shipibo Ayahuasquera   47
     Samantha Black

Dream and Ecstasy in the Mesoamerican Worldview:
An Interview with Mercedes de la Garza   53
    Osiris Gonzáles Romero

Betty Eisner: Heroine with a Hitch?   57
    Tal Davidson

Lauretta Bender: Seminal Psychiatrist and
Forgotten Psychedelic Pioneer   63
    Chris Elcock

The Wonderful and Absurd Adventures of Rosemary Woodruff
Leary: Fashion Icon, Fugitive, and Psychedelic Pioneer (Part One)   69
    James Penner

The Wonderful and Absurd Life of Rosemary Woodruff Leary:
Fashion Icon, Fugitive, and Psychedelic Pioneer
(Part Two: Freedom and Unfreedom)   75
    James Penner

Jane Osmond: The Wonder of Weyburn   81
    Erika Dyck

SECTION 2: FEMINISM IN ACTION

"A 'Dose' of Radical Christianity":
Psychedelic Therapy with Dr. Florence Nichols   91
    Andrew Jones

Psychedelic Saskatchewan: Kay Parley   99
    Geneviève Paiement

Of Mediums and Mind-Manifestors:
Eileen Garrett and the Psychedelic Experience   103
    Patrick Barber

The Cost of Omission: Dr. Valentina Wasson
and Getting Our Stories Right   109
    Amy Bartlett and Monnica Williams

María Sabina, Mushrooms, and Colonial Extractivism   115
  Osiris González Romero

Kathleen Harrison: Wisdom, Endurance, and Hope—
Reflections from a Psychedelic Woman   121
  Erika Dyck

Spotlight on Betsy Gordon and the
Psychoactive Substances Research Collection   125
  Stephanie Schmitz

Coming of Age in the Psychedelic Sixties   129
  Diana Negrín with Yvonne Negrín

SECTION 3: LIMITS OF FEMINISM

Marlene Dobkin de Rios: A Case for
Complex Histories of Women in Psychedelics   139
  Taylor Dysart

Sexual Assault and Gender Politics in
Ayahuasca Traditions: A View from Brazil   145
  Gretel Echazú and Pietro Benedito

Gurus Behaving Badly: Anaïs Nin's Diary and the Value of Gossip   151
  Alexis Turner

A Homosexual Marriage Experience in Santo Daime   157
  Ligia Platero and Klarissa Platero

Treasures of the Forest: Jarawara Women and the Plants They Carry   163
  Fabiana Maizza

Creating Awareness on Sexual Abuse in Ayahuasca
Communities: A Review of Chacruna's Guidelines   169
  Daniela Peluso, Emily Sinclair, Beatriz C. Labate, and
  Clancy Cavnar

Lola "La Chata": The First Important
Drug Trafficker in Mexico City (1934–1959)   175
  Nidia Olvera-Hernández

SECTION 4: SET AND SETTING

Decolonizing Psychedelics and
Embodied Social Change with Camille Barton   183
　Sean Lawlor

How Music Therapists Helped Build Psychedelic Therapy   195
　Stephen Lett

Women's Historical Influence on "Set and Setting"   201
　Zoë Dubus

Women Who Heal: Musicians in the Urban Ayahuasca Scene   207
　Raizza Marins

Yaminawa Women and Ayahuasca:
Shamanism, Gender, and History in the Peruvian Amazon   215
　Laura Pérez Gil

Madrinha Rita: Brazilian Matriarch of Ayahuasca   221
　Glauber Loures de Assis and Jacqueline Alves Rodrigues

The Religious Uses of Licit and Illicit Psychoactive
Substances in a Branch of the Santo Daime Religion   229
　Edward MacRae

A Bridge Between Two Worlds: Ayahuasca and
Intercultural Medicine—An Interview with Anja Loizaga-Velder   235
　Ibrahim Gabriell

Creating Communities of Healing with Fireside Project
Founding Team Member Hanifa Nayo Washington   243
　Sean Lawlor

SECTION 5: BIRTH AND DYING

*Psychedelics and Death: Transitioning
from This World with Consciousness*   253
    Jasmine Virdi

*Ayahuasca and Childbirth in the Santo Daime Tradition:
Solidarity Among Women and Psychedelic Cultural Resistance*   259
    Jacqueline Alves Rodrigues and Glauber Loures de Assis

*Abortion, Plants, and Whispered
Networks of Botanical Knowledge*   267
    Naomi Rendina

Psychedelic Motherhood: The Altered States of Birth   273
    Lana Cook

*This Is Not Native American History,
This Is US History with Belinda Eriacho*   281
    Maria Mocerino

Contributor Biographies   295

Editor Biographies   303

References   307

Index   327

Foreword

KATHLEEN HARRISON

AS I WRITE THIS FOREWORD, I IMAGINE HOLDING THIS FUTURE BOOK IN my hands, weighing it lightly as if to gauge whether its heft equals its significance.

The theme of this collection is revealing the heretofore unseen. To show the reader some of the remarkable people doing valuable work in the field of psychedelics, people who have remained largely unrecognized. It happens that all of these people are women.

Some are hidden figures, first brought to light here in this collection of profiles. These are previously untold stories of women who may have been mentioned in relation to their male colleagues, or their partners, yet their own contributions have been in the shadows. These women have been occluded from the story that we collectively like to tell about ourselves, about our social movements toward changes in consciousness, about how aware we, as a species of seekers, have become. This phenomenon is being revealed in many fields of study, yet the irony of occlusion is even greater in a field that has prided itself on its expanded awareness. It turns out that even our collective consciousness manages to subsume women, to undervalue contributions of female participants and minimize women's life experiences.

As eye-opening as psychedelics are thought to be, or as deep as a personal experience feels, they don't necessarily reveal to the explorer some of the more subterranean assumptions and gendered worldviews. Many belief systems, behavioral patterns, and cultural attitudes are clearly resistant to the profound review that the psychedelic experience can generate. Various patterns of assumption and privileged thinking may remain stubbornly unexamined. It's simply amazing that the use and sometimes abuse of power can survive intact, in relation to gender, race, and class. The roots of these dynamics run so deep that the profoundly transformative psychedelic experience often does not reach bedrock, so the power dynamics continue to operate without change. In this era of "psychedelic renaissance"—the rebirth of psychedelics in largely contemporary, Euro-descended cultures—some of us elders who lived through the "psychedelic revolution" of the '60s and '70s may chuckle or grumble at all the ironies implicit in this cartoonish framing of our own lives' work and passion. I am from that generation. Now, as then, generally speaking, women and many other humans are othered and dismissed from significance.

But, at long last, we see the stories of these intrepid originators of research, fieldwork, and ideas, along with women living today who are blazing new paths in their communities. Some of these women have spent their adventurous, exploratory, or intellectual lives being designated as muses, accomplices, or assistants, or described as primarily wives or lovers. And yet we see, reading these essays, that the women have, of course, lived their rich lives too, embedded deep in the past century of psychedelic experimentation and its myriad consequences, or carrying today's torch for a wild and promising future.

We all realize that this is the plight of many women, historically and in the present day: to be omitted, for reasons both cultural and individual. In this fictionalized history, we have all lost some richness and truth for not recognizing the accomplishments, influences, and sacrifices of these passionately lived lives. We don't see how the work of women in the field of psychedelics has also lifted up the men, and made their work better, or even possible. Women's participation and inquiries are braided throughout the pronouncements of men.

What does it mean to be a scholar who is dedicated to a path of inquiry, and yet who remains largely invisible? There are ironies in this predicament, especially when the field of inquiry—exploring psychedelics and their potential for humanity—is itself marginal at best, taboo or legally forbidden at worst. This volume of life stories reflects the role of the hidden characters in the era when psychedelics were introduced, "discovered" (although long and deeply familiar to Indigenous peoples), grown, manufactured, distributed, savored, and much discussed within the already existing systems of knowledge. That prior version was a story half told, like a great river trip when only one bank of the river is documented and described. Turn around, we point out: she is behind you, she is regarding the left bank, *le rive gauche*, the side where the bohemians live and experiment, where counterculture thrives, and creative thinking is the strongest, flowing, and more egalitarian.

Yet even as we witness the gradual inclusion of the voices of white women, we see the continued exclusion of Indigenous women, Black women, and the voices of women of color. This book uplifts women who are decolonizing psychedelic research and advocating for cultural sensitivity as a central part of psychedelic-assisted therapies. Those who are taking on expanded roles within their own traditions in cultures that have carried on shamanic work from their ancestors. Those who acknowledge that healing in colonized lands cannot begin without embodied social justice.

Through these lab assistants, psychiatrists, coauthors, refugees from US drug laws, intellectual muses, artists, anthropologists, healers, or the lives of utterly invisible women, we can begin to see patterns. Patterns within the fields of knowledge seeking, experience seeking, horizon exploring, mind expanding, heart understanding, and future viewing. If we can recognize these patterns of participation by women in the field, more such characters will come into visibility. Highlighting what has been unseen is a way to learn to see more fully.

The reader might perceive this elusive pattern by regarding each of these women as examples, as glimpses of larger networks of far more invisible humans who have been tending the plants, researching the drugs, engaging in multicultural investigations, healing with powerful rituals, birthing, writing, and sometimes sustaining those who got into the limelight. Serving tea and ideas to circles of men, taking notes and dropping insights, pointing out blind spots, and tripping hard along with the best and worst of them. Mending and ferrying egos. This is the pattern, and we are in it—those of us who dwell on, or visit and remember, that dark side of the moon, the feminine side.

Do the dead still long to be seen and appreciated, posthumously if not in life? That depends on one's worldview. I have a steel-grey, cut-velvet, floor-length ensemble that belonged to the late Rosemary Woodruff Leary, a gift to me from our mutual dear friend, Cynthia Palmer Horowitz (coauthor, with Michael Horowitz, of *Sisters of the Extreme: Women Writing on the Drug Experience*). The outfit is something one could wear to an opera, perhaps on an enhancing dose of LSD. Which is something that the undaunted Rosemary may have done, elegantly. The cascading fabric resonates with the energy of her brave and troubled life, which is told here very respectfully by James Penner.

Imagine that for each of these several dozen women, there are several dozen more (and so on and so on) doing something just as amazing in the realms of world-work that respond to such inspiration and dedication, sending ripples of good work and life choices, paths scouted and then followed, or leading to newer paths along the way. Pathfinders, all. We speak of these matters in terms of journey, or trips, as we of my generation so comfortably called them for the middle period of this seven-decade history. I still say "tripping," because each foray outward or inward, upward or downward, is indeed a journey, a quest, and when it works as we hope it will, we return with a gem, a small and persistent treasure that nourishes our insight and that we can share—to help heal and illuminate the world, to make it whole, to discover what we have collectively forgotten, or never even guessed at before.

Of course, these inspiring stories should have been told all along, but as with all stories that are hidden until we turn over a stone and peer into the unknown (or into the once-known-yet-forgotten), here they are now. Read them, savor them, imagine all the variations. Look at the women around you who are devoted to delving and uncovering. Tell their stories to each other, share this book, and the others that are now coming to light. Tell your own story too, when you can. It will be a lens for us to see the world—the fragile, broken, resilient, beautiful world.

Autumn 2023

Introduction

ERIKA DYCK, IBRAH GABRIELL, PATRICK FARRELL,
DOMENICA MEDINA SANCHEZ, BEATRIZ C. LABATE,
CLANCY CAVNAR, AND GLAUBER LOURES DE ASSIS

DID YOU KNOW THAT SUSI RAMSTEIN, ALBERT HOFMANN'S LAB ASSISTANT, was the first woman in the world to take LSD? Many people may know that R. Gordon Wasson visited María Sabina in Mexico where he learned about the magic of psilocybin mushrooms, but did you know that his wife, Valentina Pavlova Wasson, had a PhD in ethnomycology and wrote a definitive study of mushrooms in Russia? Psychedelics have attracted people from around the globe to studies of consciousness and brain sciences, but did you know that in the 1950s some psychedelic psychiatrists sought guidance from renowned psychic Eileen Garrett to help make sense of the revelatory powers of these drugs? In the case of Latin America, women have also played important roles throughout history, some names can be very well known among the psychedelic community (like the case of famous Mazatec curandera Maria Sabina) but have you ever heard about Madrinha Rita Gregório de Melo? She is a matriarch of Santo Daime religion in Brazil, currently 97 years old. Or did you know that the most famous heroin dealer for the first half of the 20th century in Mexico City was actually a woman named Lola "La Chata"? Lola's fame was such that the police called her the "empress of drugs", even William Burroughs would say that she was an "Aztec goddess". Lola became Mexico's public enemy No. 1 and a sort of Robin Hood-like character.

Psychedelics are enjoying a rebirth in the 21st century as people recognize their capacity to change the way we think. In this book we encourage readers to also adjust our thinking on the place of women in this psychedelic past as we chart a psychedelic future. The history of psychedelics has often emphasized the contributions made by leading researchers, breakthrough therapists, and champions of a psychedelic ethos. It just so happens that most of the figures whose names were on the scientific papers or political placards were men. But behind the scenes, and even in the same rooms, women and junior colleagues were working toward a psychedelic future. Whether nurses, therapists, healers, interns, wives, or subjects themselves, women's perspectives on the history of psychedelics help us to highlight a more inclusive past and perhaps a more diverse set of priorities when it comes to thinking about the place of psychedelics in the 21st century.

There has been a tendency with psychedelic histories to emphasize the colorful, albeit exciting, developments that took place in the United States and ricocheted throughout the Anglo world. Widening the frame to include women in that history at times means looking to some of the wives— whether Humphry Osmond's wife Jane, Aldous Huxley's wives Maria and then Laura, or Tim Leary's wife Rosemary (among others)—whose lives were also deeply affected by their husbands' fame. But here we also wanted to widen the geographical and linguistic context, to place psychedelics in a longer legacy of networks that move north and south, involving Indigenous women from Spanish and Portuguese communities in Latin America, and across the Atlantic to non-Anglo regions where women participated in shaping how we have come to know psychedelics. French scholar Zoë Dubus shows us how European networks of women significantly influenced how we think about set and setting. Osiris González Romero helps us to better appreciate how María Sabina became a complicated hero—a conduit for bringing mushrooms to the United States, but perhaps a traitor to her own community. Patrick Farrell shows us that while Simone de Beauvoir is famous in her own right as a French philosopher, her intimate relationship with Jean-Paul Sartre meant that she was his trusted scribe on his mescaline journey. By working with Spanish, Portuguese, French, and English authors, our collection crosses many boundaries, urging readers to reconsider some of the standard narratives in this past and to broaden their horizons when thinking about new sources of inspiration in a psychedelic future.

In this book you will read about some of the diverse and impressive contributions that women have made to our understanding of psychedelics. This is not just a story of psychedelic research and scientific progress; some of these stories serve also as reminders that these substances have a longer history and set of traditions that have at times been carefully hidden from view. Some of that history is a product of blatant sexism, which has resulted in women simply being forgotten, erased, or never fully credited for their contributions in the past. Women got married and changed their names, ended their careers, or never received credit for an idea that went to a husband or colleague whose professional careers seemingly had more at stake. But of course this was not always the case. For some women, their names are firmly connected with psychedelic history, and were it not for them, we might not be able to piece together some of these stories. Laura Huxley was a keen collector and writer herself. Betsy Gordon established an archive so that we today can review psychedelic triumphs and failures from the past, and hopefully learn from those who came before us. Nina Graboi, likewise collected her own theories and ideas, and later ensured they made their way to the New York Library, offering a vital and different perspective on a burgeoning psychedelic scene in Manhattan.

Beyond pioneering women, our authors also remind us that sometimes women faced barriers and challenges that complicated their roles in this past. Women's roles intersected with other isms—race, place, language, age, and career, to name a few. Women engaged in botanical stewardship did not always fare well in a global effort to exploit resources from the earth, especially when psychedelic plants were not considered to be of value in an industrial commercial venture. Despite colonial pressures to undermine Indigenous knowledge, plant medicines, and women's healing techniques, our authors find spaces where women persevered to protect plants, knowledge, and each other. Often women took risks, whether in careers or in expressing their sexuality, or in speaking to violence; we see these women as pioneers too. They are vital participants in this history even when they remain unnamed. We honor their contributions in this volume by highlighting how the genuine inclusion of women in psychedelics can be messy, complicated, but ultimately rewarding and necessary for developing more inclusive frameworks by first recognizing barriers to participation and differences in experience.

Music and art emerged as persistent themes in some of the contributions, reminding us of the many ways that women have influenced how one prepares for or integrates a psychedelic experience, in ways that for some time were considered ephemeral or unimportant. We might today recognize that set and setting have become critical features in a psychedelic encounter, but codifying these features initially required crossing boundaries in science. Musicians and music therapists worked in Anglo and European laboratory contexts as well as developed practices in ceremonial settings in places like Peru and Brazil. There was very little overlap between these two parallel developments in calibrating the auditory setting to the mindset, but women feature prominently in both spaces. As our authors explain, these are not merely decorative accompaniments; sonic expressions, whether drumming, singing, or orchestral selections, were part of tapping into emotional aspects of a psychedelic journey. Women like Hermina Browne and Helen Bonny in Baltimore challenged conventional musicology practices when it came to psychedelic therapy to show how music could be incorporated to elicit an emotional reaction. Latin American women honed these techniques but did so on their own terms, under different circumstances. Ayahuasca shamans and Santo Daime leaders keenly recognized the emotional power of music and singing to bring about healing and spiritual responses. Putting these women and their practices together in this volume encourages us to continue breaking down boundaries that have separated these insights across language, discipline, profession, region, and gender.

Readers are also reminded that women's networks and caring roles have been essential for beginning-of and end-of life experiences. In a section about transitions, our authors consider how older plant medicine practices, including those now considered psychedelic, are part of a longer legacy of secret knowledge that was coveted among women healers for birth control, long before feminist marches produced modern vocabulary for women's bodily rights. There was good reason to keep this information hidden from view, as the penalties for using birth control or seeking abortions carried stiff legal and social consequences for thousands of years. Despite the external pressures to keep this information from view, the relationship between psychedelics and birthing is considered sacred, intimate, and essential. It opens up another pathway of knowledge concerning psychedelic uses, which, perhaps surprisingly, has also influenced dying care. Borrowing practices, theories, and even practitioners from both ends of these life transitions, death doulas and even less formalized practices have benefitted from the wisdom of psychedelic approaches to end-of-life. In a medicalized setting, dying care has often been reduced to managing pain, and psychedelics enter into this discussion as a mechanism for addressing some of the existential and psychological pain and anxiety that accompanies the fear of dying. Our authors explain some of the complex roots of this idea in ways that borrow methods from outside clinical hospital wards, and recenter women in caring roles, while helping to humanize the process of dying.

Our book is one of the first of its kind to center women as the entry point into a history of psychedelics. We believe that this task is more than simply adding women to this history. Looking beyond our own borders and assumptions, working with a diverse group of authors and new scholars, we aim to stimulate conversations about diversity and social justice in this expanding field. We hope that by bringing these women's voices forward we can encourage more ways of changing our minds with psychedelics.

SECTION ONE

Pioneers

Susi's Tram Ride: Recognizing the First Woman to Take LSD

ERIKA DYCK AND MARIA MANGINI

SURPRISINGLY NOT MUCH IS KNOWN ABOUT SUSI RAMSTEIN, THE FIRST PSY-chedelic guide and the first woman to take LSD. The most detailed and direct information about her is available from an interview that was completed in the fall of 2006 by Susanne G. Seiler, a Swiss editor and author. Ms. Seiler is associated with the Gaia Media Foundation, a nonprofit organization established in 1993, which was responsible for the international symposium "LSD—Problem Child and Wonder Drug," held in Basel in the year of the interview, to honor Albert Hofmann's 100th birthday. Seiler sought out Ramstein, who was living a quiet life in a Basel suburb at the time, when she first learned that Dr. Hoffman's lab assistant was a woman. She was able to locate Ramstein in the local directory and wrote to her asking if she was, indeed, the right person. Ramstein called her and readily talked about her LSD experiences but was reluctant to speak at length about her history, out of fear of compromising her family. Seiler was the first to write about this female pioneer, but the importance of her report was not appreciated at the time. In about 2012, Diana Reed Slattery of the Women's Visionary Council passed on an account of this interview which Seiler had posted on Facebook in an effort to make the story known.

HOFMANN'S LABORATORY ASSISTANT

Born in Switzerland in 1922, Susi Ramstein was the daughter of an optometrist. She and her two brothers grew up in Basel, and as a teenager she went to finishing school in French Switzerland where she learned languages, deportment, etiquette, and housekeeping skills. Girls at this time were not routinely expected to attend university, but Ramstein enrolled in a training program with the Pharmaceutical Chemical Research department of

Sandoz labs as the only female apprentice. At age 20 she became the junior laboratory assistant for Dr. Albert Hofmann.

Ramstein's responsibilities in this role included preparing chemical mixtures, analyzing samples, and checking tests. Dr. Hofmann had been experimenting with derivatives of the *Claviceps purpurea* fungus—ergot alkaloids[1]—for several years already by this time. He created a number of ergot-related compounds, including LSD-25, which he synthesized in 1938 for its possible use as a respiratory or circulatory stimulant. As it seemed only to produce some mild restlessness in laboratory animals, it had been shelved, but an intuition that the substance might have additional useful effects that may have been missed led Hofmann to resynthesize it in 1943.

No one, including Hofmann himself, has ever been completely certain as to how it happened that he unintentionally came into contact with some of the chemical on April 16, 1943, when he experienced a "not unpleasant intoxicated-like condition," which he attributed to the effects of absorbing a trace amount. At 4:20 PM on April 19, 1943, he intentionally took 250 millionths of a gram in a glass of water. He considered this dose so small as to be orders of magnitude below the active threshold of other ergot alkaloids he had studied. His plan was to perform a series of experiments, gradually increasing the dose until some minimal effect could be detected. Within an hour, however, the effect of 250 micrograms was noticeable.

His somewhat serendipitous, or at least inspired hunch, about LSD-25 has been memorialized as the first acid trip, and Hofmann has been referred to as the godfather of psychedelics owing to this signature discovery.

Other than his laboratory assistant, Susi Ramstein, he did not inform anyone at the lab of his intentions, as he expected that such a tiny dose would do absolutely nothing. "Miss Ramstein" is named as this assistant in Hofmann's official laboratory report of this experiment, but his famous description of this experience in *LSD: My Problem Child* does not identify her. In the original German, however, the feminine forms used in the phrase "meine Laborantin, die über den Selbstversuch orientiert war" indicate that the assistant mentioned is a woman.

THE FIRST BICYCLE TRIP

As he reported in *LSD: My Problem Child*,[2] Hofmann asked his laboratory assistant to accompany him on the five-kilometer bicycle trip to his home.

During their journey, Hofmann later said that he felt that they made very slow progress, but Ramstein told him that she had had to pedal hard to keep up with him while also coaching him on his progress, as he was experiencing visual distortions by that time. Hofmann's wife Anita was away, having taken their children to visit her parents in Lucerne. By the time that he and Ramstein arrived at the Hofmann's empty home, Hofmann was concerned that he might have been seriously poisoned by his experiment. He asked Ramstein to summon his wife and to get some milk from the lady next door for him to drink as an antidote. In the next few hours, he drank more than two liters. When the neighbor, Mrs. Ruch, brought the milk, she had assumed the appearance of a malevolent witch with a colorful mask.

Inside his home, Hofmann felt dizzy and faint, anxious that he had caused himself permanent damage with his self-experimentation. The familiar furnishings in his home assumed threatening shapes and spun around in agitated motion. No mental effort or exertion of will seemed to alter this unpleasant mindset.

Susi Ramstein remained at his side. She could not reach the family doctor, so she called a substitute, who found nothing out of the ordinary after examining Hofmann. His vital signs were normal, and, other than anxiety, dilated pupils, and his inability to formulate a complete sentence, he seemed perfectly well.

This news reassured Hofmann who began to relax and enjoy the visual images, relieved that he was probably neither dying nor permanently insane. Ramstein notified his wife by telephone that Hofmann had experienced some kind of mysterious breakdown and stayed with him until his wife returned. We know all of this because Hofmann produced a lab report of the experience, and later described it in his well-known book. We can only guess about the thoughts and feelings of Ms. Ramstein, the first psychedelic guide, but by the late evening, when Mrs. Hofmann arrived, Susi was able to leave Dr. Hofmann in a positive and enjoyable frame of mind.

Following this auspicious self-experiment, Hofmann reported his experience to his boss, Arthur Stoll, and to Ernest Rothlin, the director of the pharmacology department at Sandoz at the time. They permitted Hofmann cautiously to continue his self-experiments, although at much lower doses. Sandoz was interested in knowing more about the potential of this mind-altering substance.

Everyone on Hofmann's Sandoz team also took part in at least one experiment, and Susi Ramstein participated in three.

THE FIRST TRAM TRIP

On June 12, 1943, 22-year-old Susi Ramstein became the first woman to take LSD. Although she was also the youngest person yet to have tried it, she took 100 micrograms, a larger dose than Dr. Hofmann's male colleagues.

She found the experience enjoyable and the effects pleasant. After her first experiment in the lab, she took the tram home, finding the appearance of the passengers and the long-nosed conductor to be comical. Ramstein discussed her ideas about the experience with her colleagues at Sandoz. Her insights helped to determine dosage levels for the medical use of LSD. She also took some of the LSD variants that Hofmann had synthesized, including *dihydro-LSD* and *d-Iso-LSD*, which seemed to be less psychoactive. About a year after her last LSD experience, she left Sandoz to marry, but she had already left her mark on the history of psychedelics.

Thinking about Ramstein's experiences at the advent of LSD takes a little guess work, piecing together details from Hofmann and a few other close-hand accounts of that time. It is fascinating to consider what a young Susi Ramstein might have been thinking as she pedaled beside her tripping boss; as it is, we know that she was an extremely helpful and observant companion/attendant. It is regrettable that we do not have a fuller firsthand account of Susi's own LSD experiences or of her subsequent experiments with other substances. Even with the few available details, we can catch a slight glimpse of this highly curious, intelligent, and courageous young woman.

Susi Ramstein Weber, the first psychedelic guide, and the first woman to take LSD, died in the fall of 2011, several years after the death of Dr. Hofmann. As is true of much of the earliest history of LSD, accidents of timing and circumstance played a role in the way that her participation and her contributions are remembered and valued. Now that April 19, "Bicycle Day," has become a well-known and joyously celebrated holiday for psychonauts, let us also remember and celebrate June 12, the date when the courage, heart, and brains of this young woman entered the annals of psychedelic history.[3]

Esther Jean Langdon: Half a Century of Research About Shamanism and Ayahuasca

ISABEL SANTANA DE ROSE

SHAMANISM AS A COSMOLOGICAL SYSTEM

During a period in which studies about shamanism were mostly dominated by male anthropologists, Esther Jean Langdon stands as a pioneer in the revival of anthropological research about this topic. In the 1970s, she was part of a generation of anthropologists who conducted their fieldwork in the South American lowlands and has contributed to a significant increase in our knowledge about the Indigenous peoples of this region.

Until the first half of the 20th century, most anthropological analyses about shamanism tried to fit this phenomenon into preconceived Western categories, resulting in only a few studies and somewhat fragmented discussions that did not contemplate the diversity of native shamanic systems. The revival of investigations about shamanism that began in the 1960s was stimulated by factors happening both inside and outside academia. By the 1980s, scientific publications and seminars dedicated to discussing this topic began multiplying. At the same time, several Indigenous groups throughout South America began revitalizing their shamanic systems.

In this context, authors such as Langdon and Jean-Pierre Chaumeil[1] questioned the inclusion of shamanism in classical anthropological debates about magic, religion, and science. According to them, shamanism is a core institution in the organization of the social and cosmological life of the Indigenous peoples from South America. They proposed that it should be seen as a *cosmological system*, associated simultaneously with several dimensions: politics, health, aesthetics, war, predation, social organization, and so on. They also proposed the idea of *shamanisms in movement*, which challenges classical anthropological analyses that consider shamanism as a static phenomenon, and instead highlights its constant transformations and reinventions.

Langdon was born in the United States and spent several years in the 1970s conducting fieldwork among the Siona peoples in Colombia. She moved to Brazil in the 1980s, where she contributed to studies in medical anthropology, Indigenous health policies, shamanism, oral literature, and performance. In spite of being North American, she describes her perspective as part of an "anthropology from the periphery," because it emerged from an approach to anthropology situated in the Global South and was influenced by her role and place as a woman scientist.[2,3] In the 1990s, Langdon edited *Shamanism in Brazil: New Perspectives* (*Xamanismo no Brasil: novas perspectivas*), the first such compilation published in Brazil.[4] The book emphasizes the relevance of shamanism as an anthropological subject and calls attention to the emergence of Brazilian research on the topic. It also highlights the importance of producing more appropriate theoretical models to understand shamanism as a system, especially regarding its dynamic character and its presence in the contemporary world.

In her writings, Langdon proposes to approach shamanism as a *cosmological system*. She highlights the connections between shamanic systems and the human necessity of expression (fulfilled by rituals, myths, symbols, and narratives), along with the search to ascribe meaning to human experience and aesthetic issues associated with this necessity. Langdon emphasizes that although there are common elements among the diverse Amerindian shamanisms, these systems are heterogeneous, constantly changing, and should be understood within their specific cultural contexts. Another important characteristic of Langdon's works are the analysis of Siona narratives regarding issues such as shamanic battles, shamanic flights in dreams or those induced by the consumption of *yajé* (ayahuasca), and illness and death caused by sorcery. She argued that in the 1970s, when the Siona were unable to conduct collective rituals with *yajé*, their narratives played a role analogous to that of the *yajé* rituals, contributing to knowledge production and to the reproduction of experiences with the invisible domains of reality. Therefore, the verbal performance of shamanic narratives expressed a cosmology and practices that reflected a shamanic vision of the world and the Siona ethnic identity.[5]

These concerns about the human necessity of expression and aesthetics are central in Langdon's 2014 study *Cosmopolitics Among the Siona: Shamanism, Medicine and Family on the Putumayo River*, which was an

Jean Langdon with Adiela at the Buenavista Reserve in 2022, in one of her recent trips to return ethnographic materials to the Siona community.

updated version of her PhD dissertation from the University of Louisiana in 1974. It is based on four years of fieldwork conducted in the Indigenous Reserve of Buena Vista, located near the city Puerto Assis, in the region of the Putumayo in Colombia. It also includes the material from four visits to the Putumayo between 1980 and 1992. In all of these visits Langdon dedicated herself to recording Siona narratives,[6] having collected more than 100 reports in the native language about issues related to shamanism. This ethnography centered on the Siona medical system, establishing connections between this system, the shamanic system, and the consumption of *yajé*. Langdon highlights what she calls praxis, that is, the interaction between symbolic meanings and concrete action in daily life, revealing the dynamic emergence of culture and the constant transformations of the shamanic systems.

CONTEMPORARY SHAMANIC NETWORKS

Reflections about shamanism have permeated the Western imagination for more than 500 years. The first records of these practices were made by travelers and missionaries in the 16th and 17th centuries. At the end of the 19th century, anthropologists started to study this topic. At this time, shamanism was perceived as restricted to specific groups that shared a common culture, history, and geographic region. Since the 1950s other social actors have started to discuss shamanism, including Western people searching for alternative spiritual experiences. More recently, Indigenous peoples themselves have become central actors in the multiplication of voices, perspectives, ritual performances, and shamanic practices conducted in very diverse settings.[7] While the concept of "shaman" was originally employed mainly in academic contexts, currently this concept is widely used by these different contemporary social actors. Therefore, in many cases, the terms "shaman" and "shamanism" have replaced the native words that traditionally refer to the diverse practices and the multiple Indigenous specialists and ritual practitioners.

In Brazil, over the last 20 years, there has been a multiplication of contemporary shamanic networks connecting Indigenous groups and representatives to diverse non-Indigenous actors, including spiritual groups, NGOs, anthropologists, and many others. Ayahuasca plays a central role in these networks and is the most popular psychoactive substance among Western spiritual groups, often explicitly associated with Indigenous shamanisms.[8] Contemporary shamanic networks are characterized by the circulation of a more or less standardized set of ritual performances, aesthetic expressions, and objects associated with generic images of shamanism and Indigenous identity. Moreover, in these settings it is common to find a series of images and concepts, such as the "ecological" or "spiritual native," "primordial knowledge," and "traditional medicine."[9,10,11] It is important to point out that these concepts give way to many ambiguous translations and are heterogeneously interpreted and used by the diverse social actors that take part in these circles. Indigenous leaders that participate in these networks often employ these images and representations in creative ways, in order to attend to their own claims and needs.

The recent growth of contemporary shamanic networks reflects itself in the increase of Indigenous rituals directed to an urban, middle-class audience, conducted in cities all over the world. In Brazil, Indigenous cultural festivals are multiplying. These are held in Indigenous villages, especially in the Amazonian region but also in other parts of the country, and include both Indigenous and non-Indigenous participants. The rise of these gatherings reflects the expansion of Indigenous social and political agency in these networks, and Indigenous representatives are increasingly participating and gaining visibility in Brazilian public discussions regarding ayahuasca and other issues that impact their communities.

As suggested by Langdon,[12] the expansion of shamanisms to non-Indigenous settings requires a reassessment of classical analytical models of shamanism. She pointed out that the emergence of contemporary shamanic networks has contributed to a renewal of the Siona shamanic practices that were apparently declining in the 1970s. Langdon suggested that her fieldwork in the Putumayo in the 1970s could be described as a situation of "shamanism without shamans." She notes that when she left the village of Buenavista in 1974, she had predicted the disappearance of the Siona shamanic system. Influenced by prevailing anthropological theories, she never could have imagined the revitalization of this shamanic system, that ayahuasca would become a popular and globally known substance, or even the rise of interest in this beverage among middle-class urban populations. Langdon highlights that, at that time, her own ideas about Indigenous cultures had stopped her from understanding the depth of Indigenous identity and the strength of Siona shamanism.[13]

By the 1980s some Siona had started to resume their *yajé* rituals, conducting sessions directed to their mixed-blood neighbors and to non-Indigenous visitors. They also began to participate in the regional healing (*curandeirismo*) networks that are part of the Colombian popular medical system. Further, at the end of this same decade, some Siona became visible and valued in contemporary transnational shamanic networks. In these settings, the new *taitas* performed *tomas de yajé* for an audience composed of anthropologists, journalists, and other urban professionals.[14]

Most of the research about these contemporary shamanisms indicates that these rituals are directed especially to individual, psychological, and therapeutic issues. In this sense, they are very different from Indigenous rituals that tend to prioritize public and collective aspects. Moreover, these ritual performances tend to reflect a "much more loving shamanism,"[15] displaying aesthetic expressions that represent a generic Amazonian shaman and not the particular Indigenous shamanisms. Thus, in these performances and discourses oriented to a mostly urban and non-Indigenous audience, ambiguity and aspects connected to cannibalism, sorcery, and predation are usually absent.

There are several recent ethnographic reports from Brazil about dialogues and alliances between Indigenous groups and non-Indigenous spiritual groups. The current investigations about this subject highlight the creativity and the dynamic nature of these contemporary movements. Shamanisms today are characterized by dialogues, controversies, and equivocations between several Indigenous and non-Indigenous groups. It is also important to emphasize the increasing Indigenous leadership in these networks, as well as creative Indigenous agency more broadly. According to author Jean-Pierre Chaumeil, in many cases these Indigenous reactions and the new versions of shamanism resulting from these processes are surprising and even contrary to anthropological images and expectations.

The concept of *contemporary shamanic networks*[16] moves past these dichotomies, emphasizing the extremely dynamic and creative features of these current movements. Contemporary shamanic networks are phenomena characterized by the constant construction and multiplication of ritual practices and symbolic systems. These practices cross several boundaries—geographical, symbolic, political, and conceptual—inviting us to question rigid Western dichotomies such as "forest/city," "Indigenous/non-Indigenous," and "traditional/modern."

Langdon has argued that the anthropological studies about shamanism reveal a history of anthropology itself.[17] The anthropological concerns, concepts, and questions in the 1970s and today are completely different. Jean Langdon's works about shamanism for over half a century reflect these transformations and also trace the changes that have happened to Indigenous shamanisms and their connections with the so-called non-Indigenous world. However, in spite of these changes, some topics remain constant in her writings about shamanism and ayahuasca, such as the emphasis on the associations between shamanic systems and the human necessity of expression; the analysis of aesthetic issues associated with this necessity of expression; the focus on creativity and constant reinvention; the dynamic character and heterogeneity that characterize Amerindian shamanisms; and the concept of praxis, which calls attention to the relationship between symbolic meanings and concrete action in daily life.

Mescaline Scribe

PATRICK FARRELL

SIMONE DE BEAUVOIR'S DESCRIPTION OF JEAN-PAUL SARTRE'S ENCOUNTER with mescaline in 1935 is a striking account of a psychedelic experience gone wrong. The episode appears in the second volume of her memoirs, *The Prime of Life* (1960),[1] and describes a time in their lives long before their rise as two of France's most famous philosophers. By mid-century, they achieved global fame: even independent of her landmark feminist work *The Second Sex* (1949), Beauvoir was an accomplished novelist (her 1954 novel *The Mandarins* won France's prestigious Prix Goncourt prize) and a founding editor of the influential periodical *Les Temps Modernes*. Together with Sartre, Beauvoir became a leading figure not only of French existentialism, but also prominently engaged in postwar political activism.

Sartre's bad trip was vividly captured by Beauvoir's economical prose: "faces acquired monstrous characteristics . . . just past the corner of his eye swarmed crabs and polyps and grimacing Things." The experience resulted in a period of depression for Sartre, but Beauvoir was reluctant to blame the mescaline itself. Indeed, there were many reasons to be depressed at this time, not least (in their eyes) the impending prospects of "turning thirty"— Beauvoir had just turned 27, and Sartre would soon cross the threshold. Socially, France and Europe more generally continued to reel in the years after World War I, which saw the rise of authoritarian and fascist political movements. Perhaps as importantly, Beauvoir's account of Sartre's bad trip highlights the extreme disconnect from emotional, spiritual, and ceremonial considerations that often occurred in this early stage of psychedelic use in the West.

BEAUVOIR AND SARTRE: YOUNG WRITERS IN LOVE

At the time of Sartre's mescaline experience, it had been five years since they made a pact to be one another's "necessary other"—neither married, nor monogamous, they nevertheless remained devoted to each other until

Sartre's death in 1980. They had met in 1928 and became close the following year after ranking first (Sartre) and second (Beauvoir) in philosophy in France's prestigious national exams. They were inspired by literature, art, music, film, history, and philosophy; they wanted to be writers—of essays, plays, short stories, novels, it didn't matter, as long as they wrote.

Quite amazingly and without exaggeration, Beauvoir read and edited everything Sartre ever published, all the while maintaining her own formidable writing output. As a teenager, Beauvoir had earned the nickname *Castor* (Beaver), so notorious was her industry among her classmates. Her unremitting studiousness resulted in works we are still assimilating, not least her masterpieces *The Second Sex* (1949) and *The Coming of Age* (1970). But these monumental achievements were, at this point, far in the future.

ALCOHOL AND AMPHETAMINES

Beauvoir relished the freedom afforded her as an instructor at the girls' school Jeanne-d'Arc in Rouen, northwest of Paris. Sartre took a teaching position nearby in the coastal city of Le Havre, but felt oppressed by his situation. He feared his best years were behind him, that, as she writes, there

Beauvoir at café Deux Magots in 1944. (Robert Doisneau/Gamma-Rapho/Getty Images)

would be "no more fresh and blinding revelations": "We were both still the right side of thirty, and yet nothing new would ever happen to us."

Beauvoir had a long and complex relationship with intoxicating substances. A cheerful drinker, at the time she was drinking quite a lot, and Sartre complained that when she drank too much, she got too sentimental and poetic, and conflated these states with an intuition for truth. She disagreed and appreciated wine and spirits' ability to reduce her defenses. Anyway, it was somewhat hypocritical and ironic of him to be so critical of her drinking, as he had his own excesses with alcohol and substances.

Sartre regularly consumed the amphetamine orthedrine and later corydrane (a mixture of aspirin and amphetamine), which were available over the counter in France until banned in the 1960s and early '70s. Discussing his speed use later he said, "The doctors said it's dangerous now. Too bad, because I loved it . . . It made my hand move so fast, I couldn't write faster." Beauvoir also found occasion to use these substances but never to the extent of Sartre, who was said to be addicted. She stopped using them altogether by the 1950s.

PHENOMENOLOGY AND FASCISM

Like many young intellectuals at the time, they were excited about phenomenology. Phenomenology placed the emphasis on each individual's direct subjective experience; the aim was to focus on one's experience without prejudice—free of conceptual categories, abstractions, and ideologies. Emphasizing direct, embodied experience, phenomenology would provide the basis of Beauvoir's and Sartre's emerging existentialism. "The novelty and richness of phenomenology filled me with enthusiasm," Beauvoir wrote. "I felt I had never come so close to the real truth."

Beauvoir visited Sartre in Berlin where he was studying. The Nazi party had recently come to power, and the two were in disbelief that such a hyper-nationalistic, militarized, and violent ideology had ascended to power. They saw parades of brownshirts in Hamburg; Beauvoir was berated in Dresden for wearing lipstick. She remarked, though, that the country "doesn't feel like a dictatorship" and that, at least in the bars and cafes, socializing was "incredibly debauched."

CRUSTACEANS, PAREIDOLIA, AND DEPRESSION

Back in France, Sartre tried mescaline after a friend suggested it "induced hallucinations" but warned that it "would be a mildly disagreeable experience, although not the least dangerous." Beauvoir records that Sartre thought it might be useful to try mescaline as it would produce an abnormal state of consciousness, in keeping with his present interests in "dreams, dream-induced imagery, and anomalies of perception."

Michael Jay's recent study of mescaline[2] describes how at the time of Sartre's experience, mescaline was widely sought by artists and intellectuals for use "neither as a spiritual epiphany nor a model psychosis, but as a zone of aesthetic, creative and existential possibility." The severe "de-spiritualizing" of mescaline use at this time is also noteworthy as Jay describes how the pharmacist Alexandre Rouhier's book *Peyote: The Plant That Fills the Eyes with Marvels* (1926) had popularized knowledge in France about Indigenous peyote rites of several traditions, and criticized the growing and commonplace assumption that mescaline independent of the cactus and its rituals was an equivalent experience. Rouhier thought of peyote as a "divinatory palaeo-pharmacy," something to be respected and revered—not merely as a chemical to induce changes in brain function and perception.

When Sartre visited his psychiatrist friend Daniel Lagache at Saint-Anne Hopital in Paris that chilly winter morning to be injected with mescaline, it was in a highly clinical setting, bereft of the ritualistic, ceremonial, spiritual, or even medical elements. The object, Lagache had said, was to hallucinate, which is what Sartre did. As arranged, Beauvoir would wait at a friend's apartment and call the hospital after a few hours. When she called, Sartre said in a "thick, blurred voice, that my phone call had rescued him from a battle with several devil-fish." She went to Saint-Anne's to retrieve him. In the train car on the way home Sartre was silent, speaking only to tell Beauvoir about the "dung beetles" on her shoes and about a "leering" orang-utan he believed was hanging by its feet outside the train gazing in at them.

Over the next few days, Beauvoir and Sartre were uncharacteristically incommunicative; she records being "irritated" by his "surliness." Later she learned that Sartre was in a state of severe depression. He had been deeply affected by his mescaline experience and was anxious and fearful. He saw faces everywhere: "houses had leering faces, all eyes and jaws . . .

every clockface . . . the features of an owl." Beauvoir considered it likely that Lagache's warning of possibly bleak experiences primed Sartre in that direction. It likely did not help that Sartre's vision had been severely compromised since losing sight in his right eye following a childhood illness.

Most famously, he was regularly accompanied by some sort of crustacean; Beauvoir refers to a "lobster trotting behind him," though in a later interview he describes a plurality of "crabs and lobsters." The situation got so dire that Sartre genuinely thought he was in danger of psychosis. When Beauvoir tried to calm him, he was dismissive: "'Your only madness,' I told him, 'is believing that you're mad.' 'You'll see,' he replied gloomily."

LEAVING A LEGACY

Reading Beauvoir's account of Sartre's bad trip is important for several reasons. In the first place, Sartre had very little to say about it; what little he did, in the eventual text *The Psychology of the Imagination* (1938), does not mention the crustaceans nipping at his heels. However, in a 1972 interview with John Gerassi, he did revisit the experience:

> Never tried coco, opium, or heroin. Or LSD for that matter, although I gather that it has some of the same effects as peyote, you know, mescaline, which I used to take. I think that's how I first started hallucinating my crabs and lobsters. But it wasn't nasty. They would walk along with me, on my side, but not crowding me, very politely, I mean, not threatening. Until one day I got fed up. I just said, OK beat it, and they did. I liked mescaline a lot. As you know I am not a nature lover.[3]

Beauvoir's account is perhaps most valuable, as it records a moment in time before either writer had taken on their larger-than-life reputations. Beauvoir describes their engaged struggle for those trademark Beauvoirian/Sartrean themes of "freedom," "responsibility," and "choice" at a time of rising radicalization and polarization in French and broader society. It is not difficult, if a little speculative, to imagine that the marching lobsters and crabs were in some way associated with the boot-stomping fascists they had seen in Germany just months before.

Further, coupled with his fatalistic sense of his own failures, that turning 30 amounted to a personal crisis, it is not surprising that Sartre's mescaline experience was so disturbing. It shows the extent to which a person's "head space" can impact a psychedelic experience, to say nothing of set and setting.[4]

Finally, Beauvoir's engrossing account of this episode in their busy lives is a literary treasure in its own right. Perhaps the only thing that could improve it from this perspective would have been if she had taken mescaline—or better yet, peyote—herself. Her words are vivid enough describing the experiences of others; we can only imagine what she might have written had she been the one to lead the lobster parade.

Heroines of Mescaline

IVO GURSCHLER

IN 1905, SEVERAL WOMEN (AND ONE MAN) DETAINED AT A PSYCHIATRIC institution in Breslau, now Poland, were administered extracts of the peyote cactus intravenously.[1] At least two of them had, as it seems, full-blown "mystical" experiences. In 1920, a student of medicine, Leni Alberts, did the very first experiments with pure mescaline at the University Clinic in Heidelberg, which was to become the hotspot of psychedelic studies (avant la lettre) during the interwar period. Her experimental subjects were trained psychiatrists, who appeared to be extraordinarily cheerful while under the influence. What makes these two historic instances of investigating the plant and its main psychoactive substance exceptional is that they documented aspects that were generally either ignored or even suppressed in the scientific exploration of psychedelics' original conception: 1) the *entheogenic* dimension of the cactus-induced experiences and 2) the therapeutic potential of mescaline, useful for the treatment of depression.

I. INVOLUNTARY EPIPHANIES (1905)

> *What if He came back,*
> *What if He came back as a plant?*
> *Would you let Him in*
> *Would you let Him into your heart?*
> —Guy Mount, "Peyote Song"

It is widely known that the very first Western "psychonauts" who explored the effects of the peyote were US and British physicians, and the first series of medicinal experiments with *Anhalonium lewinii* (*Lophophora williamsii*) were conducted at Columbia University by D. W. Prentiss and Francis P. Morgan. The first, albeit involuntary, *female* psychonauts, however, were research subjects in a small series of mescaline experiments performed by the influential psychiatrist Dr. Johannes Bresler (1866–1942) in Breslau, then part of the German Empire.

In 1898, Arthur Heffter[2] concluded his pharmaceutical analysis of peyote by isolating four different alkaloids and identifying "Mezkalin" (C_{11} H_{17} NO_3) as its main psychoactive ingredient: obviously, it was this substance that was solely responsible for the "beautiful color visions" (*schöne Farbvisionen*), which were regarded as the distinctive feature of the cactus taken as a whole. Because of the uncomfortable physiological side effects (nausea, headache, etc.) he endured, he doubted that mescaline would ever be of therapeutic value. His uncomfortable experience in part explains why it took more than two decades for mescaline research to take off.

The pharmaceutical company E. Merck kept a very close eye on the latest findings; in 1912 "Mescalin sulfuricum" was offered for the first time as a research chemical. Therefore, when Bresler did his mescaline experiments in 1905, he used extracts of the plant as a whole. Bresler, who would soon turn out to be an ardent admirer of Adolf Hitler, ensured his readers that he informed the test subjects about the unpleasant physiological effects of the serum, "but of course not about the occurrence of visions."

EARLY MESCALINE EXPERIMENT SUBJECTS WERE MOSTLY WOMEN

Little is known about the experimental subjects except their initials, their age, gender, and a short sketch of their diagnoses: Mrs. Sch. (female, 47 yrs., paranoia), B. (female, 29 yrs., epileptic), L. (female, 25 yrs., epileptic), F. (female, 24 yrs., epileptic), R. (male, 43 yrs., psychotic). Two of them, Sch. and B., had (or were allowed?) to take two turns each. Mrs. Sch., and, for her second session, Mrs. B. had religious visions. After meeting both of her deceased daughters, Sch. perceived sacred paraphernalia, encountered three white virgins, and finally even the holy mother of god herself, Jesus on the cross, and a number of guardian angels who spoke to her (Bresler did not note what the angels said to her). After hearing bells ring, B. also came across the holy virgin, in the guise of the (Black) Madonna of Częstochowa: "I am in the celestial empire," B. reports. "I saw Holy Mary, it is as if I want to die," adding "I thank god for this beautiful viewing, which I've had while

I am in my right mind; others might think that I am not in my right mind, since I am perceiving such things."

Bresler seems to have dismissed the significance of these visions, concluding that "the content of the visions is in accordance with the life of imagination (*Vorstellung Leben*), which was to be expected." It was largely thanks to the candid nature of the reports of these fearless women, who had nothing to lose and could speak freely, that Bresler had the idea that *Anhalonium lewinii* might prove useful "for patients suffering from persistent agonizing optical deceptions, with the mescal-visions pushing them into the background at least temporarily."

II. LENI ALBERTS'S FARSIGHTED OBSERVATIONS (1921)

In a recent article, neuroscientist Robin Carhart-Harris stated: "We can no longer ignore the potential of psychedelic drugs to treat depression." In many ways Carhart-Harris is repeating a claim that Leni Alberts made almost 100 years earlier, when she said:

> The occurrence of a euphoric state [. . .] in all experimental subjects makes me think that mescaline may be useful for overcoming melancholic mind states, provided the unpleasant side effects may be reduced. The visions, which only appear in the dark or with eyes closed, would not necessarily be in the way of this therapeutic treatment.

When Alberts identified this feature, she did so almost as an aside. To discover the effects of mescaline, she asked her test subjects to fulfill a number of tasks, like simple arithmetical exercises, anagrams, reading tests, and weight estimations. She then compared the outcomes of their tests while under the influence to their sober results. Alberts observed a general slowing down of cognitive processing capabilities, but mescaline did not seem to have an overall negative effect on their reasoning or problem-solving skills. Despite the small trial, Alberts's work revealed a hidden promise and inspired further mescaline studies.

Following Viennese chemist Ernst Späth's fully artificial synthesis, mescaline became a proper scientific "working object." The mescaline experiments at the University Clinic in Heidelberg precipitated an international

From the appendix of Leni Alberts's thesis on mescaline (1921).

research boom. Alberts's doctoral thesis kicked off this pioneering phase of psychedelic studies.

Alberts struggled to get test subjects to concentrate on their respective tasks and noticed their cheerful moods during the mescaline experiments. The contrast with their usual behavior was striking enough for her to describe some kind of euphoric state. Other contemporary researchers, however, did not follow up on this observation.

WHY DID IT TAKE SO LONG FOR SCIENTISTS TO RECOGNIZE THE SALUTOGENIC EFFECTS OF MESCALINE?

There is no simple answer. Yet there are likely five interrelated reasons for modern science's failure to recognize the true nature of peyote and its derivative mescaline:

1. An overestimation of the significance of the imaginary, visionary effects as *the* most decisive pharmacological feature of the drug, classified as hallucinogen.[3] Alberts, however, realized that these visionary appearances might obfuscate its therapeutic properties.
2. The way that mescaline allegedly mimicked psychosis resulted in a strange epistemological loop, in which the mind-*set* of the psychiatrists and the institutional *setting* led them to consider the effects as pathological.
3. Mescaline was withheld from patients as well as persons with a history of mental health issues (a taboo even today).
4. Science is supposed to be a serious business, and psychiatrists "tripping balls" would have seriously undermined the scientific character of their explorative investigations.
5. Finally, science in general is an agnostic endeavor, and it can, for structural reasons, not take recourse to some "deus ex botanica" to explain its results. Hence, it was only after peyote, mescaline, LSD-25, etc., became *popular* drugs, consumed outside the "safe space" of psychiatry and the straight jacket of reductionism, that their therapeutic benefits—arising from their euphorant or spiritual qualities—could be fully taken into account on a broader level.

Perhaps, if Leni Alberts's observations were followed more closely from the beginning, some of these features would not have taken 100 years to resurface.

Mrs. Amada Cardenas:
Keeper of the Peyote Gardens

STACY B. SCHAEFER

DEEP IN THE HEART OF SOUTH TEXAS, WHERE PEYOTE (*LOPHOPHORA WIL-liamsii*), the mind-expanding cactus sacrament grows, is a place known by many as the "Peyote Gardens." Here stands the modest white house of the late Mrs. Amada Cardenas, the first federally licensed peyote dealer in the United States. This article is to honor Mrs. Cardenas; the telling of her story is intended to provide readers with a sense of inspiration, and encourage living with heartfelt compassion, as Amada did throughout her life, following the peyote way.

Amada was born in the hot, brushy terrain of the Peyote Gardens in 1904. She was brought up in a community where folk Catholicism was a way of life. She also learned the peyote trade from her father at an early age. When Amada married, she and her husband, Claudio Cardenas Sr., took on the livelihood of peyote dealers, *peyoteros*. For decades, they devoted their work day to harvesting peyote and making it available for sale to members of the Native American Church (NAC) from across the United States and Canada.

A number of these Church members made the pilgrimage to South Texas to pray with the peyote, visit with the Cardenases, and purchase a supply of this plant sacrament to take home to their Church and family. Those that could not make the journey bought dried peyote from Amada and Claudio, who shipped it in the mail.

The NAC is a syncretic religion that combines Christianity with pan-Native American beliefs. Peyote and its consumption is a vital part of this spiritual tradition. In 1918, the United States government recognized the NAC as a bonafide religion. Despite this legal status, members of American Indian tribes who worshiped in the NAC way endured numerous injustices and persecution regarding the use of peyote. In more recent years, federal legislation guarantees the right for registered members of the Church to use peyote in their religious practices.

Around the same time that the NAC was established, Mexican Americans from Texas, *Tejanos*, who worked primarily as cowboys or *vaqueros* on land that had formerly been part of the Spanish land grants, began to provide peyote to Native Americans who traveled to South Texas. The Cardenases became sought out by people from Indian Country for their role as *peyoteros*. Their kindness and generosity extended beyond their relationship as peyote dealers; Amada and Claudio Cardenas genuinely cared about their visitors and participated in the prayer meetings that began to take place on their property. They were also highly respected and admired by many Native Americans who came to their home.

One Navajo NAC member, Geri Arviso, recounted her experience as a little girl visiting the Cardenas' home in Mirando City:

> And I remember there was a lot of peyote in the backyard; they were really big. . . . My mother really took it to heart that this was a sacred place, a really holy place, on the premises, and she was touched by the fact that there were people that lived way out here that respected the peyote just as we do. . . . Everyone knew that Mr. and Mrs. Cardenas are the people who took care of the medicine out there and they would pray for them.[1]

Mrs. Amada Cardenas with peyote.
Courtesy of Stacy B. Schaefer

The Cardenases also experienced legal challenges with state and federal government officials over the interpretation, as well as implementation, of laws regarding the regulation of peyote. Nevertheless, Mr. and Mrs. Cardenas always stood strong in their support of Native Americans' rights to acquire and use peyote in their religious ceremonies. On several occasions, the Cardenases risked prosecution and incarceration for providing peyote to NAC members. Leaders of the NAC recognized the Cardenases' dedication to the Church and as caretakers of the peyote. In 1957, Claudio and Amada were appointed to be Texas Delegates-at-Large for the Native American Church of North America. Later on, in 1987, Amada was appointed as an officer of the Native American Church of the United States.

After Claudio's untimely death in 1967, Amada was determined to continue on in the peyote trade, which she did for more than a decade. In the 1970s, the Texas Department of Safety (DPS) became the regulating agency of peyote for the federal government; Amada was one of the first peyote dealers to obtain the official peyote dealer permit. Over the years she realized how difficult it was to carry on the business alone, and eventually retired. For the rest of her life, she continued to open her door to generations of NAC members, many whom had become dear friends. She also extended her hospitality to others that were newcomers who wanted to meet her, as she had become legendary near and far. Anyone who came to her house, Native American or not, she welcomed warmly, offering her visitors food, a place to stay, a place to pray, and she allowed tipis to be put up on her property for specific meetings.

Through her example, Amada demonstrated the beauty that humanity is capable of expressing. In her elder years, she prayed the moment she woke up every morning, throughout the day, and at night in bed before she slept. Amada prayed for family and dear friends who were facing difficult challenges in their lives. She prayed for her neighbors, for Native Americans and non-Indians from afar who confided in her about their problems. She prayed for politicians, religious leaders, even people suffering in countries she had only heard about in the news. Everyone was significant in her eyes and worthy of love. And first, and foremost, she prayed over the peyote.

At an early age, Amada learned from the Indians who came down to South Texas, and from her father and her husband, how to make "Peyote Chiefs." The Peyote Chief is a large peyote top chosen for its size and numerous sections. After her husband Claudio passed away, she began to make Chiefs for people who requested them or for whom she wanted to gift such a powerful talisman or central ritual object. Amada selected these peyotes and spent days, even weeks, working with her fingers to form each one so that it dried with a flat bottom and fuzzy areoles on top that looked like a crown. Over the course of preparing a Chief, Amada put her good thoughts and healing prayers for its future owner into each Chief, blowing sacred tobacco smoke over each one in the process. Few people are deemed worthy to have such powers to make Chiefs, and Amada usually had a long list of Road Men who had requested her to make them.

Amada earned the reputation of being a healer. She attributed her good health and long life to eating a little peyote every day; she passed away one month shy of 101 years old. But she was also known to have healed others. One powerful example of her healing powers was shared by Loreta Afraid of Bear Cook, Lakota from Pine Ridge Reservation. She had come with her husband and others to Amada to acquire peyote, and for Amada to heal her husband, who was deathly ill with a festering boil about the size of a fist. Loreta recounts:

> She reached in the back of his leg and touched it, and knew where it (the boil) was. She blessed him and prayed for him . . . and she gave him peyote, she told him, eat this and you will get well from it, you'll get home and you'll be okay. And so we wanted to believe.
>
> And so early the next morning, as the sun was coming up, she took the medicine and she showed it to the sun, and let the sun's rays hit it, and we had to lift him out of the bed . . . she was saying in her own language prayers with this peyote and she gave it to him . . . so he forgot his pains for those moments and for me it was like she had performed a miracle because that thing (puss) that came out of his wound, it exploded, it's just like it perforated the skin, just right as she is saying these prayers . . . so she told us to believe in the medicine and to believe in that prayer the power of prayer. And we did. . . . he survived it . . .[2]

Amada showered all of her visitors with blessings and sprinkled holy water upon them and their vehicles as they would take their leave. She explained about her actions that, "My prayers are ancient . . . I say prayers . . . for all the world, for everyone who is alive . . . that God lends them a hand, that He watch over them on the road . . . for their families, all of my friends, for all the world."[3]

Indeed, the world would be such a kinder, more humane place if more people followed Amada's example. Amada wanted to keep her property open as a refuge, a sacred place, for future visitors, regardless of their cultural heritage, religious traditions, or nationality. She saw that what united them all was that they respected and worshipped in the peyote way of hope, faith, love, and charity.

After her passing in 2005, Amada's only son, Claudio Jr., has tried to honor his parents' tradition in accommodating visitors who have come to pray with the peyote. It has been a challenge for him, since he has lived in Minnesota with his family for many years. Several *Tejanos* have helped as caretakers, and some NAC members have helped with repairs and upkeep, but it remains a challenge to manage the property from afar.

The Peyote Gardens encompass less and less land as the terrain is altered with root plows for turning the brush into grazing lands for cattle. The oil drilling rigs, and now wind turbines, also disrupt peyote habitat. Peyote is also being overharvested—the number and health of the peyote populations are dwindling precariously. On the US side of the border, the Cactus Conservation Institute is working to address this crisis. Additionally, the joining of several organizations has created the Indigenous Peyote Conservation Initiative, which is intended for Indigenous communities that practice peyote traditions on both sides of the US–Mexico border.

These developments for conserving and protecting peyote in South Texas are promising. Amada's place still remains a unique sanctuary that honors her wishes to keep the doors open. One can feel her presence as she watches over everyone who comes to the Peyote Gardens to heal, learn, pray, and honor others, as they commune with this sacred, awe-inspiring plant.

Another Aspect of Reality: Maria Nys Huxley's Influence on Psychedelic History

ANDREA ENS

ALDOUS HUXLEY'S 1954 CLASSIC *THE DOORS OF PERCEPTION* IS ONE OF THE most famous texts in the history of psychedelics. In this book, Aldous describes his first time taking mescaline with Dr. Humphry Osmond in May 1953 and highlights the important mystical component of his psychedelic experience. Many people see this book as foundational to the development of American scientific and countercultural interests in psychedelics. What many people do not know or realize is that a third participant was also present: Maria Nys Huxley, Aldous's first wife.

MARIA NYS HUXLEY

Maria's friends, family, and loved ones consistently described her as a charming, whimsical woman who deeply cared about her husband, often to the point where she prioritized his well-being and success over her own. The Belgian refugee was 17 years old when she first met Aldous in 1915 while residing at Garsington Manor near Oxford, England. The two married in 1919, and had their son, Matthew, the following year. In 1937, the Huxley family relocated to Hollywood, California. Maria's tendency to dote on Aldous continued up until her death from breast cancer on February 12, 1955.

But Maria was not just Aldous's wife. She was a psychedelic pioneer in her own right. She was a direct participant in one of the most famous historic drug experiences in the United States, was instrumental to her husband's thinking on psychedelics and his professional development, and ultimately helped influence the artistic, intellectual, and cultural dimensions of psychedelic culture in postwar America.

A great deal of Aldous's professional success in his 35 years of marriage to Maria was indeed helped along by her actions. Maria, for example, managed

Maria Nys Huxley in October 1934.

a large proportion of Aldous's correspondence, served as his typist and secretary, arranged house parties which allowed him to network with prominent thinkers, artists, writers, and scientists, looked after his often ill health (which included managing his diet and shopping for doctors), and taking him to his appointments. Much of this work would have been more difficult or even impossible for Aldous due to his poor eyesight.

AN AMERICAN WIFE

Maria's experiences as a wife were common for many American women in the postwar period. It is therefore important to briefly recognize the sort of gendered expectations Maria would have found herself enmeshed within while participating in the United States' psychedelic culture and broader society, despite the Huxleys' consideration of themselves as European expatriates. After the Second World War, many Americans looked toward the home for comfort and stability during this otherwise chaotic era. The most stable homes, many people believed, were patriarchal nuclear family units: households headed by a breadwinning father who worked outside of the home, with a subservient wife who reared the children and took care of the family's domestic needs within the home. Even Sigmund Freud's popular psychoanalytic theories drew from the idea that men were the proper leaders of civilization and that it was a woman's place to support—not challenge—these social hierarchies.

However, not all of Maria's labor was simply done for her husband's benefit. Her house parties are a good example of this point. Maria was in charge of the guest lists for these events. Some notable names from her parties included, for instance, Christopher Isherwood, Jiddu Krishnamurti, Anita Loos, and Edwin Hubble. But by inviting distinguished people to her home on the premise of a meal—and by screening out people she felt she and Aldous would have no interest in meeting—Maria showed a level of control over Aldous's professional networking and also created opportunities for her to learn from and educate experts in various fields herself. Maria's position in the household allowed her to contribute to the intellectual dimensions of postwar psychedelic culture in unexpected ways.

MARIA'S INFLUENCE

Maria's ideas about psychedelics also influenced *The Doors of Perception*'s content as well as scientific ideas about mescaline's effects. Aldous's book describes the differences between sustained schizophrenic madness and the temporary madness one might experience through psychedelics. "The schizophrenic is like a man permanently under the influence of mescalin," Aldous writes, "and therefore unable to shut off the experience of a reality which he is not holy enough to live with."

This understanding of different kinds of madness parallels Maria's thoughts as expressed in a letter to Humphry Osmond from July 21, 1953 (the year before *Doors* was published): Maria states that "the difference between real madness and induced madness I am quite sure is that in real madness the fear is 'Will it get worse? Will it stop?', whereas in mescal you are there to remind us, which I never forgot, that it was induced *artificially*, that there is a time *limit* and that it will not affect one permanently."[1] Osmond responded enthusiastically to Maria's observations in this letter. He immediately asked her to write more about her own mescaline experience, recognizing that her views reflected leading scientific understandings of this drug's effects by Osmond's peers.

They also reflected "another aspect of reality," Osmond writes in a responding letter, that was "just as important as Aldous's from the point of view of what it reveals." Osmond was especially interested in how Maria might compare "mescal madness" to the sorts of madness she had reportedly experienced under the influence of the malaria-treatment drug Atabrin. We do not know whether Maria wrote a response, but it is clear that she was regarded as an independent thinker and important participant in these early discussions about the power of psychedelics to mimic madness.

Unfortunately, it is difficult to know what Maria herself might have thought about her contributions to psychedelic history. A house fire in 1961 destroyed the Huxleys' Hollywood home, and among the items lost to the flames were all of Maria's diaries and letters Aldous had saved over the years. Only five of Maria's letters survived. But, even so, the lack of remaining sources[2] does not fully explain why Maria Nys Huxley has been largely left out of discussions about mid-20th century "psychedelic pioneers." While postwar gender politics may have caused her initial absence from early histories of psychedelic culture, Maria's continued exclusion from these historical narratives speaks to a broader reluctance to acknowledge women's participation in psychedelic spaces into the present day.

"Please Write Up Your Work!": Laura Archera Huxley as a Psychedelic Pioneer

ANDREA ENS

"IF A PERSON DOESN'T DO SOMETHING EITHER USEFUL OR BEAUTIFUL, then one doesn't have any right to take the oxygen of people and the food of people." These words were spoken by Laura Archera Huxley, lay therapist, researcher, and second wife of British intellectual and novelist Aldous Huxley. She said this during a 1988 "Pioneers in Research Series" interview recorded as part of the Institute for Noetic Sciences' Gathering of the Elders conference. This brief quote speaks volumes about Laura's hardworking, ambitious character, as well as her broader perspectives on life, labor, community, and happiness: all crucial concepts related to her decades-long interest in psychedelic therapies.

Yet, despite her inclusion in a series on psychedelic pioneers, Laura is rarely credited with this status in studies of American psychedelic culture. It seems there is real truth in historian Mike Jay's observation that the public faces of psychedelics have typically belonged to college-aged white men, and that limiting our understanding of drug users and researchers to this narrow group hides the important role of women like Laura within these historical spaces.

LAURA ARCHERA HUXLEY

Laura was born in Turin, Italy, in 1911. In her youth, she was a prodigious concert violinist; she had even once played for the queen of Italy, Marie José of Belgium, before debuting at Carnegie Hall in 1937 with the New York Women's Symphony Orchestra. Laura moved to the United States shortly before her New York performance. When World War II began, she decided to quit music to instead learn about psychology and alternative medicine. Laura's interest in film eventually led her to Los Angeles, where she first met Aldous and then-wife Maria in 1949. The three became close friends,

Laura Archera Huxley.
Photo by John Engstead

but Aldous and Laura's relationship became a romance after Maria passed away from cancer in 1955. They spontaneously married the following year at a drive-in wedding chapel in Yuma, Arizona.

DEFYING EXPECTATIONS

Laura defied expectations of what it meant to be a proper wife right from her wedding day. Friends of the Huxley family initially assumed Aldous's new wife would assume the same sort of caretaking responsibilities Maria had previously shouldered for Aldous's benefit;[1] after all, postwar American women were generally expected to dote on their husbands inside of the home instead of pursuing their own careers and interests outside of it. That Laura refused to play the role of Aldous's caretaker shocked some of her husband's peers, and several of them made comparisons between her and Maria as a result.

For example, in 1957, the Huxleys' longtime friend Dr. Humphry Osmond privately described Laura as "very much like a large and self-contained cat in human form: decorative and Aldous likes having her around. She does not devote herself to Aldous as Maria did, but this may perhaps be just as well. If anything she errs in the other direction." Laura, it seems, rejected the idea that she should limit herself to simply being Aldous's housewife despite what others thought.

These sexist social expectations certainly did not discourage her interest in psychedelic therapies. Compounds like LSD-25 and mescaline fascinated Laura for how they allowed users to rapidly and intensely explore the deep recesses of human consciousness. However, Laura was highly critical of casual psychedelic consumption. These compounds, she believed, were substances that must be treated with the greatest therapeutic respect, not "something to be distributed like a cocktail." Her first exposure to psychedelics' therapeutic potential took place in October 1955 when Aldous asked her to guide him through a day-long psychedelic experience to help him recover buried memories from his childhood. The couple shared between six and eight more psychedelic experiences from 1955 to 1963. Laura even administered Aldous 100 mcgs of LSD to ease him through his death on November 22, 1963.

YOU ARE NOT THE TARGET

All of these shared psychedelic experiences—in addition to ones she observed or underwent without Aldous's company—culminated in the publication of her 1963 self-help therapy book, *You Are Not the Target*.[2] This book offered its readers 33 strategies (or "recipes") for changing oneself, finding one's purpose, acting with and seeking out love, and dealing with anxiety, sadness, anger, self-doubt, and other emotions in a productive, positive manner.

You Are Not the Target's success launched Laura into the public realm while also giving her the opportunity to network with leading scientists and countercultural figures interested in psychedelic remedies.

Sanford Unger, Ram Dass (then Richard Alpert), and Timothy Leary all expressed interest in Laura's therapies and findings before and after her book was released. Leary even wrote to Laura on November 18, 1960, urging her to "please write up your work!" since he and others were eagerly "awaiting the promised publication."

Not everyone approved of Laura's recipes, though. Countercultural spiritual leader Jiddu Krishnamurti argued with Laura about her approach due to his concern that her recommendations would encourage people against finding the answers to their problems themselves. Researchers also levied critiques in Laura's direction as psychedelics became increasingly controversial among medical and scientific experts. Often, though, simple misunderstandings shielded her from professional backlash. Laura had difficulty pronouncing the letter "r," so, when some people believed her therapies used dogs instead of drugs, Laura later recalled they were "quite nice and not upset." The fact that figures from postwar psychedelic culture's conflicting research and spiritual sides took issue with Laura's work reflects her important, but understudied, position within this space. Laura's self-help therapies could be understood as a sort of middle ground between objective, scientific psychedelic studies on one hand and the more subjective, mystical component of psychedelic culture on the other.

LAURA'S INFLUENCE

Laura's influence on psychedelic history is not just limited to her own research: she also had a major impact on Aldous's final novel, *Island* (1963). This was no secret. Aldous clearly stated as much in his foreword to *You Are Not the Target*, where he explained that Laura's work was crucial inspiration for this famous text's understanding of "moksha-medicine" and healing. Even Laura herself was surprised at the extent to which Aldous drew from her work in writing this text. But it is important to note that Laura's influence is significant here because Aldous's book, like the previous *The Doors of Perception* (1954), was highly influential within American psychedelic countercultural circles. The fact that Laura's findings were so instrumental to *Island* sheds further light on her important role within the development of American psychedelic culture.

Overall, Laura Archera Huxley was an active, ambitious, and controversial participant during psychedelics' early years in the United States. Her personal drug experiences and her resulting therapies pushed her into the public limelight, prompting a variety of actors to respond to her findings in positive and critical ways. Laura's actions mark her as a postwar psychedelic pioneer worthy of further historical consideration.

Nina Graboi, a Forgotten Woman in Psychedelic Lore

CHRIS ELCOCK

NOVEMBER 2012. I HAVE JUST STARTED MY RESEARCH ON THE HISTORY OF LSD and this is my first time in the US. I'm heading to the University of Santa Cruz library where I will be examining a collection at the archives. I am greeted by Nicholas Meriwether, better known for directing the local Grateful Dead collection. I have informed the staff about my visit, and there is an air of anticipation on his smile. "I'm here to look at the papers of Nina Graboi," I tell him. His face lights up and he addresses me as a true Californian. "Dude, she had such an amazing life!"

The collection is unsorted and time-consuming—I may well be the first researcher to plow through it. Out of one box comes a colorful piece of clothing that belonged to Timothy Leary. "Goddam amazing," whispers Nicholas, as we carefully study it. For me this is the first contact with an icon of the psychedelic Sixties. I do get a slight buzz, but I still don't really know who Nina Graboi was. Nicholas tells me to grab a copy of her autobiography. Little do I know that her book *One Foot in the Future* is going to be a major source for my project.

A JEWISH REFUGEE IN NEW YORK CITY

Nina Graboi was born in Vienna at the end of World War I and brought up in the thriving Jewish community of Leopoldstadt. After the Nazis annexed Austria, she escaped to London, where she took up various low-paying jobs. Part of her family had relocated to Belgium, and during a visit she met her husband Michel. Then the war broke out and the Maginot Line crumbled. After a year living under German occupation, the newlyweds were smuggled into Free France. Eventually they boarded the SS *Wyoming* in Marseilles and, after an unfortunate six-week spell in a Moroccan detention camp, they finally reached New York City.

At last the horrors of fascist Europe were behind them. They quickly set up a textile business that was soon employing dozens of people. Their successful venture enabled them to have their own spacious house built on Long Island. They had two children, Dan and Nicole. They hired a nanny for the kids, a housekeeper, a gardener, and a butler who brought her breakfast in bed every day. "In short, it was the American dream," Graboi wrote.

But something was amiss. The move to the suburbs created distance from her siblings who had emigrated to Manhattan. While Michel commuted to run the business in the city, Nina became a model housewife and entertained her new friends with lavish parties. After all the time on the run in Europe, she had not really gotten to know her husband. It turned out he was not really the man she hoped he was. The boredom and emptiness of postwar conformity slowly settled in. "I teetered on high heels, wore my hair in the casual-seeming Italian style that was the result of nights spent with fat rollers pinned to my head," Graboi remembered.

There had to be more to life than this. In her quest for greater meaning, she had turned to alternative spirituality and meditation. But in the early '60s, psychedelics started appearing in the pages of *Time* magazine. She was thrilled by the possibility of experiencing exceptional states of consciousness, even as a woman who had always looked down on "drugs." Eventually she met and befriended Timothy Leary, the former Harvard professor turned LSD proselytizer and countercultural icon of the decade. The two of them became collaborators in the American psychedelic movement.

Graboi's psychedelic odyssey offers an intimate account of a woman who fully grasped the transformative power of the psychedelic experience. Before experimenting with psychedelics, she freely admitted being middle class and conforming to the gender stereotypes of her time. But after taking LSD in 1966, her perspective on postwar society was turned upside-down. "What I had once taken for reality now looked like flim-flam. The hypocrisies and delusions in which I, like most people, had spent my life stood naked before me." In the aftermath of the experience, she closed her bank account and divorced her husband, Michel.

THE PSYCHEDELIC MOVEMENT AND THE CENTER OF THE LEAGUE OF SPIRITUAL DISCOVERY

The transformative psychedelic experience led Graboi to become actively involved in New York's vibrant psychedelic scene. In September 1966 Graboi accepted Leary's offer to direct the newly founded Center of the League for Spiritual Discovery in Manhattan, which was set up in a dilapidated Greenwich Village storefront. The League is best remembered for being part of Leary's own brand of psychedelic religion.[1] At the time the High Priest of LSD was facing a lengthy jail sentence for cannabis smuggling. In an attempt to beat the charges,[2] he presented psychedelics as spiritual adjuncts that should be protected by religious freedom.

But what actually happened behind the walls of the Center? Enthusiasts and non–drug users alike could have access to information about psychedelics and join the daily meditation sessions. All this would not have happened without Graboi's dedication: "As head of the New York Center I could do much to prepare those who were determined to try [psychedelics], discourage those to whom it would be detrimental, and counsel those who were trying to integrate the experience."

Psychedelic artist Martin Carey once walked into the Center and was taken with its supportive environment:

> There was a light machine going in the front and soft Indian music playing, and there were candles and incense . . . All of a sudden, I felt I was tripping. For a moment I was really scared, and I thought, well, if it has to happen, this is the place for it. Of course as soon as I stopped being scared, it stopped. Richard Alpert was speaking, and there were pictures of Timothy Leary along the wall. The whole room—the whole environment—there was a sense of a Catholic martyr trip about it. I sat way in the back. It was a very large, narrow room . . . Sitting in a room like that with a lot of other people who were turning on to a very high level and being drawn together because of it.

The Center was more than a place for psychedelic spirituality. As a hotspot for New York's counterculture, the League's attendees were invited to sit on the floor rather than on chairs, which were "as much a badge of the straight world as short hair." Graboi purposefully decided against a poster telling folks not to litter because it "would bring visions of the police state to the young dropouts' minds and provoke them to contrary acts." Instead a staff member drew a psychedelic goddess that featured a much gentler caption—"Don't be a litterbug."

Graboi's involvement with the League was not confined to managing the Center, however. On one instance she gave a talk on psychedelic spirituality at the Riverside Drive cathedral. But the diversity of the crowd made her a little nervous: "The faces that scrutinized me as I stood behind the lectern were young, in their twenties and thirties. Some were open, but reserved. Others betrayed the closed hostility I was familiar with from some of the visitors at the Center."

But she gradually grew into it and openly joked about her drug use: "Until a year ago I was law-abiding citizen. Then I smoked marijuana and became a criminal." She eloquently presented the psychedelic experience as a way of easing the perennial fear of death. She made a good impression on some of the attendees who then asked her where they could get their hands on some acid.

NINA GRABOI'S PSYCHEDELIC LEGACY

The story of Nina Graboi's involvement with the psychedelic movement is significant because it challenges the idea that the psychedelic countercul- ture of the 1960s was strictly a man's world[3] and that women were periph- eral figures who were supposed to reproduce gender stereotypes and to be sexually available for men—as Leary's appetite for womanizing aptly illus- trates. To be sure Leary's influence loomed large at the Center, which was decorated with mandalas and pictures of the High Priest.

But Graboi was unimpressed by his cult of personality. On one occa- sion two young men were in the process of repainting the ceiling but they had uncovered large bronze plaques under the plaster. Although Graboi thought that the plaques gave the room a unique charm, the countercul- turists wanted to paint over them because Leary had once told them that "all metal should be returned underground." She laughed so hard that tears ran down her cheeks.

This anecdote points to another popular misconception surrounding the counterculture of the Sixties, which was supposedly young, naïve, and oblivious to work.[4] The League certainly drew its share of criticism from the outside for supposedly encouraging illegal drug use—in fact it strictly pro- hibited drugs on the premises. But some of those critics were confounded upon seeing enthusiastic volunteers helping her refurbish the storefront:

"It was a pleasant sight: four long-haired teen-aged boys wearing beads, colorful shirts and patched pants, cheerfully wielding screwdrivers, hammers and saws." Several critics ended up tempering their views on psychedelics and the League thanks to a woman who was far older than the baby boomers.

TOWARD A HISTORY OF WOMEN AND PSYCHEDELICS?

The international psychedelic community is becoming increasingly aware of the male-dominated narratives of the history of psychedelics. To be sure psychedelic stars like Leary, Aldous Huxley, and Ken Kesey, along with all the male psychiatrists undertaking psychedelic research at the time, are the main actors in most accounts. Is this the product of male bias in the process of history writing? The reality of the gender relations of the time? An unfortunate absence of primary sources? A combination of all the above? In any event, the story of Nina Graboi is proof that these stories are there if we bother look for them.

Wilma Mahua Campos, Shipibo Ayahuasquera

SAMANTHA BLACK

HELLO FRIENDS, I WOULD LIKE TO SHARE SOME EXPERIENCES I HAVE HAD during my many years in traditional medicine. My name is Wilma Mahua Campos; I am the daughter of an Elder healer named Don Benjamin Mahua Ochabano and Señora Celandine Fields Gordon. We are from the native community of Paoyhan on the Ucayali River in Peru. I am 44 years old, mother of five children, and I am of the Shipibo ethnic group. We are part of the Shipibo-Conibo-Xetebo community and our land is the upper, middle, and lower Ucayali region in the Peruvian Amazon.

For my people, it is normal for certain ancestors, parents, and relatives to pass traditional teachings to their children from an early age. I do this

Wilma Inkan Kena Mahua Campos in front of her icaro.

now with my children, and this is how my parents taught me traditional medicine practices from a very young age, with the help of my grandparents, uncles, and other relatives. Those of us who value our ancestral lineage from ancient times to the present are very careful to preserve and develop our culture.

Since I was a small child I took a lot of interest in studying Shipibo medicine[1] with my parents, grandparents, uncles, and other relatives. I spent my childhood surrounded by Elder healers and took close notice of all that they did in their traditional works. I learned to prepare medicines with leaves and plants, and how to make salves, teas, and poultices. From a young age I participated in the ayahuasca ceremonies together with the Elders in my family[2] and saw how they treated the people who visited our ceremonies for healings. In this way, I became familiar with traditional medicine since I was a very little girl.

When I was 12 years old, I fell seriously ill, and together with my family I made the decision to use traditional plant medicine diets to heal me.[3] I started the traditional plant diets for my health and also to continue learning traditional medicine. Through the plant diets I cultivated my relationship with the plants that my people use for healing. The energies of these plants began to form in my body and mind as I dieted as a young teenager. I was cured of my illness within a year and spent the next five years with a renewed desire to learn about traditional medicine; I started to make medicine and to participate in the ceremonies again. At this point I became a mother with my first son. The birth of my son humbled me, and I made a new commitment to stay very humble, and to make the right decisions about the course of my life. I spoke with my father and with my uncle who raised me, and they thought about this. After a few months, they held ceremonies for me, where they sang prayers for me to start with my life's mission and to fulfill my purpose in life.

Those were wonderful ceremonies, and I finally understood that it was time to realize my dreams within the world of plants. As I sat with my family, I listened to each person share their own songs in their own voice. The melodies they sang to me were *icaros* (medicine songs) in my Shipibo dialect so I understood everything that was said about me, as my family handed over to me the healing power and energy of our central healing plant, the *Noyarao*.

With the energy of this sacred plant, the *Noyarao*, I saw many lights, flowers, and different visions, so I started the traditional plant medicine diets again. I did not know when to end my diets, so I spent a while more. As I continued dieting, my mind changed, and I became new. I had a vision of this change: I saw a white cape full of beautiful designs, and the cape was surrounded by my family, both the living and the ancestors. In my vision, my family was creating beautiful designs on the cape, designs that were meant for me to have and to use as a healer. Then I saw myself in the middle of the white cape, surrounded by the healing designs. I saw that in fulfilling my purpose, I am a design of my family, too.

My first diet was *Marrusa*, the famous Incan plant which I was named after. My Shipibo name is Inkan Kena, which means "a hospital or healer who carries Incan plant medicine." After *Marrusa* I dieted with *Chiricsanango, Noyarao, Bombizana*, and others.

There was another vision that I will never forget. I saw that my arms, hands, fingers, and feet grew into many green living, flowering leaves and branches that transformed my body. When I was not in ceremony I saw the same thing in my dreams, and once while I was inside one of these lucid dreams, I called to my parents to ask them what this vision meant. From inside my dream, they responded to me that this vision was part of my diets, and that the healing power of the plants was adapting in my body and blending with my spirit, to become one with my energy; they also told me that from my mother's womb I was chosen to become a healer, by the plants. My father dieted with the plants for two years before I was born, to pray for a child to join the family lineage of healers.

Plants become people in dreams and plant spirits become family to us who are healers. Plants are spirits that teach us how to heal the spiritual mind and the physical mind. Plants teach us their songs which we call in our language *icaros*. Since I first dieted I now have almost 23 years of experience with natural medicine, and I am very happy to be the woman I am.

This is how my father and my uncle Pascual gave me the power and energy to continue my mission of traditional medicine as a legacy of their wisdom. I prepared myself to be a healer together with my parents, uncles, and grandparents, some of whom have since departed and find themselves in the glory of the Lord Our Father God. Thanks to the teachings of my family, now I am a woman, a daughter, and a mother in the world of plants. Learning is not easy; it is very strict. This way of healing and becoming a traditional healer is not learned in one year. It takes time. It takes months, days, and years of going hungry, thirsty, and not talking to anyone. During these years I did not go out to the street and I did not walk with fast steps—I walked very slowly and carefully. I ate food without taste: no salt, no sugar, no spice, no oil. But little by little I became accustomed to the diets and I mastered everything that was asked of me by the plant spirits.

Everything I did during that time strengthened me. I took that time to learn from my parents, while they were still present with me. I learned to help cure many kinds of sick people with plant diets, singing *icaros*, teaching and learning traditional medicine. I adapted to hold and express a lot with light when I became one with the energies of *Noyarao* and other curative plants. These are my experiences for many years and I continue to learn more and more. It is never enough—there is always a new challenge, always more to learn, and I have to keep discovering new things every day and continue to have new experiences.

Thirteen years ago I discovered the *Noyarao* tree, which we also call the "flying tree" (*palo volador*). I lived with and studied this tree not only in visions but in its physical form with the bright sunlight. Its leaves retain the sunlight so at night the tree glows, and very beautiful lights shine through its leaves and its branches. We are able to smell its flowers, touch the tree with reverence, and take its extract. We smoke its leaves with *mapacho* (Amazonian ceremonial tobacco, *nicotania rusticana*) and in this way we continue to learn from this tree. I continued to drink the tree in my traditional plant diets, until I could overcome my lower energies more, and come into contact with the angels of God, their prayers, their gifts, wisdom, intelligence, and above all the light of peace, love, and many other qualities.

Both men and women are called on this path. In our ancient minds, our ancestors were very wise; they had no schools or hospitals to learn in but they knew how to do their activities correctly, and they developed their arts, their medicines, their families, and their communities. They knew that just as humans have rights in life, plants also have rights.

Our ancestors took the natural medicine ayahuasca to diagnose their health problems. They used this natural medicine to cure their sick people and to discover the causes of physical, psychological, and spiritual diseases. That was the only way they had to diagnose and heal their sick. They knew how to treat the sick by giving them specific plants to drink, saunas with the steam of plants, vomitive purges, plasters, and salves, all using the spirit and the body of the plants. In this way they cured. They knew the right time to give the medicine, and how to stay in a good relationship with the plants and the people. They saw the signs and drew information from the sun, the moon, and the other heavenly bodies. They were such geniuses that they did not ever doubt their skills. They used native plants to hunt animals and eat well, to catch fish, and for their work on the farm. They did not wear shoes or sandals; they walked with bare feet on the earth and made their own clothes from cottonseed.

In the past, our culture was very different. For one thing, we used to have a big festival every year where people met, gathered, shared skills, and traded. This was called the *Ani Xeati* festival where many original peoples were gathered from different tribes, to celebrate. These festivals took months to prepare and lasted for over a week. The people would gather to hunt, raise houses, and plant fields together. The women would take this time to weave new clothing such as Shipiba skirts (*chitonti*), Shipiba blouses (*caton*), ankle straps (*jonxe*), and Shipiba belts (*chinexete*). The women would prepare special clothes for the *Ani Xeati* party such as the *mustarchilla* or *teote*, which is a short cape used during the festival. They would also prepare a feast-time ceremonial spear painted with designs (*wino*), and ceremonial crowns woven with macaw or heron feathers (*maiti*).

There was always a fun encounter—a first haircut, an initiation for teenagers, a marriage, a new home, or canoe built. There were games held between women and men so that single people could meet one another. They would do ceremonies to help the people in the year to come, under the direction of the *apus* (mountain shamans), the *ayahuasqueros* (river valley shamans), and the authorities of different peoples. The unique presentation of each group of people was celebrated and honored.

Now, in our present times, culture continues to live but is not honored. The larger society does not value Indigenous peoples such as the Shipibo-Conibo-Xetebo. We must recognize original peoples around the world, because they have ancient knowledge. There are people who make fun of Indigenous people and call them nothing more than peasants, without realizing that they have a whole and distinct culture; they live life in their own way. Indigenous people have many cultures with many different values, traditions, and ancient knowledge.

Culture adds value and meaning to the rural life of a peasant. They develop and supply markets, which are valued by consumers, such as medicinal plants and products of the countryside. I am Indigenous and know the value of my people. We are as human as anyone else in the world. Nature is full of life and we must learn to care for and value the healing qualities of the plants and trees—they give us the way to live, to exist, to heal, to eat, and to care for ourselves. There is much more to discover from Indigenous peasants. Let us pay attention, because we can learn many things from the peasant people.

Interview and translation from Spanish by Samantha Black.

Dream and Ecstasy in the Mesoamerican Worldview: An Interview with Mercedes de la Garza

OSIRIS GONZÁLES ROMERO

THE FOLLOWING IS AN INTERVIEW WITH DR. MERCEDES DE LA GARZA, PRO-
fessor emeritus of the National Autonomous University of Mexico. She is
one of the most recognized researchers on shamanism and the ritual uses of
plants and mushrooms with psychoactive properties. Her research consti-
tutes one of the most valuable contributions to Indigenous plant knowledge,
most broadly due to its methodology and the study of primary sources such
as epigraphic texts, codices, sculptures, and manuscripts, together with ethnographic works and interviews.

This interview offers a general overview of her research. I inquired about
the reasons that prompted her to conduct this path-breaking research.
I sought her opinion about the contributions made by other women. Finally
I asked for her advice to new generations of researchers dedicated to the study
of the ritualistic use of plants and mushrooms with psychoactive properties.

This interview serves as a cordial invitation to our readers to come and
learn firsthand about the work of Dr. Mercedes de la Garza. She is one of the
pioneers in the Global South. The interview comprises 10 questions focused
on specific issues within her vast work.

1. How did you become interested in researching sacred and psychoactive plants' ritual and therapeutic uses?

I am a historian of religions. Among my topics on Nahuatl (Aztec) and
Mayan religions, I decided one day (around 1985) to investigate shamanism from pre-Hispanic times until today. I relied on several sources: plastic
works and other pre-Hispanic vestiges; epigraphic readings of Mayan hiero-
glyphic writing; pre-Hispanic (Maya) and colonial codices; texts written in
colonial times by Indigenous people and Spaniards; and research conducted

by anthropologists in present-day Indigenous Nahua and Maya communities. I also conducted some interviews with shamans from both cultures.

And in the course of the research, I came across sacred plants with psychoactive powers. From pre-Hispanic times, the preclassical Period (1800 B.C. to 300 A.D.) until today, shamans have used them. The most ancient vestiges of Mesoamerican shamanism are precisely those that reveal the use of plants and mushrooms, both by the representations of shamans in ecstasy or trance, as well as of the plants themselves.

2. How have you approached your research; what kind of methodology was necessary to carry it out?

The central object of my research is shamanism, with all that it implies: the characters, their roles in the community of doctors, diviners, counsellors, dreams, initiations, sacred stones, and healing and psychoactive plants and mushrooms, which allow the externalization of the soul toward other dimensions of reality, according to their conception of the world. The temporal scope that I cover is from pre-Hispanic times to today.

Shamans are ritual specialists recognized as having received a gift from the deities and chosen by them in their dreams. They act individually and perform private rites.

My methodology is the history of religions, which considers the religious phenomenon as a historical creation, and approaches it objectively. It is grounded in the comparative analysis of the data provided by different sources to find the meaning of the religious phenomenon and to understand it.

3. You are a professional researcher in history; could you explain the importance of the study and analysis of primary sources?

Any historical research has to be based on primary sources. It is necessary to carry out a hermeneutic study of them to understand them and not simply collect information but interpret it with attention to historical context. However, it is also essential to keep up to date with the progress of research by other authors when it supports or clarifies an interpretation or provides new data. Likewise, when the subject requires it, it is necessary to appeal to data provided by other disciplines, both humanistic and scientific.

4. As a woman dedicated to science, did you experience any difficulty, obstacle, or discrimination during your research process?

I have not been discriminated against as a woman, but there are always anti-feminist or competing male critics.

5. Could you explain women's main contributions to research with sacred plants and psychedelics?

Mercedes de la Garza.
Wikimedia Commons

I can mention the following: in the United States, Marlene Dobkin de Ríos, in 1974, was the first to discover data that spoke of the use of these plants among the Mayas of the classic period. She was harshly criticized by several male researchers locked in their dogmas. I studied her proposal, considered it valid, and quoted her, recognizing her contribution.

Another outstanding anthropologist dedicated to shamanism and sacred plants is Antonella Fagetti, from the Benemérita Universidad Autónoma de Puebla, Mexico. She and I, along with several other researchers, are now working on a project on psilocybin.

Also dedicated to studying sacred plants is María Bencioli, who looks at the use of peyote. Lilián González has delved into the use of tobacco. And also María Gabriela Garrett Ríos and María de Lourdes Baez Cubero have published their research on the Santa Rosa, the Indigenous name for marijuana.

6. What do you consider your most significant contribution to the study of sacred plants with psychoactive properties?

My book *Sueño y éxtasis: Visión chamánica de los nahuas y los mayas* (Mexico, Instituto de Investigaciones Filológicas and Fondo de Cultura Económica, 2012).

In this book, I talk mainly about sacred plants in shamanism. But I include a table of all those I found mentioned in the sources. With their scientific names and their names in the different languages, as well as their primary uses.

In 1990, I published at the Universidad Nacional Autónoma de México the book *Sueño y alucinación en el mundo náhuatl y maya* (*Dream and Hallucination in the Nahua and Mayan World*), a predecessor of the previous one, which was translated into French and published in Paris under the name of *Le Chamanisme nahua et maya*.

7. Based on your experience, how would it be possible to make a kind of history that recognizes the work done by women in the research on sacred plants and psychedelics?

Perhaps by the initiative of a female historian, or perhaps a male historian respectful of women's contributions, of which there are some.

8. What is the role of Mexican researchers and institutions in the context of the so-called psychedelic renaissance?

I don't know what the so-called psychedelic renaissance is.

9. What would you recommend to the new generations of researchers dedicated to studying the ritual and therapeutic uses of sacred plants with psychoactive properties?

They do not leave their subject of study to live experiences with sacred plants, losing objectivity. It has happened to several scholars, and I have friends who know a lot about sacred plants but have not written anything because they have strayed down that path.

10. What is your opinion about the initiatives presented to regulate and decriminalize sacred and psychedelic plants in Mexico?

I am not aware of such initiatives.

Betty Eisner: Heroine with a Hitch?

TAL DAVIDSON

TIMOTHY LEARY, RAM DASS. THESE TWO WERE AS FORMATIVE FOR ME AS they were for the worlds they were a part of; and yet, I had grown very tired of the saga of psychedelic history beginning with their names. When I was a teenage Deadhead, their use of psychedelics to critique and reimagine society started off my thinking about the ways that our reality was socially constructed. Later on, as a psychology student steeped in social constructionism and interested in the history of psychedelics, I began to spot a place that their theories about the social fabrication of reality did not reach— namely, I noticed how their celebrity repeated the white male heroics of a patriarchal society, crowded out the participation of people at marginalized intersections of identity, and ultimately, showed that psychedelics may not have unstitched the social fabric to the full extent they thought was possible.

This is how I came to focus my historian-energy on American psychologist and pioneer of LSD-assisted psychotherapy Betty Eisner (1915–2004).

Betty Eisner.

The subject of my MA thesis, Eisner was a voracious innovator and networker, laser-focused on developing psychedelic psychotherapy in repertoire as well as in professional legitimacy.[1] She was piercingly curious and intuitive about the inner workings of the psyche, but also deeply disciplined; for all the methodology and metaphysics she invented, Eisner grounded her practice in the psychoanalytic tradition and knew how to present her discoveries to tweeded-out men in mahogany rooms. She helped codify the basics of the clinical psychedelic toolbox, enhancing and theorizing the "set and setting," such as the use of music, art, and mirrors.[2] She participated in landmark conferences and took an active role in building professional cohesion among an international group of psychiatrists and psychologists who worked with LSD.

When psychedelics were banned, Eisner continued to work on cutting edge psychology, including transpersonal psychotherapy, group therapy, and the formation of intentional communities based on psychotherapeutic principles. It's hard to read Eisner's biography and not be struck by the life force she poured into the psychedelic revolution and its spillover into the psychotherapeutic counterculture. Or, to say it another way, Betty Eisner was every bit as deserving of glorification as the 1960s' all-male cast of psychedelic deities, and I expected that promoting her story could help start to rectify the identity-based exclusions that haunted the history of psychedelics.

But there was a hitch. In 1976, a client died in her care, and the circumstances of his death revealed an alternate story about her that was difficult for me to reconcile with the psychedelic champion she had become in my mind. Eisner does not discuss this tragic event in her memoir—her clinical career simply ends in June 1978 after a fruitful decade exploring Ritalin, ketamine, and bodywork as legal alternatives to LSD. Buried in the legal files from her hearings with the Board of Medical Quality Assurance of California, I learned that Eisner's client died after experiencing an extreme physical response to a session that involved Ritalin, bodywork, and "blasting" (a technique for releasing emotions through screaming, related to primal scream therapy) while taking a mineral bath.

According to Eisner's testimony, the client had been uncooperative throughout the session (perhaps even suicidal), but at a certain point his energy level dropped, and she and her assistant helped him out of the tub and into a bed. As people began to arrive for that evening's group therapy session, the client's condition became worse, and Eisner coordinated the group in calling an ambulance and assisting the client. When the medics arrived, they could not resuscitate him. But as they took him away, Eisner and her therapy group were hopeful that he would nonetheless recover to full health.

An occupational hazard? It didn't look that way to me. As I read through her client testimonies, I learned that everything Betty Eisner described as cutting-edge care was enveloped in boundary transgressions, medical recklessness, and warped client-therapist power dynamics. In that particular session, clients alleged that Eisner was afraid of calling the paramedics and handling the investigation that would follow, going as far as instructing clients to perform CPR while she thought of a cover story for the police. Before getting to that point, she led the group through chants and energy medicine, which they did despite their insistence on calling for help, because to do otherwise would be to act "out of authority" (paramedics corroborated this, reporting that they walked in to a scene of "15 to 20 people ranging in age from their late teens to late 50s, standing around the victim holding hands [in what appeared] to be some type of occult ritual").

Examining these testimonies, it became clear that Eisner had cultivated a group dynamic that centered her as an absolute authority and, according to one client, rendered disobedience to her as "heresy." This dynamic was years in the making. Her group clients lived together in homes she managed, and she used relocation and eviction as leverage over them. She barred them from seeing medical doctors, instead insisting that their health problems were psychogenic and would best be treated by her. This was especially dire when clients experienced therapy-related injuries such as broken ribs as a result of heavy-handed bodywork under ketamine anesthesia or unconsciousness as a result of an asphyxiation-based "treatment" Eisner called "containment." She also established power hierarchies among clients themselves, in one case ordering members of one of her client group homes to restrain one of its residents to a bed for days, restricting the resident's meals and bathroom visits. Clients complied because their dissent would undo years of therapy—or at least that's what Eisner told them.

This dark episode in Eisner's career reframed my impressions of her as a feminist activist, or a pioneering figure in psychology. It drew my attention toward the social systems into which Eisner was embedded. More than her personal achievements, I became curious about how Eisner's professional communities in psychology and psychotherapy would respond to her situation, and how these responses reflected expectations about gender and the politics of psychotherapy of the time. Paying attention to her surrounding context taught me an important lesson about the nuance of feminist history. Beyond recovering the stories of marginalized individuals, a feminist approach to history can help undo the mode of historical storytelling that centers the ingenuity of individuals in the first place, instead shifting emphasis onto their social embeddedness.

My supervisor, Alexandra Rutherford, recently sent me a short piece by science fiction writer Ursula K. Le Guin called "The Carrier Bag Theory of Fiction." In it, Le Guin makes the point that a hero's story rarely makes room for all the details of life in which the hero is embedded, but in reality, the hero's background is full of understated activity that makes their story possible. Le Guin also continually refers to the hero with the pronoun "he," because in our history as in our present, social conditions make it most likely that it will be a cis man who makes big gestures from visible places. What if instead, the context itself was "the hero"? To Le Guin, this would look like less cycling between triumph and tragedy, and more attending to the richness and subtlety of the worlds that carried the lives of folks like Betty Eisner.

This last thought is especially important for reclaiming Eisner's place in the history of psychedelics. She made lasting contributions and deserves credit as an innovator, networker, and agent of cultural change. But more interestingly, the shape of her successes, adversities, and mishaps reflect a world that was poised to respond to her with particular assumptions about gender and who has the right to challenge authority. Eisner's story is complex, and to make sense of her life, we need to pay attention to the social context in which she was embedded: What does her navigation of professional spaces reveal about how the disciplines of psychology and psychiatry were gendered, and how were psychedelics therefore gendered? What do her interactions with professional authorities reveal about conventional attitudes toward psychedelics, and how were these attitudes laden with power? And what does her inventive thinking as a therapist reveal about changes to notions of selfhood and well-being in the countercultural era, and what did women have to contend with while working at the crux of such profound change?

Contextualizing Eisner within these structural power dynamics encourages us to think beyond her personal triumphs and tragedies, to challenge the common notion that psychedelics were championed into existence by scientific renegades, and to instead explore how psychedelics were constructed in dialogue with an array of social norms. This is particularly crucial for the history of psychedelics, as these substances are often suggested to help us look behind the veil of society and to expose the tyranny of hegemony. While there is truth to that, a contextual look at Eisner's life shows that psychedelics are also socially constituted, shaped by people and institutions to satisfy their own complex intentions. So yes, Betty Eisner deserves to be remembered alongside other psychedelic pioneers for her ingenious shaping of clinical practice to meet the therapeutic potential of psychedelics—but also to show the ways that psychedelics themselves were shaped by the people and societies with which they coexisted.

Lauretta Bender: Seminal Psychiatrist and Forgotten Psychedelic Pioneer

CHRIS ELCOCK

AS HISTORIANS GRADUALLY SHED MORE LIGHT ON WOMEN'S PERSPECTIVES in the rich history of psychedelics, we are slowly beginning to see the under-appreciated role women played in the rise of psychedelic science in the postwar era. Unsurprisingly, very few women were official members of the research teams (nevermind team leaders) in major hospitals and universities, and they were almost never credited for the thousands of scientific publications that resulted from research into LSD and other psychedelics. The cultural climate of the time, which confined women to the sphere of domesticity and gendered stereotypes, was largely responsible for this imbalance.

Notwithstanding Betty Eisner, whose work has finally been chronicled and placed alongside the research of Sidney Cohen and Timothy Leary,[1]

Lauretta Bender, 1951, New York University. School of Medicine. US National Library of Medicine Digital Collection

a notable and virtually undocumented exception to this trend is Lauretta Bender. Her story is fascinating not just because she is yet another woman whose psychedelic legacy has been obscured by other narratives, but because it reveals a series of triumphs against adversity that led to her rise as a maverick and highly regarded psychiatrist.

Bender's childhood suggested anything but a fantastic career in medicine. Born in 1897 in Butte, Montana, she experienced serious difficulties at school to the point where she repeated first grade three times. Her teachers concluded that she was mentally deficient, but it turned out that she was merely, if acutely, dyslexic. Fortunately, her father recognized that she was an extremely bright child with learning difficulties who needed empathetic support instead of punishment. His strong faith in his daughter was well justified and years later Bender underscored how critical this intervention was: "Had my father not been superintendent of public instruction during my grammar school years, I doubt that I would ever have graduated."

Bender showed how wrong her instructors had been by going on to study medicine at the University of Chicago and receiving her MD at the University of Iowa in 1926, at a time "when it was rare for women to be physicians." Subsequently she remained keenly interested in the study of reading and writing disorders and arguably her greatest legacy is the Bender-Gestalt Test (also known as the Visual Motor Gestalt Test), a widely used tool she developed to diagnose learning difficulties among children. Her approach to the issue was radically innovative, as noted by psychologist Rosa Hagin: "At a time when learning problems were frequently dismissed as minor symptoms of emotional disturbance, she placed them in a neurodevelopmental context, devised examination methods that have won universal acceptance, and recognized and valued the contribution that teaching made in remediation."[2]

Between 1929 and 1930, Bender conducted research into schizophrenia at Johns Hopkins by studying 90 women diagnosed as such. Many of the subjects were mute and Bender developed nonverbal ways of communication that she continued to use in her subsequent work. Moreover, she became a well-respected authority on the study of autism, even though her legacy has been obscured by Leo Kanner's 1943 paper,[3] which is often referred to as the seminal article that turned autism into an identifiable clinical syndrome. In fact, Kanner and other experts in the field frequently looked to her expertise on the matter, and it was Bender who first called childhood schizophrenia (which was often the name given to autism back then) a pathology of the central nervous system.

In 1930, Bender began working at Bellevue Hospital in New York City and a few years later she became the first director of the children's inpatient ward. A guiding principle to her supervision was the maximization of child welfare and the creation of a supportive learning environment for them. Teachers were recruited as part of the medical team and implemented in-hospital tutoring services for children with language issues. Such provisions are nowadays taken for granted, but by the standards of the time they were groundbreaking.

During her time at Bellevue, she used amphetamines to treat children suffering from hyperkinesia and other forms of mental illness. She had posited that the illness stemmed not from increased motor activity or physical energy but rather from a problem of perceptual disorganization, including self-image concepts. In the 1940s, Bender and her team found that amphetamines were effective in the treatment of hyperkinesia as well as narcolepsy and sexual problems among children under the age of 13.

Bender's stellar career and pioneering accomplishments have granted her a special place in the history of psychiatry, as illustrated by some of her peers' superlative praise in *The Women of Psychology* (1982), published a few years before her death in 1987: "Lauretta Bender undoubtedly has been the preeminent woman psychiatrist of the second half of the twentieth century. There is some justification for naming her the preeminent living psychiatrist in the world, period." What is less known about Bender, and that further illustrates the incredible breadth of her contribution to psychiatry, is her research into psychopharmacology and in the use of psychedelics to treat mental illness.

In 1956, she was appointed Director of Research of the newly created children's unit at Creedmoor State Hospital in Queens in 1956. Five years later she was among the few physicians to begin treating children with mental illness by giving them psychedelics. Around that time, she discovered LSD, and as someone subject to migraines, she used the drug to treat her condition and "found it a very effective preventive."

Initially, Bender and her colleagues struggled to win approval of the New York State Commissioner of the Department of Mental Hygiene, Paul

Hoch. Hoch balked at the prospect of provoking a temporary psychotic episode, which was the prevailing theory of what the psychedelics were doing, as a method of therapy, until Bender, citing prior work, convinced him that by inhibiting serotonin, LSD would increase responsiveness to sensory stimulation along with skeletal and muscle activity.

Bender's team started with low doses of 25 μg (micrograms)[4] on mute children and children diagnosed with autism and schizophrenia between 5 and 11 years of age. They found that the majority of them were subsequently able to interact with the medical staff and engage in motor play, which was accompanied by improvements in well-being and elevated mood. They gradually increased the dosage until they reached 150 μg per day and noted "an improvement in their general well-being, general tone, habit patterning, eating patterns and sleeping patterns" within the autistic population, while some children improved their vocalization. The boys diagnosed with schizophrenia (without autism) "became more insightful, more objective, more realistic" even though they soon became depressed because they realized that they were in a hospital cut away from their families.

Bender and her colleagues came to similar "normalizing" results using psilocybin and the more obscure methysergide, better-known as UML-491 and marketed by Sandoz Pharmaceuticals as *Sansert*, for the treatment of migraines. By 1965, however, there were mounting controversies surrounding psychedelic drugs, and Sandoz, the patent holder of LSD, ceased its distribution to protect its brand image. Bender's team did not turn to the National Institute for Mental Health for supplies because by then there were (unfounded) rumors linking LSD with irreversible chromosome damage.[5] Three years later, her last known involvement with psychedelic science was to publish a paper that did not corroborate those reports, after closely examining their 89 child subjects.

According to parapsychologist Stanley Krippner, Bender purposefully withdrew from the debates surrounding LSD in order to protect herself and preserve her reputation as a medical doctor, even though in private she was very enthusiastic about psychedelics—tellingly, she had read Huxley's *The Doors of Perception* (1954) and was using the word psychedelic by 1966. In this respect, it is worth noting that in spite of the 1970 federal prohibition of these drugs, she managed to have her New York State license to acquire and administer psychedelics renewed in 1971.

What Lauretta Bender did with that license is a matter of speculation, but in any event, further, in-depth historical research may be warranted to answer this question and shed more light on Bender's role in pioneering the treatment of children's autism with psychedelics, at a time when anecdotal evidence suggests that she undertook significant psychedelic research in the 1960s.

The Wonderful and Absurd Adventures of Rosemary Woodruff Leary: Fashion Icon, Fugitive, and Psychedelic Pioneer (Part One)

JAMES PENNER

WHEN ROSEMARY WOODRUFF LEARY DIED OF CONGESTIVE HEART FAILURE in 2002 in Santa Cruz, she left behind photographs from her years in exile, rejection letters from various publishers, journals, newspaper clippings, court papers from various trials, and a notebook with 57 prison love letters from Timothy Leary. Her collection of fake IDs and forged passports had been destroyed many years prior. Of all the memorabilia, the most important document[1] was her unfinished memoir, *The Magician's Daughter.*

Rosemary had spent some three decades writing this manuscript by "kerosene and candlelight in Asian hotels, unheated European farmhouses, and South American jungle hut[s]." This manuscript documents her countercultural odyssey through the 1960s and '70s and features a candid and often unvarnished account of her tumultuous marriage with ex-Harvard professor Leary. Although they were together for only six years (from the spring of 1965 to the fall of 1971), during those six years and after, Rosemary lived a life that seems unreal to readers today: there were three weddings to Leary (at Joshua Tree, at Berkeley by a Hindu priest, and a final one at Millbrook); Off-Broadway theatre productions; drug busts in Laredo Texas, Millbrook, and Laguna Beach; public trials and incarceration on several occasions; and an epic jailbreak from the California Men's Colony, followed by a descent into the revolutionary underground that would take her to France, Algeria, Switzerland, Afghanistan, Canada, Colombia, Costa Rica, multiple Caribbean islands, and finally Cape Cod where she hid in broad daylight as "Sarah Woodruff" the innkeeper.

Although Rosemary lived one of the most unfathomable lives of the 20th century, when she passed away in 2002, it looked like the memoir that documented her extraordinary life would never be published. Fortunately,

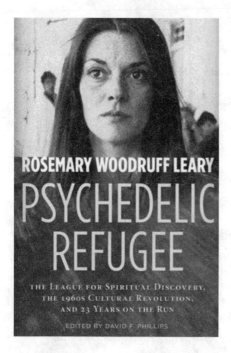

Psychedelic Refugee is the retitled memoir of Rosemary Woodruff Leary, compiled and edited by the late David E. Phillips.

due to the tireless efforts of her close friend and editor, David E. Phillips, we finally have Rosemary's account of her own life in her own words.

For nearly a decade, Phillips, an attorney and librarian by training, managed to resuscitate her manuscript by assembling the incomplete chapters and by locating fragments and a detailed unpublished interview with Rosemary that was conducted in 1997. Phillips's restored version of *The Magician's Daughter* was retitled *Psychedelic Refugee* when it was published by Park Street Press, a Vermont-based publishing house that specializes in titles that chronicle psychedelic history. Regretfully, Phillips did not live long enough to hold the published copy of *Psychedelic Refugee*[2] in his hands. He passed away in March of 2020, and the book was published in March of 2021.

When we look at the images from the newsreels of the 1960s and early '70s, Tim and Rosemary appear to have lived a charmed life of romance, rebellion,[3] LSD trips, and political activism. But another narrative lurks behind the images that appeared in the press. The book explores the highs and lows of Tim and Rosemary's fraught relationship and a different perspective of certain key moments in psychedelic history. The posthumous publication of *Psychedelic Refugee* allows Rosemary to emerge from the

Timothy Leary and Rosemary Woodruff Leary at a Press Conference (circa 1969).

shadow of her famous husband. In the larger narrative of Rosemary's life, psychedelics function as her rite of passage: they changed her life forever and ushered her down a path that she never could have anticipated. Rosemary likely never intended to be a soldier in the struggle against the War on Drugs; however, before she realized, she found herself in the trenches of the conflict. *Psychedelic Refugee* is a record of not only her experiences, but a life lived in extremis.

At the beginning of her memoir, Rosemary writes, "I have regained my freedom and now can tell my story." The truth is that Rosemary was never able to fully write her story because the fear of self-incrimination hung over her head like a Damoclean sword. Although she was "legally" free to write her story, she was forever burdened by the weight of the past. Rosemary was determined to protect the people who helped her when she "aided and abetted" Leary's escape from prison in 1970, and who sheltered her during two decades of exile. That said, *Psychedelic Refugee* is her Sisyphean effort to reclaim her story. Although some episodes (e.g., Tim's jailbreak) have been omitted, she left behind a powerful and moving narrative that gripped me each time I read it. In my case, the incompleteness of the tale—what some might call the lack of closure—presented a historical challenge: I had to fill in the omissions, and also figure out why these episodes had been elided in the first place.

Stylistically speaking, LSD plays a central role in the narrative of *Psychedelic Refugee*; it influences the author's prose style and stream of consciousness narration. For Rosemary, the past is viewed as a series of powerful and magical images that resemble the lived experience of an LSD trip—surreal, humorous, unpredictable, and often absurd. The earliest images are from her childhood. Rosemary's story begins in a middle-class home in St. Louis in the 1950s, where she was a precocious child who enjoyed reading and performing in plays while in high school. She dreamt of leaving St. Louis and ended up engaged at 17 when Brad, an air force officer, presented her with a beautiful diamond ring.

After a wedding and a honeymoon in Las Vegas, Rosemary moved to an isolated air force base in the Pacific Northwest. Rosemary's new life was disappointing to say the least: "I was uncomfortable with the major's wife and officers' club dinners. Unwilling to learn bridge or patience. Beaten when I answered back, swore, or got angry." Much like Stella in Tennessee Williams's *A Streetcar Named Desire*, Rosemary endured domestic violence when she was pregnant. Many women in the 1950s were forced to "suck it up" and accept an abusive marriage because there didn't seem to be any way out. However, Rosemary would not. One day when Brad was at work, Rosemary packed her clothes and caught a train bound for St. Louis. Brad returned to an empty house and found Rosemary's discarded wedding ring in the sugar bowl.

The experience of a failed marriage pushed Rosemary in exciting new directions. She adopted the life of a seeker and the idea that life can be an adventure. After moving to New York City, she quickly immersed herself in the burgeoning jazz scene of the late 1950s and reinvented herself as an interior decorator, model, and a "beatnik stewardess" who enjoyed hosting flights to Havana and San Juan. In 1965, two events altered her life forever: she began experimenting with LSD in January and met Timothy Leary at an art gallery in New York City a few months later. Rosemary had taken LSD earlier in the day and she was transfixed by Leary's lecture on psychedelic art and the "audio-olfactory-visual alterations of consciousness." After the lecture, Rosemary and Leary went for a drink and the psychologist invited Rosemary to Millbrook, the enormous mansion in upstate New York where Leary lived with his associates and followers. Although Rosemary was enamored with Leary, she declined his invitation to Millbrook because she was then living with a jazz musician. A few months later, Rosemary met Leary a second time, and this time she accepted his invitation.

Although Rosemary and Leary slept separately during her first night at Millbrook, she remembers feeling the professor's presence as she slept: "I felt him through the night, footsteps pounding the maze of corridors, bare feet in the final rounds." For Rosemary, "[Leary] was exhilarating, like the first draft of pure oxygen after a trip in the dentist's chair," continuing "he perceived the world with the knowledge that [his training] in psychology gave him the unfettered imagination of an Irish hero, a combination that produced a fey charisma, a likeable madness, and an outrageous optimism . . . the magic of loving and being loved by such a man would keep me enthralled for many years. I could not imagine loving anyone else. Everyone was boring compared to him."

Rosemary's romance had several phases. First, there was the honeymoon period that lasted five months, followed by what could be described as the police harassment phase. As Leary became a popular public figure in the media, the federal government identified him as a "threat." There were three confrontations with law enforcement ultimately resulting in Leary's imprisonment in 1970.

The first confrontation occurred when Leary, Rosemary, and Tim's two children, Jack and Susan, were driving to Mexico. After mysteriously being turned away from the Mexican border, they were busted at the American border in Laredo, Texas. The incident put Leary back in the headlines and his legal case became a cause célèbre. Before Laredo, Rosemary had no criminal record. Afterward, she too became a target of police surveillance and harassment.

When Leary and Rosemary returned to Millbrook in the winter of 1966, they were subjected to the infamous Millbrook raid orchestrated by G. Gordon Liddy, a Dutchess County prosecutor who was "cracking down" on drugs. Rosemary testified before a grand jury where she pled the Fifth Amendment (the right to not bear witness against oneself in a criminal trial) in order to not incriminate Leary and her Millbrook friends, but the judge rejected her request for immunity and she was charged with contempt of court. Rosemary served a month in jail before the charges were finally dropped because Liddy had an invalid search warrant. The full account of Rosemary's trial and her decision not to testify are dramatized in *Psychedelic Refugee*. It was the first public trial in the US that examined if LSD, as a religious sacrament, could be protected by the First Amendment. The Millbrook trial was another moment in the memoir when Rosemary stuck to her principles and refused to be bullied by the judge and the prosecution.

The third and final confrontation occurred when Leary drove to a Laguna Beach suburb in 1969. He was busted for having two roaches of cannabis in his station wagon ashtray, and the Orange County judge, determined to make an example out of the counterculture icon, doled out a hefty 10-year sentence. Ben Connally, a US District Judge in Texas added another 10 years to his sentence for the earlier Laredo bust in 1965. Leary now faced a 20-year sentence for possessing a small amount of cannabis on two occasions.

The third trial is a turning point in *Psychedelic Refugee* because Rosemary faced a key dilemma: should she let her husband remain in prison for a decade, or should she attempt to organize his escape? Rosemary and Tim's experiences with psychedelics led them to be bold and write their own "movie": the script they devised could be described as a psychedelic version of *Bonnie and Clyde*, albeit a version where the hero and heroine do not die in a hail of bullets. Would their grandiose escape plan actually work?

The Wonderful and Absurd Life of Rosemary Woodruff Leary: Fashion Icon, Fugitive, and Psychedelic Pioneer (Part Two: Freedom and Unfreedom)

JAMES PENNER

HER DECISION TO PARTICIPATE IN A JAILBREAK WAS ARGUABLY THE BIG-gest of Rosemary's life. No matter what the outcome, there would be severe repercussions that would affect the rest of her life. If the plot failed, Tim would probably be moved to Folsom or San Quentin where he would remain for many years and the prison authorities would probably uncover her participation in the plot. If the jailbreak succeeded, Rosemary would be deemed a high-profile criminal for "aiding and abetting" his escape. She would be aggressively pursued by the FBI and the Bureau of Narcotics and Dangerous Drugs (BNDD). Rosemary was on parole from previous charges, so her participation was very risky to say the least. Despite the serious consequences, Rosemary embraced the plot even though she was not convinced that it would succeed.

Psychedelic Refugee emphasizes that Rosemary's optimism seemed to stem from her experiences with psychedelics. It is hard to explain or quantify, but experimenting with psychedelics makes certain people bolder than they normally would be. Through her experiments with altering her consciousness, Rosemary had learned to embrace a state of fearlessness. The jailbreak plot was yet another test of her will power and inner strength.

Rosemary was a key player in the escape plot. She raised $20,000 from the Brotherhood of Eternal Love, an entity that was often generous with whatever financial resources they possessed. Rosemary also acted as a go-between with the Weather Underground who provided a getaway car, false identifications, and several safehouses in San Francisco and Washington State. The plot itself contained multiple risks. The 49-year-old ex-psychology professor who smoked too much would have to climb a large tree and then scutter across a roof of two cell blocks to reach a telephone cable that he would have to grab with hand-ball gloves and carefully wrap his ankles around; once all of his weight was resting on the telephone cable, he would then have to inch along it like a caterpillar until he reached the other side of the 12-foot barbed-wire fence. If at any point he fell from the telephone wire, he would certainly break many bones and probably be Folsom-bound for the rest of his life. He would definitely lose his right to remain at California Men's Colony in San Luis Obispo, the most "humane" prison in the state.

When the night of the jailbreak finally arrived, Leary did one last tarot card reading—we are not sure what the cards suggested—and then some yoga in the prison yard. As he settles his pose, the psychology professor focuses on the telephone pole and the telephone cable that he can see in the distance. He then visualizes himself crossing to the other side of the barbed-wire fence. Later that night he would successfully execute this escape plan and be whisked away to Washington State where he would finally be reunited with Rosemary.

Breaking Tim out of prison was certainly a bold gesture, but ironically it resulted in a state of unfreedom because both constantly worried about being apprehended by the FBI and the BNDD. Tim and Rosemary altered their appearances in order to escape detection. Leary became "William J. McNellis," a midwestern businessman and Rosemary became "Margaret Ann McCreedy."

Their altered identities replaced the alteration of consciousness. However, Rosemary's quest for autonomy extended into her personal life. In exile, Rosemary became increasingly depressed and alienated; it was difficult to live out a suitcase, and the mounting pressure of increased surveillance weighed on her psyche and on her marriage. When the FBI, the BNDD, and the Nixon administration made Tim and Rosemary prime targets for capture, Rosemary struggled to maintain her sanity.

The post-jailbreak section of *Psychedelic Refugee* (1971 to the 1980s) focuses on Rosemary's quest for inner peace and personal autonomy. As Rosemary is pulled further and further into Leary's orbit, she found herself slowly losing her sense of individuality.

The theme of losing her sense of self had been observed during earlier parts of her memoir. As early as 1966, Rosemary had also witnessed Tim's curious response to the Millbrook bust: "Tim was released on bail later in the day. Unscathed, good-humored, and unworried, he seemed almost to enjoy this new confrontation with the law. It was as if he thrived on the response of the press, the need for more lawyers and funds, the threat of trial and prison, the invitation to climb onto the cross, the myth of the tragic hero: a sweet dream of oppression. It was his movie."

Rosemary's marriage to Leary gave her an intimate view of her husband's fondness for self-mythologizing and the fact that he never met a microphone that he didn't fall in love with. Although Tim seemed to relish playing archetypal roles for the counterculture—wise man, high priest, and anti-establishment rebel—Rosemary, while in exile, longs for a peaceful life where she and Tim can write books and escape from the sycophants and the publicity machine that Tim cannot resist.

By the spring of 1971, Rosemary begins to seriously consider breaking away from Tim. At first, she sought a separation, but it became a permanent rupture. Rosemary's account of their relationship in *Psychedelic Refugee* offers a more nuanced view of their marital politics. Rosemary was determined not to be a passive victim. Although she feared that she would be demonized by some in the counterculture for leaving her husband, she proceeded anyway.

"Wandering and Return," the final chapter, is perhaps the most fascinating of all; it covers Rosemary's odyssey in the underground of the 1970s and her Homeric return to the United States in 1976. The narrative of this chapter is based on an interview she gave to Robert Greenfield in 1997. Rosemary spoke openly about her experiences in exile and was less concerned about incriminating herself and others. Here she mentions John Schewel, her handsome lover and companion in exile, for the first time. Rosemary describes how John successfully ushered her into the underground when she left Timothy in the fall of 1971. For two decades, John and Rosemary traveled the globe, living in Canada, Afghanistan, Sicily, Colombia, and Costa Rica, completely under the radar of federal US authorities.

Rosemary and John eventually reentered the US by posing as water skiers on a cigarette boat that safely came ashore in Fort Lauderdale, Florida. The couple eventually decided to settle in Provincetown, Massachusetts, which turned out to be a safe haven for Rosemary for nearly two decades. Although she enjoyed living on the edge of Cape Cod, she reminds the reader that she

Rosemary Woodruff Leary lived underground in Provincetown, Massachusetts, for nearly two decades. She rode her bicycle because she didn't want to get a driver's license with a false name (a federal crime). Courtesy of Gary Woodruff

always slept with her suitcase packed and her tennis shoes next to her bed. When she and John go their separate ways in the 1980s, she embraces her newfound independence: "I learned how to be myself and how to live without a man, how to cook for myself, and how to be alone."

Psychedelic Refugee symbolically ends with Rosemary's reunion with Tim some 20 years after their breakup in Switzerland. At this point, Rosemary was living underground and Tim was single after Barbara Chase, his fifth wife, had left him a few weeks earlier. Rosemary describes meeting at the Asian Art Museum in Golden Gate Park in December 1992: "Both of us were so physically altered as to be unrecognizable as who we had once been. But as always when we got together after an escape or when he had gotten out of jail, it was a movie. In Vista Vision and Technicolor. Wide Screen. Tim was so good at creating drama and he so loved to play and he was brilliant at it." Tim even had ace up his sleeve: "He asked me to marry him [and] I said no. And he said, 'Well then, I will have to cross you off my list.'"

After reading *Psychedelic Refugee*, I get the impression that there are many versions of Rosemary Woodruff Leary that circulate in the public imagination. For some, she was the svelte and beautiful wife of Timothy Leary who often appeared at his side during interviews for the press; for others, she is a fashion icon whose influence was recently lauded in *Vogue* magazine.[1] For the psychedelic community and the counterculture, she is a heroic figure in the War on Drugs who stuck to her principles and steadfastly refused to name names to federal authorities. Each of these versions of Rosemary are accurate, but for me what stuck out the most in *Psychedelic Refugee* was the author's robust sense of humor and her generosity of spirit in the face of adversity. After all, she had every right to be upset about the enormous sacrifices that she had to make during the last three decades of her life. Who would have thought that the vibrant and fun-loving narrator—a person who clearly loved life and being in the company of others— would end up living a solitary and Kafkaesque life in the underground for 23 years? Although Rosemary frequently found herself in precarious and absurd situations during her last three decades, *Psychedelic Refugee* is not the memoir of a bitter and angry person. Instead, it features the voice of a magnanimous heroine who lived long enough to tell her story.

Jane Osmond: The Wonder of Weyburn

ERIKA DYCK

STABLE. CLEVER. LOVING. CREATIVE. SUPPORTIVE. ELEGANT. STRONG. Caring. Intolerant of extreme weather.

These are some of the ways that Fee (Euphemia) and Julian Osmond described their mother, Jane, wife of Humphry Osmond. Jane was a nurse and a widow when she met Humphry during World War II at a hospital where he was working as a psychiatrist. Within a few years they married, and had a daughter, Helen. In less than two years after Helen was born, Humphry was offered a job in Weyburn, Saskatchewan, Canada—far from the picturesque south shores of England where the two had grown up.

Jane Osmond, circa 1950s.

A NEW HOME ON THE WIND-SWEPT SASKATCHEWAN PRAIRIE

The Osmonds moved to Canada in 1951. On the Canadian prairies, Humphry Osmond soon became the superintendent of the provincial mental hospital, described as the largest asylum in the British Commonwealth. It was here that he focused on research into hallucinations that led him to famously coin the word "psychedelic," and where Jane had her own mescaline experience. While Humphry launched into a career studying psychedelics, Jane kept her own experience more private. Over the next decade Humphry encountered a colorful cast of researchers, politicians, and scientists eager to engage in psychedelic explorations. Jane meanwhile felt stuck in a windy, cold, even desolate agricultural community, starved of cosmopolitan features.

As Humphry's career soared, Jane nonetheless provided consistent support. An excellent typist, a consummate host, a sophisticated source of intellect, and a devoted reader herself, Jane had typed up Osmond's now-pioneering studies in schizophrenia: "John Smythies and I were pushing poor Jane on the last draft of 'Schizophrenia: A New Approach' as she was doing the last bit of our packing" as they prepared to move to Canada, Humphry recalled. She brought stability to the home and support to Humphry's budding ambitions to explore psychedelics. Helen's childhood in Weyburn was an important focal point.

Humphry described one such tender moment in a letter on April 23, 1954: "Here we are bereft on the prairie. Snow still on the ground and our little Helen far away in England, having left us about 42 hours ago. I have two parting pictures in my mind's eye. An indomitable little figure dashing up the gangway to the plane determined that she and my sister should have a seat and disappearing into the flank of the silver brute. Then a little face pressed against the plane's port with a Teddy Bear clutched close and waving the other hand briskly. Then the huge plane roared into the night leaving Jane and me weeping bitterly."

ESCAPE THROUGH TRAVEL

Sometimes Jane accompanied Humphry on trips to New York, Los Angeles, and, of course, home to England. For Humphry Osmond, the "megapolis" of New York City was a bit intimidating, but Jane relished these opportunities to soak up the urban culture, replenish their library, and shop. Humphry sought advice from their good friend Aldous Huxley about frugal accommodations, leaving "enough money for visits to bargain basements which Jane is keen to see." For Jane, thrift shopping brought its own hidden rewards. On one trip to New York City, Jane returned to Weyburn with a golden coat, and later sewed herself a dress to match. Humphry remarked to Aldous that Jane and her elegant new coat would be the talk of Weyburn. Her son later recalled that people commented on her beauty, likening her to Katherine Hepburn and Deborah Kerr.

But shopping was merely a brief bit of entertainment. Jane accompanied Humphry to lectures and met with people who were curious about the psychedelic research world. Jane was there when Bill Wilson spent hours with them inquiring about LSD. She became friends with Matthew Huxley (Aldous and Maria's son) and his wife Ellen as they embarked on their own psychedelic experimentation under the Osmonds' watchful eyes. Jane and Helen had their own adventures with Al and Rita Hubbard when they escaped Saskatchewan for visits to an island in British Columbia. Humphry Osmond records that Al had given mescaline to Jane; unfortunately, nothing further is said about Jane's experience.

COMMUNITY ENGAGEMENT

While Jane may have relished these brief escapes from the wind-swept prairies, local women in Weyburn remember coveting her influence in their community. Friends and nurses at the Provincial Mental Hospital recalled Jane's generosity and erudition. She hosted teas and dinners, inviting staff and families from the hospital who were permitted a glimpse into their lives and a sample of their record collection. For some of these invitees, Jane was a model of elegance and culture and they looked forward to these dinner parties. She befriended Amy Izumi, wife of architect Kiyoshi Izumi who recommended redesigning hospital spaces after experiencing LSD. In 1959 Jane gave birth to Euphemia (Fee). Amy Izumi was named one of her godmothers. Jane later gifted her maternity clothes to one of the wives of a local psychologist, who recalled treasuring these clothes—the most beautiful and stylish maternity wear in the region.

The Osmond household must have been quite the standout in the small community; undisputed master of the domestic sphere, Humphry often notes Jane's various home beautification projects, often carried out when he was away. When he was home, her concerns may have been drawn elsewhere. Humphry was an adventurous "kitchen chemist" and on at least one occasion he felt close to death after consuming a homemade concoction. Writing to Aldous after the fact he notes: "I very prudently did not call Jane (this was from midnight to 04:30) because I feared anxious colleagues might give me morphine or something and kill me . . . I only dared tell Jane the other night!"

"TOO GOOD A CAREGIVER"

Jane seems to have made friends easily and made caring seem natural. Her nursing training combined with her sense of duty made Jane a constant source of strength for those around her. When Maria Huxley[1] succumbed to a cancer diagnosis, Humphry wrote to Aldous suggesting that Jane could come to help Maria. This pattern of caring for others, perhaps at times at her own expense, seems to be lifelong; both Fee and Julian remember her often taking responsibility for the well-being of those around her.

As Aldous's first wife Maria's health rapidly declined in early 1955, Humphry Osmond writes: "I am naturally very sad to hear that Maria is not well. Jane and I have discussed the matter and if you would be agreeable she would be glad to come down to look after Maria until it is clear how things are going. Jane has done a great deal of nursing. It might be nicer for Maria than having someone to whom she would have to adjust. I would be glad to know that Maria had someone near her whose kindness and competence is proven . . . we love you both very much."

Before Jane and Helen could come to California, Maria's conditioned worsened and she had her last psychedelic experience on her deathbed. Aldous later wrote to Humphry Osmond: "I think you know how deep was her affection for you. She always regretted that she had not had the opportunity of getting to know Jane better."

In 1961, Humphry Osmond left his position in Saskatchewan and the family returned to England where their son, Julian, was born that same year. Jane was once again in south England, surrounded by extended family and more familiar surroundings. But Humphry was not one to sit still, and he was soon invited to a new post in the United States. In 1963 he took the position of director at the Bureau of Research in Neurology and Psychiatry at the Psychiatric Institute in Princeton, New Jersey. With a teenager and two young children, Jane decided to remain in England with a more extensive network of friends and family close by.

For the next 15 years, Jane and Humphry maintained a long-distance relationship at a time when letter writing was the most cost-effective form of communication. Fee and Julian still remember the sound of her typewriter most evenings, as Jane and Humphry wrote to each other daily, and enjoyed biannual visits.

Humphry and Jane had an incredible network of friends who stopped by for visits. During this period Fee and Julian were busy with their studies. Fee, a "day girl," recalls their daily drives to and from school, while Julian attended boarding school, where he recalls his mother writing to him and visiting weekly. Jane and the children continued to host a long list of intrepid travelers and friends who would come by their home, sometimes unannounced. Fee recalls her godmother, Eileen Garrett, driving up their county lane in her Rolls Royce, arriving with glowing red nails and matching lipstick. Julien recalls visiting godmother Garrett at her French villa and being enchanted by the stuffed tomatoes, strawberry tarts, Coke in a bottle, and wonderful visits by the poolside. Sir Julian Huxley visited their home in England, after becoming close with Jane and Humphry. Young Julian Osmond was named after Aldous's brother, Julian, and his visit left an impression on the young boy: "he was very tall and thin" to which Fee helpfully corrects "Aldous—tall & slim. Julian—not so much!" With family friends that included psychic mediums, knighted biologists, and CIA operatives alongside a host of researchers, writers, and politicians, Jane often felt pressured to ready the house for guests and engage in meaningful conversation. Unexpected guests could be a cause for irritation, but Jane would always make guests feel welcome and wanted.

"JANE SENDS LOVE"

But Fee and Julian have fond memories of quieter moments with their mother, who also seemed to relish more simple pleasures: family picnics, long walks, reading, and flying kites on the South Downs. They remember their mother as the very backbone of the family, nourishing the children and sustaining a relationship with Humphry across the Atlantic. Brighton was another favorite spot, and Jane would take the kids on day trips where they would fly kites by the sea. The time spent in far-away Saskatchewan would arise occasionally, and Fee and Julian were aware of "Dad's word"—psychedelic—which might be said on the radio from time to time. Long walks in nature were common; Jane loved the natural beauty of Surrey and especially nearby South Downs, where her ashes were later scattered after her death in 2010.

In 1975, Humphry Osmond left for Tuscaloosa, Alabama, to become the superintendent of the Bryce Hospital, another large psychiatric institution. This time, after more than a decade of letters, phone calls, and holiday visits, Jane, Fee, and Julian boarded a ship and made a journey across the ocean to join Humphry in Alabama. Helen, now an adult, remained in England and followed in her mother's footsteps, taking up nursing. Once more, leaving the rolling hills and ocean breezes behind them, Jane arrived in Tuscaloosa to the blazing heat and stench of a pulp and paper mill. Jane was not impressed with the heat, which seemed to have replaced the frigid cold of the Canadian prairies and the damp of England. By this time, Humphry's work with psychedelics had changed too.

While in Saskatchewan, psychedelic science was in its ascendency, but by the mid-1970s that work was tarnished by claims of it being unethical, risky, or even damaging. Humphry's focus shifted once again back to his patients with schizophrenia, and less on the potential for psychedelics to bring insights or relief in this field. His children recall knowing that "Dad had invented a word," but the specter of psychedelics was very different by the time they entered high school in the mid 1970s, and perhaps like typical teenagers, the comings and goings of their parents were not of particular interest.

Ever the caregiver, Jane resumed her position in the family home after more than a decade of living apart. It seems that both partners had developed their own patterns of coping in the intervening years. Fee and Julian remember Jane reading, sewing, taking long walks, and resuming her work with "Dad" as a sounding board, typist, and listener. She also worked part time at an emporium selling antiques and fine collectables. Humphry had a real appetite for linking people and ideas, and his children remember him sitting in his living room chair, talking to Jane, or quietly reading. They vividly recall him constantly scribbling notes and cutting clippings out of newspapers and magazines to attach to letters to his friends and colleagues, often with a scattering of them at his feet—dad's "memos"—much like the crumbs of toast he'd leave in the kitchen, Jane's perennial bane.

As we enter into another psychedelic moment in history, we are grateful for those clippings, and for the care that Jane took to nurture relationships, record meetings, and nourish a network of thinkers who helped to lay foundations for a psychedelic science. Humphry's letters to Aldous routinely ended with "Jane sends love." Indeed, Jane's support is a reminder to all of us that we should acknowledge the people in our lives who encourage us to promote radical ideas. Fee suggests that, "without her, Dad would not have had the freedom to do all that he did."

With thanks to Fee Blackburn and Julian Osmond for generously sharing their thoughts of their mother with us.

SECTION TWO

Feminism in Action

"A 'Dose' of Radical Christianity": Psychedelic Therapy with Dr. Florence Nichols

ANDREW JONES

WHEN WE THINK OF THE HISTORY OF PSYCHEDELICS IN CANADA,[1] THE work of prominent men such as Abram Hoffer, Ewen Cameron, Humphry Osmond, and "Captain" Al Hubbard comes to mind. Almost unknown is Dr. Florence Nichols, a Canadian psychiatric physician and missionary who, throughout her fascinating career, used LSD to treat mental illness on three different continents.

Florence Nichols circa 1950. Courtesy of the General Synod Archives, Anglican Church of Canada

MEET FLORENCE NICHOLS

Colorful, radiant, electrifying, vigorous. These are words that have been used to describe Florence Nichols. She was known to infect others with her enthusiasm for spirituality and psychiatry. As a psychiatric missionary, Nichols tended to cross boundaries, whether they be gender, national, ethical, or disciplinary.

Seeing herself as the first female psychiatric missionary, Nichols ignored prescribed gender roles and pursued training in a psychiatric context dominated by men. Driven by her passion to help others, she left for India in 1946 to establish a psychiatric unit at the Christian Medical College in the city of Vellore. India had long been a destination for Canadian women missionaries,[2] but Nichols's particular emphasis on psychiatric issues was quite novel. This openness to new places and experiences, and passionate devotion to her spiritual mission, led her to employ a variety of physical and psychological treatments in her psychiatric practice. When LSD came to her attention in the 1950s, Nichols saw it as an effective and efficient tool for helping patients.

FOLLOWING DREAMS TO INDIA

Born in 1913, Nichols had dreamed of becoming a missionary since she was a child. "I never breathed a word about my desire to be a missionary to anyone, not even my Mother or Father," she later said. "It was my private, treasured secret . . . But I knew it was what God wanted me to be." Knowing that her parents did not approve of this path, she quietly pursued medicine while hoping that one day this would allow her to follow her dream. She received her Bachelor of Arts from the University of Toronto in 1934 and her medical degree in 1937. During a surgical internship, Nichols realized that she was more concerned with her patients' mental lives and decided to pursue psychiatry. After earning a Diploma in Psychiatry in 1941, she worked at the Ontario Hospital in Toronto until she finally mustered the courage to apply to the Missionary Society of the Church of England. By 1946, she was on her way to India to help build a new department of psychiatry at the Christian Medical College in Vellore.

Psychiatry was not a priority for physicians in Vellore, and the College lacked infrastructure and funding for mental health treatment. They were

Women medical students carry the jasmine chain on Graduation Day at Christian Medical College, Vellore, 1932. Courtesy of Reena Mary George (CC BY 4.0)

not quite sure what to do with Nichols at first. She spent her initial years in Vellore struggling to learn the local language, Tamil, and familiarizing herself with local customs. To this end, her colleagues suggested that she visit the small village of Mattathur, near Vellore. She spent a happy five weeks living there in a small earthen hut while assisting as a nurse. The Christian Medical College did not have beds dedicated to psychiatric patients, and Nichols used a nurse's pantry as her office. Over time, she carved out a niche for psychiatry at the College and was given more rooms and assistants.

Florence Nichols returned to North America in 1950 to receive further psychiatric training at the University of Philadelphia and to find more funding for the Christian Medical College. In 1955, she traveled back to Vellore, and finally began her goal of setting up a fully developed psychiatric department at the College. As the head of the department, Nichols sought to reduce the stigma surrounding mental illness by showing kindness to patients, while also enhancing treatment options. The department came to offer a wide range of treatments that were common in psychiatry at the time, effectively blurring the lines between biological and psychological approaches to mental illness. Nichols practiced psychological therapies rooted in insight, such as psychoanalysis and family therapy, and employed physical therapies such as electroconvulsive therapy (ECT) and insulin coma therapy. She also used barbiturates to facilitate psychoanalysis.

LSD: A NEW WAY TO HELP PEOPLE

This familiarity with a variety of psychiatric practices put Nichols in a good position to recognize the unique value of psychedelic medicine. Nichols was introduced to LSD through a colleague in the late 1950s. Like many psychiatrists at the time, she took the drug herself. During her first LSD experience, she relived an episode from when she was four months old. Her mother had mistakenly left her out on the porch in the winter, and she was very cold. The story was confirmed by her mother, and Nichols became enthusiastic about the therapeutic potential of this new experimental drug. LSD "makes you relive things almost from birth, and I mean re-live," she later said. After her first experience, Nichols felt that LSD had taught her more about herself in four hours than she had learned in 700 hours of psychoanalytic training. She began to use it to treat certain patients in Vellore.

RELIVING BIRTH IN NOTTINGHAM: FRANK LAKE AND CLINICAL THEOLOGY

Unfortunately, Florence Nichols did not publish about her work with LSD. She had planned to write a long article and even a book about her use of psychedelic therapy, but it seems this plan did not come to fruition. Her approach to LSD therapy, though, would have been heavily influenced by her collaboration with Frank Lake, a British physician who, in the late 1940s, was the superintendent of the Christian Medical College. In turn, she introduced him to her unique combination of Christianity and psychiatry, which incorporated Christianity into her psychiatric practice, based on her conviction that "a firm Christian faith increases ego-strength."

In the early 1950s, Lake returned to England where he pursued psychiatric training, including with Ronald Sandison and his work with LSD at Powick Hospital near Worcester. While using LSD in his practice throughout the 1950s and 1960s, Lake became astonished to find that, as Nichols had experienced, many of his patients reported reliving their birth trauma under LSD. Skeptical at first, he eventually started taking these experiences seriously when details from the reports of patients were later confirmed by mothers and other witnesses. He also learned that other psychiatrists, such as Stanislav Grof, made similar observations with LSD. Certain psychoanalysts, such as Otto Rank, had previously argued that being born constituted a significant trauma for infants that impacted their subsequent personalities. Picking up on this tradition, Lake came to understand LSD's therapeutic value in terms of its ability to reveal how one's birth trauma resulted in particular behavioral patterns.

When Nichols's mother became ill in 1959, she left Vellore to return to Canada. The next year she travelled to England to work with Lake. Together they developed "Clinical Theology," a framework for educating clergy members about mental health. While psychotherapy was becoming more socially acceptable in the 1960s, many people still relied on church leaders to ease their mental distress. Clinical Theology was a response to the growing realization that clergy members were often unequipped to handle more pressing psychological problems. Lake felt that the advice of ministers and the medication of psychiatrists served only to temporarily tranquilize a person's worries, leaving the deeper roots of mental illness intact. The aim of Clinical Theology was to provide the tools to recognize and address these deeper roots. Lake travelled around England giving seminars to members of clergy and he established a Clinical Theology Association in 1962.

In addition to serving as an educational program, Clinical Theology evolved into a complicated mixture of existential philosophy, Christian theology, and psychoanalysis. In 1966, Lake published *Clinical Theology: A Theological and Psychiatric Basis to Clinical Pastoral Care*, which outlined the practical and theoretical dimensions of Clinical Theology. The 1,160-page volume drew on his observations from LSD therapy to articulate the relationship between birth, psychiatric disorders, and Christian faith. Many of these observations came from LSD sessions with clergy members. Recognizing the importance of building a trusting relationship and a comfortable set and setting, Lake started these LSD sessions with prayer and Christian ceremonies.

For Lake, psychiatric therapy was about confronting one's deepest and most painful emotions, and he identified these painful encounters with Christ's crucifixion and resurrection. By "lifting the veil of repression," LSD helped patients experience the roots of these emotions in birth. Lake also noted his own ecstatic LSD experience, in which "'God' in the ground of

[Lake's] being was sheer bliss," but he did not think that LSD caused spiritual experiences. Rather, the drug merely allowed one to relive positive or negative experiences from birth.

A MISSIONARY AT HOME

When Nichols moved back to Canada in the early 1960s, she continued to practice LSD therapy and teach Clinical Theology. In Toronto, she took a position at the Bell Clinic, a private hospital that centered on treating addiction. By early 1963, she had used LSD to treat over 100 patients suffering from alcoholism. According to Nichols, the majority of these patients had obtained sobriety, while others were making progress.

In Canada, Nichols was not shy about promoting LSD to the news media. In 1962, she appeared on a Canadian TV program that documented a woman's experience of LSD therapy at Toronto Western Hospital. "No case is hopeless with LSD," she told a reporter in 1963. "It brings not only awareness but also revelation, insight, reintegration, and a lessening of anxiety." Nichols also used psilocybin in her practice to help patients recover memories from birth and infancy.

In addition to her work at the Bell Clinic, Nichols organized and conducted seminars in Clinical Theology throughout Ontario. Sponsored by the Canadian Mental Health Association, the seminars featured lively reenactments of encounters between pastors and those seeking advice. The goal of these reenactments was to help clergy members recognize specific psychiatric disorders. Apparently, Nichols was a very convincing performer.

By the mid 1960s, negative publicity surrounding LSD use in Canada led the director of the Bell Clinic to end the LSD program. LSD became illegal in Canada in 1968, and Nichols stopped using it in her psychiatric practice. Continuing her missionary work, she traveled to Singapore in 1968 to provide psychiatric training to clergy members. In the mid-1970s, she moved to British Columbia where she treated sex offenders in a maximum-security prison.

Nichols had a creative side too. She wrote engaging memoirs about her experiences in India. In her later years, she wrote a book that examined her life from the perspective of her poodle, Barney. She passed away in 1987.

A CANADIAN PSYCHEDELIC PIONEER

Florence Nichols had an adventurous and productive career as a psychiatrist. She clearly achieved her dream of helping others. But due to her role as a Christian missionary, her story raises complicated ethical questions about situating her desire to help people within the larger context of colonialism. Still, by treating over 100 patients with LSD at the Bell Clinic and by working to publicize LSD's therapeutic benefits, Nichols was an early proponent of psychedelic therapy in Canada. We should therefore remember her name alongside the male Canadian pioneers[3] of psychedelic therapy.

Psychedelic Saskatchewan: Kay Parley

GENEVIÈVE PAIEMENT

To anyone and everyone
who fights the stigma

THIS IS THE SIMPLE, HEARTFELT DEDICATION THAT GREETS READERS OF Kay Parley's remarkable 2016 memoir *Inside the Mental: Silence, Stigma, Psychiatry, and LSD.*[1] The dedication reflects Parley's ethos throughout: the book feels like a beguiling conversation with a compassionate, straight-shooting friend who happens to have a razor-sharp memory and a treasure trove of stories. To say that Kay Parley has lived a remarkable life would be a laughable understatement.

Kay Parley's memoir,
Inside the Mental.

ALL IN THE FAMILY

Born in 1924 and raised on a farm in southeastern Saskatchewan, Canada, Parley grew up having never met her maternal grandfather, who was institutionalized in the nearby Weyburn mental hospital with a diagnosis of paranoia. When she was six, her father, diagnosed with manic-depressive psychosis, was committed to Weyburn too.

A recent graduate of Lorne Greene's Academy of Radio Arts, in 1948 Parley was an aspiring actress and working as a secretary at CBC radio headquarters in Toronto. She was 25. That's when she began to hear voices. The voices would natter on about prophecies or command that she walk across the city and back until her feet bled.

Her symptoms worsened until she had her first full-on breakdown. Her mother flew out, brought her home and delivered her to Weyburn too. It would take until 1972 (and four more breakdowns, which arrived precisely every six years) for her to be diagnosed with manic-depressive psychosis (MDP).

Though it felt like the end of the world, Parley's entrance into "The Mental" (as locals called it) was the beginning of a life-changing journey that saw her transform from a frightened young patient into a psychiatric nurse, teacher, artist, freelance writer, memoirist, and novelist.

KAY PARLEY: FROM PATIENT TO NURSE

Weyburn Mental Hospital sowed the seeds of Kay's rebirth and healing. During her nine-month stay, she started painting again; she met her grandfather for the first time; she reunited with her father; she even edited the hospital newspaper, *The Torch*. After a few years bouncing around various secretarial jobs and between Regina and Toronto (where she had another breakdown), a letter from a friend informed her that a new superintendent had taken over at Weyburn and was making improvements. She was intrigued and felt something pulling her back. The letter felt like a sign. "It began to look as if I was destined to be involved with psychiatry," she writes.

Parley returned to Weyburn in 1956 as a trainee psychiatric nurse, a burgeoning profession at the time, and set out, as she puts it, to "learn something concrete about mental illness, to find a new and worthwhile interest in trying to help those who were sick like me." By then, British psychiatrist Humphry Osmond[2] had overseen the (newly renamed) Saskatchewan Hospital at Weyburn for five years, and radical change was in the air.

Osmond had joined forces with biochemist and psychiatrist Dr. Abram Hoffer (both believed that the cause of mental illness was biochemical, a relatively new theory) and the two were well advanced in their groundbreaking LSD trials aimed at understanding and treating schizophrenia, psychosis, and alcoholism. Osmond is famous for having coined the term "psychedelic," in a letter to his good friend, author, and fellow Englishman Aldous Huxley (by then living in California) in 1956.

Dr. Osmond had introduced Huxley to mescaline three years prior, prompting Huxley to write *The Doors of Perception*. In the journal she kept from this time, Parley writes, "I admire Dr. Osmond so much. He is so bubbly and interesting and kind, and so concerned with treating the mentally ill like deserving human beings."

Into the early '60s Parley became known among her colleagues as an excellent "sitter," tirelessly guiding patients through their all-day LSD therapy sessions with utmost care, dedication, patience, and understanding. In an essay she wrote for the *American Journal of Nursing* in 1964, she explained why she and her colleagues derived so much satisfaction from working these sessions.

"The psychiatric nurse appreciates a situation that provides an opportunity for her to form constructive personal relationships with her patients," Parley wrote. "She likes to be involved in treatments that give her patients the most benefit with the least mental or physical discomfort, and she enjoys seeing results from her work. Anyone who has watched LSD properly used knows LSD is rewarding in all these areas."

One of Osmond's major theories was that LSD could provoke an experience akin to a psychotic episode and, when administered to doctors and nurses, he posited that it could help them to understand their patients, to see the world through their patients' eyes. In conversation with CBC radio host Anna Maria Tremonti in 2016,[3] Parley said she noticed that staff who took LSD did connect more with patients.

"Groups of staff were taking [LSD], they were trying to find out how their patients felt, and they were learning a lot because it upset your perceptions so badly," Parley said. "I think they got a lot more empathy for patients.

I noticed when I worked with nurses that had had LSD, they always seemed to understand their patients better."

For many years Parley worked as a freelance journalist, writing about any number of subjects related to psychiatry and mental illness. She pursued two bachelor's degrees (in sociology and education), taught at the Saskatchewan Polytechnic college for 18 years (retiring in 1987), and continued to paint.

And she's kept as busy as ever. Parley's first fantasy novel, *The Grass People*[4]—all 480 pages of it—launched in 2018. Her paintings were exhibited at Regina's Government House, the former residence of the lieutenant-governor of the North-West Territories, in 2019.

Though she only ingested LSD once, the insights gained from her experience she believed helped fuel her decades of service and creativity.

TEA? OR LSD?

Aldous Huxley's nephew Francis Huxley,[5] a social anthropologist, came to Weyburn to study interaction among the wards to help with Osmond's project to redesign of the institution. One night in 1958, Huxley invited Parley over to the Osmonds' place[6] where he was housesitting. As she recounts in her memoir, "He asks me for a cup of tea, and when I accept he suddenly seems to change his mind and says, 'Or would you rather have LSD?'"

That fateful night, as Francis walked her home, he told her, "You may as well face it, you're one of the strong ones." Dr. Osmond had banned Kay Parley from trying LSD because of her history of breakdowns, but in the end, that trip (and the conversation that followed) was the gentle but fateful nudge that shifted her self-perception from frailty to courage.

"No wonder people reported achieving insight when under LSD," she recounts. "I got a totally new impression of myself in that instant, and it was to strengthen me many times through the years. I, who had considered myself a weakling, was one of the strong ones. It was a revelation."

Present-day psychiatry—indeed, any one of us—can learn much from Parley's life. From the central roles community and creativity play in maintaining mental health, to the value of being open to change and experimentation (especially in finding unique, individualized pathways to healing), her story reaffirms that the hardest, scariest, and most circuitous roads are often the very ones that hit upon our deepest hidden treasures.

Of Mediums and Mind-Manifestors: Eileen Garrett and the Psychedelic Experience

PATRICK BARBER

EILEEN J. GARRETT (1893–1970) IS REPUTED TO HAVE BEEN THE GREATEST psychic and trance medium of the 20th century. Less known is her role as one of the unsung women influencers[1] behind the golden age of psychedelic science. Working with some of the leading psychedelic researchers of the 1950s and '60s, Garrett was a pivotal guiding force. Along with a host of psychedelic revolutionaries, she formed an integral part of a pioneering network of investigations into psychedelic drugs and parapsychology while also helping to map out the "other world" of psychedelic experience. In the process, she did more than most to bridge the gap between spiritual and scientific worldviews.

Eileen Garrett, circa late 1950s.

PSYCHIC PHENOM

Eileen Garrett's Early Years

Born in County Meath, Ireland, in 1893, Eileen Garrett endured significant personal tragedy and illness as a child and young adult. She lost both parents to suicide shortly after her birth; all three children from her first marriage died in infancy; her second husband, an army officer, perished in World War I in an explosion in Ypres; and she was plagued by chronic respiratory problems.

Garrett's early years also marked the discovery and refinement of her paranormal gifts. From a young age she had the ability to read the energy fields (or the "surround" as she called them) that encapsulated living things. She displayed powers of extra-sensory perception (ESP) such as precognition, telepathy, and clairvoyance. She could also see and communicate with the dead.

In the 1920s, Garrett underwent her first encounters of mediumship, where she would enter into trance and channel discarnate entities via the assistance of her spirit controls. Garrett participated in the burgeoning spiritualism movement in Europe and the US and had a regular spot on the séance circuit.

Of course, many people dismissed Garrett's psychic feats as an elaborate hoax or a sign of some unraveling madness. Even Garrett doubted herself at times. Her skepticism eventually resulted in a sustained period of mentorship where she honed techniques at the hands of various psychical professionals. In order to satisfy her own and others' curiosity, Garrett offered herself up to the endless tests of scientific experts in the field of psychical research (later to become parapsychology).

Eileen Garrett Rises to International Fame

Garrett rose to international prominence when the British R101 airship crashed on its maiden voyage in 1930, killing nearly all of its 54 passengers. Mere days after the disaster, Garrett channeled the spirit of the R101 captain and claimed that he had communicated specific technical details of the reasons behind the crash. These fantastic claims erupted into the sort of controversy one might expect; nevertheless, they sealed Garrett's reputation as the most renowned psychic-sensitive person of the modern era.

Prominent scholars, artists, politicians, scientists, philosophers, and philanthropists sought Garrett's attention. Throughout the 1930s, she split her time between psychic residencies in London and the US, the most famous of which were the ESP experiments of J. B. Rhine's team at Duke University's parapsychology laboratory. Famously she conversed with the deceased mother of filmmaker Cecil B. DeMille, whose spirit was trying to advise her son about his movie while on set. DeMille, by then already a cinema legend, responded rudely to Garrett, but left the encounter in tears upon hearing his mother speak through the medium embodied by Garrett.

At the beginning of World War II, Garrett assisted with the French resistance, only to be driven out of the country by the Nazi occupation. She immigrated to New York City in 1941 and became a successful author, publisher/editor, and entrepreneur, writing several books (many of them autobiographies), before founding the Creative Age Press and the literary magazine *Tomorrow*.

In 1951, Garrett returned to her psychic calling, partnering with wealthy benefactor and US Congresswoman Frances Bolton to launch the Parapsychology Foundation (PF). The PF served to advance the field as a scientific and academic enterprise, providing a source of much-needed research grants and hosting annual international conferences.

PSYCHICS AND PSYCHEDELICS

Psychologist C. S. Alvarado once lamented the inherent gender bias in the history of parapsychology, concluding that "instead of focusing on women as auxiliary figures in the work of men, we need to start writing a different type of parapsychology history in which we represent women's viewpoints and women's work in their own right, not only in relation to the work of men." In some ways, Eileen Garrett was the rare exception to this tendency towards male-centric histories. Indeed, it would be impossible to overlook or diminish her place in parapsychology.

Garrett is one of the more intriguing entries in the pantheon of psychedelic explorers. Why would a psychic and medium of her stature get involved in psychedelic research in the first place? She was already wired in such a way that she could naturally access the altered states of consciousness sometimes brought on by psychedelics.

It was not like Garrett, or other investigators of the time, were the first to connect psychedelics and paranormal phenomena either. Hundreds of years before, Indigenous shamans were safely and effectively incorporating substances like ayahuasca, peyote, and psilocybin into their daily existence: as medicines, as sacraments, as aids to access spiritual realms and receive guidance from ancestors, and even for more mundane tasks such as finding a lost object.

Eileen Garrett Joins the Psychedelic Community

Garrett's initiation into the psychedelic community came through her relationship with author Aldous Huxley, which began following a first meeting at the tearoom Garrett operated in London during World War I. As Huxley's interest in mysticism, visionary states, and various psi phenomena grew, his interaction with Garrett increased. He wrote essays and reviews for her *Tomorrow*. She was a frequent participant in the paranormal sessions held at Huxley's home in California. She even communicated with Huxley's first wife Maria after the latter's death from cancer.

As most psychedelic history buffs will know, Huxley is regarded as one of the icons of psychedelic culture, remembered most for his mescaline-inspired *The Doors of Perception* (1953). Through Huxley, Garrett became a close confident to Humphry Osmond, the psychiatrist who administered that famous mescaline trip and coined the term psychedelic. And through Osmond, Garret became attached to the psychedelic research team in Saskatchewan, Canada, including Osmond's psychiatric partner Abram Hoffer and psychologist Duncan Blewett (coauthor of the first-ever therapeutic manual on LSD).[2]

Osmond and his Saskatchewan colleagues' belief in psychedelics' vast potential may not have happened were it not for the knowledge and experiences shared with them by the women and Indigenous groups with whom they collaborated. Garrett was a case in point.

Psychedelics and Parapsychology

When it came to psychedelics and parapsychology, Osmond, Hoffer, and Blewett were attracted to the possibilities the drugs held for developing psychic openness. Flowing from their experience with the Native American

Church in 1956, they connected with Huxley, "Captain Trips" Al Hubbard, Huxley's anthropologist nephew Francis, Garrett, and others within their tightknit circle to carry out various psychedelic group experiments. Of particular interest was the possibility of the group experience in certain set and settings to foster increased communication and understanding, and even empathic bonding, among participants. Osmond, for example, drew attention to one instance of nonverbal communication that bordered on telepathy.

Garrett proved an ideal partner because she personified the kind of cosmic consciousness that was so characteristic of genuine mystical "psychedelic" experiences. While she conceded marked differences between mediumship and psychedelic experience (a fact which had to do with her having no memory of trance encounters), Garrett confessed psychedelics gave her unique insight into psi phenomena and her abilities: "I have had psychic experiences which occur at the height of the LSD experience. I believe the drug has made me a better, more accurate sensitive when I perceive, hear, think and feel."

Garrett created a dedicated platform for research in psychedelics and parapsychology. The PF trialed its own LSD experiments with other well-known mediums, the premise being that the drugs might trigger ESP activity. It also held the first international conferences on the subject, one in New York in 1958 and the other one at Garrett's retreat in La Piol, France, in 1959.

For Osmond, who cochaired and presented at both conferences, the forum was momentous because it put psychics and scientists on an equal playing field. "The sensitives," as he put it, "became assistant investigators rather than guinea pigs." He continued: "The records do not suggest that sensitives were seriously questioned by scientists in the past. It seems to me that, sixty years ago, they were trotted out so often, looked at, pried at, then they performed and were put away again. All the respectable ladies and gentlemen went off in one direction and the sensitives in another."

It was clear at the conclusion of these conferences that investigators had only scratched the surface of psychedelics' implications for psi phenomena. Preliminary data had been gathered but hypotheses were few. Investigators also lacked an appropriate methodology for more controlled testing. The opportunity for sustained inquiry never arrived.

In May 1967, Osmond wrote Garrett a lengthy letter, tracing a timeline of developments from the early '60s on and detailing his opinion of where things went wrong. As he observed, "It is curious looking back to realize that many of those who now play a large part in the psychedelic movement had never heard of the word."

Eileen Garrett passed away during a PF conference in France in 1970.

The Cost of Omission: Dr. Valentina Wasson and Getting Our Stories Right

AMY BARTLETT AND MONNICA WILLIAMS

STOP US IF YOU'VE HEARD THIS ONE: AMBITIOUS, BRAVE, AND PIONEERING white man travels to Mexico in the 1950s and is invited to a mushroom ceremony with a *curandera*. He has a profound personal experience and brings his account of this adventure back to a major publication in the United States, heralding the introduction of the psilocybin mushroom to North America and the world.

For those who regularly engage with research in the field of psychedelics, we have likely all heard this version of the story of R. Gordon Wasson a hundred times. Except we keep telling an incomplete story, again and again . . . until recently. Scholars are just beginning to pay more attention to the women behind these stories too.[1]

This Week *cover featuring*
Valentina Wasson (May 19, 1957).

OUR COLLECTIVE BLIND SPOTS

This mis-telling happened recently (and ironically) in an article on the importance of fairness and inclusion in the psychedelic renaissance.[2] Specifically, while highlighting the often under-cited contributions of Mazatec native healer María Sabina, Gordon Wasson is nevertheless credited as "the most notable Westerner to intentionally ingest psilocybin in Mexico" as well as the only author of the book *Mushrooms, Russia, and History*.

In fact, Gordon's wife, Dr. Valentina "Tina" Pavlovna Wasson, had as much—if not more—influence in bringing the psilocybin mushroom to the attention of North Americans.

LET'S TALK ABOUT DR. VALENTINA WASSON

In many ways, the stories we tell around R. Gordon Wasson and other "founding fathers" of psychedelic studies are universally accepted as canon within the psychedelic community. But when we accept repetition over rigor and fail to question the stories we tell, we fall prey to the same misogynistic assumptions of the time that made figures like Dr. Valentina Wasson invisible to researchers, writers, and historians in the first place.

Valentina was a pediatrician and scientist and a passionate mycology enthusiast—a hobby she had cultivated as a child in Russia. She was also a prolific enthomycologist and researcher. The "real" story of the West's "discovery" of psilocybin is that after Valentina had led several previous expeditions to research traditional uses of mushrooms in Mexico, María Sabina introduced Valentina and her husband (who was a banker, not a scientist by trade) to her psilocybin mushroom-based practice. The Wassons together gathered mushroom spores during this visit, which were subsequently cultivated and analyzed by psychedelic researcher and chemist Albert Hofmann, thereby directly facilitating his isolation of psilocybin.

Valentina developed a deep professional and personal passion for the psilocybin mushroom, and she made important and influential contributions to its popularization across the Western world, such as her belief that psilocybin could be used for therapeutic purposes, including to support the dying process, another insight that put her ahead of her time.

While we update this story, let's clear up two other often overlooked misattributions: Gordon did indeed write up his much cited experiences in a famous *Life* magazine article entitled "Seeking the Magic Mushroom."[3] However, Valentina's personal account was also published just a few days later in a very popular magazine at the time, called *This Week*. *This Week* was a nationally syndicated Sunday magazine supplement that was included in American newspapers between 1935 and 1969.

At its peak in 1963, *This Week* was distributed with the Sunday editions of 42 newspapers for a total circulation of 14.6 million. This wide public exposure to her account of their time in Mexico shows that Valentina's contributions were not overlooked at the time—she had a voice and she was using it. Instead, that voice was not given an ongoing place in the collective consciousness of psychedelic studies, and she has been largely forgotten by those who came after.

The second misattribution relates to the omission of her written contributions to the field, as it was Valentina who was the ethnomycology expert, and in fact the lead author of the two-volume text *Mushrooms, Russia, and History*, not her husband Gordon, as is frequently cited. The books include a dense and vibrant account of the world of mushrooms in Russia and eastern Europe, weaving local mycology and botany with historically significant myths and historical events in the region. In volume II of the collection, Valentina also details their experience in Mexico, including pictures and art from their visit. These books capture Valentina's lifelong passion for mushrooms and honor the influence her fungi-filled Russian childhood had on her important contributions to the popularization of psilocybin mushrooms and growth of the psychedelic field.

WHY CORRECT ATTRIBUTION MATTERS

The prevalence and problematic legacy of these oversights and misattributions is something we should all be working to dismantle. Unfortunately, while Gordon is lionized in the story of psychedelic history, Dr. Valentina Wasson and her many accomplishments are forgotten, obscured, and pushed into the background, much like many other women of this time.

The reality for those doing research in this space is that it is simply easier to find references about white men—and in this case, this evidentiary bias has resulted in an inaccurate and marginalizing oversight that has been replicated hundreds of times in academic articles and research. The phenomenon of being obscured in the research is well documented among many key female commentators in the psychedelic movement.[4] And as the case of Valentina shows us, we can and must do better.

The implications of this oversight—and many more like it—should not be taken lightly. Valentina's story is similar to many dozens of marginalized people whose contributions have been undervalued and underreported in the literature and in popular culture around psychedelics. As the psychedelic renaissance unfolds and as more people learn about psychedelics, it is essential that we build a collective understanding and awareness of the diversity and complexity that has led us to where we are today.

As Valentina's story shows, those of us committed to building and growing an inclusive psychedelic movement have a collective responsibility to ensure that the voices and contributions of historically marginalized groups are given equal and enthusiastic place in the present. Her story also shows us that these influential forgotten figures of the past should be remembered and celebrated for their contributions to this moment, and to the inclusive and vibrant future we are creating together. Psychedelic work is most impactful when it embraces the inherent diversity and complexity of the journey.

In addition, Valentina's story reminds us that you never know where your passions will lead you—or lead others. Valentina Wasson spent her childhood in Russia loving mushrooms, and she nurtured that love throughout her life. At its core, it is that simple, earnest childhood passion that changed the world for all of us. Her story therefore also shows us the power of following our life's passion with humility, curiosity, and an open heart. And this is a story that is definitely worth remembering.

As the psychedelic renaissance unfolds, we can continue to remember what we have forgotten. With intention, we can correct our past mistakes and hold each other and ourselves accountable for the stories we tell as we build the future of psychedelic studies. We must create a strong culture of curiosity: questioning our assumptions with a critical and intersectional eye, and dismantling the stories and practices that keep replicating social and cultural inequalities in psychedelic research and history.

Whether we are talking about the legends we have collectively woven together about the foundations of psychedelic research, or whether we are accounting for race, gender, sexuality and culture in clinical trials, studies and psychedelic community-building in modern times: inclusivity, attribution, and accountability matter.

Psychedelics teach people to question what they think they know about themselves and the world around them. This lesson also applies to the psychedelic community and the stories we tell about ourselves and to each other.

Get curious. Ask questions. Seek truth.

María Sabina, Mushrooms, and Colonial Extractivism

OSIRIS GONZÁLEZ ROMERO

"WHO WAS MARÍA SABINA?"

"What kind of wisdom is necessary to find healing in the sacred mushrooms?"

No doubt these are questions that many people have asked themselves. To satisfy that curiosity, I share with you the ideas and experiences of María Sabina. She is undeniably the best known Mazatec sage, but despite her notoriety she remains poorly understood.

Indigenous knowledge about mushrooms is not a pearl of isolated or fortuitous wisdom, but is deeply rooted in ancient Mesoamerican tradition. Archaeological evidence and written historical sources have demonstrated the use of sacred mushrooms by the Maya, Mixtec, and Aztec civilizations.

THE ENCOUNTER WITH THE SACRED MUSHROOMS

María Sabina's first encounter with sacred mushrooms occurred when she was six or seven years old (circa 1900) when one of her uncles became ill. To cure him, his family called for a sage (*Chotá-a-Tchi-née*). This physician-sage had the power to diagnose the sick person, to whom he would feed several pairs of mushrooms. The mushrooms were distributed in pairs to represent the idea of duality and the archetype of the primordial couple. The purpose of having the patient ingest the mushrooms is to learn the origin of his condition so the patient can contribute to the healing process. "A Mazatec 'shaman' guides through prayers and chants the one who has decided to 'realize' the cause of his ills, and to watch over the good development of the ritual."[1]

The physician-sage performed a ceremony or *velada* to cure María Sabina's uncle. She watched as he lit the candles and spoke with the "guardians of the hills" and the "guardians of the springs." She saw how he distributed the mushrooms among the adults and her uncle. Once in complete darkness, she heard the wise man talk and sing, although it was different from the language he used every day.

These cultural traits belong to the ancient Mesoamerican tradition, which recognizes that the mountains, springs, and plants are endowed with life and personality. They are sacred entities with which it is possible to communicate through a ritual language.

A few days after the healing ceremony, María Sabina was with her sister María Ana tending the family's chickens to protect them from foxes. Sitting under a tree, she recognized some mushrooms just like the ones eaten by the physician-sage who cured her uncle, and little by little, she began to gather them.

On that first occasion, she ingested the sacred mushrooms together with her sister. After experiencing some dizziness, both girls began to cry; however, once the dizziness disappeared, they both felt fine and were very happy.

María Sabina reports that she felt a new lease on life. In the following days, she says that when they felt hungry, they ingested the mushrooms and felt a full stomach and a happy spirit.

Together with her sister, they continued to eat the mushrooms as they went into the bush. Sometimes their mother or grandparents would find the girls lying down or kneeling. Then, finally, the adults would pick up the girls and take them home. Still, they were never scolded or beaten for eating the sacred mushrooms because the Mazatec people knew it was not good to scold people who had ingested them. After all, it can provoke mixed feelings in them. For example, they may feel that they are going crazy.

THE ENCOUNTER WITH THE PRINCIPAL BEINGS

It was not until she was widowed for the first time that María Sabina got closer to the wisdom of the sacred mushrooms. During the first years of her widowhood, she began to experience discomfort in her waist and hips due to childbirth. She decided to retake the sacred mushrooms to cure herself. However, the decisive moment for reaffirming her vocation was when her sister María Ana became ill. Among the most severe symptoms were pains and spasms in the belly. To relieve her, she called other wise men and healers, but these efforts were unsuccessful.

María Sabina knew that the Mazatecs used sacred mushrooms to alleviate illnesses, so she decided to do the ritual herself. According to testimony recounted by Mazatec writer Álvaro Estrada, she said: "To her, I gave three pairs. I ate many, to give me immense power. I can't lie, I must have eaten thirty pairs of *derrumbe* mushrooms." According to scientific literature, contemporary Mazatecs know and use at least 10 different species of psychoactive mushrooms.[2] The most well known are *derrumbe* (*psilocibe caerulescens*) and *pajarito* (*psilocibe mexicana*).

Undoubtedly, this experience was crucial because, in addition to achieving the purpose of relieving her sister, María Sabina had a vision in which six to eight characters appeared that inspired tremendous respect in her. "I knew they were 'the Principal Beings' my ancestors were talking about," she stated.

Ancestors are the bearers of knowledge, wisdom, and experience for Indigenous peoples. Consequently, they are the front line of teachers, facilitators, and guides, and are distinguished for having left a legacy. In the case of María Sabina, her legacy is directly related to the power of healing with the help of sacred mushrooms.

A remarkable fact is that this legacy of wisdom appeared to María Sabina in the form of a book. According to María Sabina's testimony, the Principal Beings surrounded a table on which an open book appeared, which grew to the size of a person. It was white, so white that it glowed, and on its pages were letters. It was not just any book, as Estrada reports: "One of the Principal Beings spoke to me and said: María Sabina, this is the Book of Wisdom. It is the Book of Language. All it contains is for you. The Book is yours, take it to work with."

This revelation was decisive in consolidating María Sabina's vocation. The news of her sister's healing spread among the inhabitants of Huautla, the village where she lived, who sought her out more and more frequently to help them heal their sick family members.

Another remarkable aspect of María Sabina's story is her recognition of Western medicine. For her, there was no opposition between traditional medicine and Western medicine, but rather a complementary relationship. She also held this to be the case with the spirituality coming from the Mesoamerican tradition and the tradition coming from Christianity. On one occasion María Sabina was shot twice and was taken to the village doctor, a young man called Salvador Guerra. He used anesthesia and removed the bullets; she was amazed and grateful to the doctor, and they later became friends, and she even performed a mushroom ceremony for him.

THE ENCOUNTER WITH ROBERT GORDON WASSON

It was her prestige within her community that led to María Sabina's encounter with Robert Gordon Wasson in 1955. Wasson had been in Oaxaca before, and even to Huautla inquiring about the ritual uses of sacred mushrooms. Their encounter marked a critical moment for studying and understanding sacred mushrooms' ritual and therapeutic uses.

In both writings for a general audience and in scientific literature of Western culture, there was a belief that these rituals had disappeared with colonization, which was inaccurate. That is why the meeting between María Sabina and Wasson is of particular significance. According to Wasson's testimony: "There is no indication that any white man has ever attended a session such as the one we are about to describe, nor has he ever consumed the sacred mushrooms under any circumstances."

In this encounter, it is worth highlighting the asymmetry of power. Wasson was a banker who became vice president of J. P. Morgan, with abundant resources to finance his expeditions. At the same time, María Sabina was a recognized sage in her community. Still, she did not charge a fixed amount of money when she performed her ceremonies with sacred mushrooms. Instead, she was under pressure to accept a meeting with Gordon Wasson by the municipal trustee of Huautla. In an interview with Alberto Ongaro in 1971, Wasson admitted that the Mazatec sage had been asked to perform the ceremony by the trustee, Don Cayetano. She felt she had no choice. "I should have said no."

The pressure put on María Sabina was later corroborated in an interview she gave to Álvaro Estrada in 1976: "It is true that before Wasson, no one spoke so freely about children [sacred mushrooms]. None of our people revealed what they knew about this matter. But I obeyed the municipal

María Sabina and Robert Gordon Wasson.

trustee. However, if the foreigners had arrived without any recommendation, I would also have shown them my wisdom because there is nothing wrong."

The encounter between María Sabina and Robert Gordon Wasson represents one of the most critical events in the history of research on the uses of psychedelic plants, mainly because of its cultural repercussions, which are far from being understood or even acknowledged. Their encounter represents an opportunity to learn about the scope and depth of the wisdom of the Indigenous peoples whom María Sabina's gift represented. It also provides a chance to reflect on some ethical aspects, such as cultural extractivism, that a decolonial approach cannot leave aside.

Their meeting also gives us an opportunity to reflect on the role of women in psychedelic research, notably the frequently overlooked expertise of Valentina Pavlovna Wasson.[3] She earned a PhD and had a broad knowledge in the field of mycology. Unfortunately, she was not present in the first encounter with María Sabina according to the available information. In her *This Week* magazine article in 1957, Valentina only briefly mentioned her husband's encounter with a "shaman," and her goal was to describe the mushroom experience in a non-ceremonial context. Furthermore, due to Valentina's premature death in 1958, it is highly possible that these women never met.

Although María Sabina surpassed Wasson in wisdom, she did not have the same recognition during his lifetime. While he obtained recognition, prestige, and worldwide fame for "discovering" the sacred mushroom, María Sabina lived with the stigma of "revealing" their secrets to an outsider. There was much anger toward her in her community. Some unknown people burned her house, and a drunk man murdered her son. Years later, in 1985, she died in impoverished conditions, which did not reflect her contributions to the knowledge of psychedelic plants. That is why it is essential to insist on "historical reparations"[4] for the expropriation of mushrooms from Indigenous communities, as Mazatec researcher Osiris García Cerqueda has proposed.[5]

Recognizing the "colonial traces" in the psychedelic renaissance is essential to reflect on these persistent ethical issues, which should not be forgotten or left aside.[6] Confronting these historical legacies is necessary to reverse the undesirable effects of discrimination, cultural appropriation, and lack of recognition.

It is no exaggeration to say that from the perspective of Indigenous peoples, psychedelic research on the therapeutic properties of psilocybin, and the development of related pharmaceuticals have a history linked to extractivism, cultural appropriation, bio-piracy, and colonization.

Let this small text serve as a tribute and recognition of the wise women of all of Mexico's Indigenous peoples.

Kathleen Harrison: Wisdom, Endurance, and Hope—Reflections from a Psychedelic Woman

ERIKA DYCK

AFTER A GENEROUS TWO-HOUR CONVERSATION WITH KATHLEEN HARRI-
son, I felt inspired, blessed, and above all, that I understood what it was
like to *be* psychedelic. Kathleen is a teacher, a nurturer, a traveler, a family
member, an ethnobotanist, a photographer, and a wise voice with important
insights on how psychedelics help us to heal in this fraying world. Her life
itself has been psychedelic—she is a healing life force, connecting people,
ideas, and plants, and stimulating new ways of seeing outside ourselves.

At one point she told me that she had never met a psychedelic she didn't
like. I was excited and nervous to learn more from this wise psychedelic
traveler.

Coming of age in the 1960s, Kathleen arrived in San Francisco during
the summer of love and recounted precious memories of mind expansion,
music, and relationships that formed against this iconic backdrop of a psychedelic moment in time.

But there is so much more to being psychedelic than Grateful Dead
memories, or even anecdotes about her years of collaboration with Terence McKenna—years that included research, marriage, children, and
publishing.

Kathleen explained that psychedelics have been critical teachers in her
life, and, most importantly, they opened her eyes to new ideas, reinforcing
the need for investing in people and the kinds of values that come from
interpersonal relationships. She described herself as being an anthropologist from a young age, always curious about people, their relationships,
ancestors, customs, and interests. She fondly remembered traveling to
Mexico as a young girl with her family and living along the coast, soaking
up the atmosphere and learning about the people who lived there—not to

study, just to live. This experience planted an important seed of curiosity that blossomed into a lifelong interest in people, plants, and the relationships among them.

Today, in my academic world, we are encouraged to do community-engaged research and to develop reciprocal relationships with our research subjects. Kathleen immediately saw through this window dressing and explained that true reciprocity is not something that is transactional. It is about deep relationships that evolve over time with mutual respect, making families and familial connections that extend over generations. This takes time. There is no roadmap for how to do it; you need to learn to listen, care, and it helps if you are empathetic.

This kind of insight and reflection comes from her lifelong interest in psychedelic plant medicines and the cultural knowledge about their use that emerged from studying people who live among psychedelic plants around the world. However, her work is also focused on local contexts where she has created deep connections with specific families for over four generations. We can visit other places, but we need to be grounded and present in our own communities in order to fully appreciate how we interact in our ecosystems.

For Kathleen, studying psychedelics in this way is ultimately both frustrating and rewarding. Some of the people with psychedelic knowledge live in dire conditions—in poverty, with limited access to education, food shortages, barriers to owning property, etc.—factors that make it easy on the surface to recognize vast differences in resources and privilege. It is frustrating because one often feels helpless to shatter the bonds of poverty.

Yet, as she explained, in some Indigenous cultures in Mexico amongst the communities where she has worked and developed close relationships, the idea that someone could own psilocybin mushrooms or profit from them is wrong. She told me that one Indigenous elder explained to her that he knows the world needs this medicine. Considering that for some healers, they live in communities cut off from the internet or many outside influences, the recognition of our collective suffering is all the more poignant. The plant world is rich. It is diverse and magical, and despite economic conditions, some feel lucky to be rich in knowledge about these plant medicines.

In 1985, Kathleen initiated and cofounded Botanical Dimensions[1] with her husband Terence. It functioned as a nonprofit for 34 years and is now functioning under a fiscal sponsor. Under Botanical Dimensions she carried out projects in Peru, Ecuador, Costa Rica, and California, with ongoing projects in Hawaii and Mexico. She is now working on a documentary film, *Almost Visible*, about the interfamilial friendship with a Mazatec healer's clan. The private Hawaii Forest-Garden continues. The Ethnobotany Library is still in Northern California, but its survival is in doubt, due to the inability to run educational programs during the pandemic, which is what had supported it previously. Kathleen was the visionary and the energy behind Botanical Dimensions; today, she continues that work by writing a book about the principles of living a psychedelic life.

I asked Kathleen, then, does she see the psychedelic renaissance as an opportunity to face global challenges head on? To gain access to psychedelic plant medicines and perhaps confront colonialism along the way?

Her answer surprised me, until I listened more and understood better.

She said no. In fact, she said that despite the shortcomings of the psychedelic movement in the 1960s and '70s, that it was more hopeful.

Today, we have lost our critical edge, and above all, we are losing our critical thinking skills as a species.

I thought back to my training as a historian, watching the civil rights marches, the feminist campaigns, and the Stonewall protests—all of which brandished banners of equality and collective action, in a mantra that together, "we shall overcome." But, gazing at my 21st century reality, especially during this pandemic, we again see marches for Black Lives Matter, #MeToo, and the Truth and Reconciliation efforts to identify mass graves of children from Canadian Indian Residential Schools. These, along with daily news reminders of violence and discrimination continue to reveal the ugly remnants of a broken system, one perhaps that will accelerate a need to look inward and focus on ourselves. But, surely, there has also been some progress? How could the 1970s have been better, when those same struggles persist today?

Kathleen summed it up in a word: hope. In the 1970s, she said, we had more hope. Today, we are saddled with many of the same injustices, while flooding and fires remind us that the earth itself is suffering. The relationship between plants and humans is even further strained today than it was 50 years ago, or at least we are exposed to more and more images of suffering around the globe in our digitally connected modern lives. Yet, the exposure to more information has dulled our capacity to critically analyze that information, and our ability to reach around the world may have also diminished our willingness to think about our local circumstances and our responsibilities as a collective force for change.

We need to, she explained, each individually and collectively learn about the gift of plants, but also to be wise in our choices and be tuned into the collective suffering of others. In other words, we need collective action that is genuinely sensitive to the needs of others, and is grounded in our local realities. The goal, it seems, is not simply to decriminalize psychedelics, but to continue to nourish the relationship between plants and people that give psychedelics their meaning.

We need to slow down. Reflect. Pay attention. Be critical.

Our modern world has created a dizzying pace of information gathering and knowledge production—research goals and markers of success. But, what psychedelics can help teach us is about the power of slow learning, or cumulative knowledge that takes time, and takes the form of prayer, song, appreciating the varieties of species, magic—a rich tapestry woven from different threads of knowledge. If we can learn to see all these threads at the same time, and marvel in their collective beauty as a whole, we might begin to appreciate the deeper knowledge that psychedelic plants have to offer. And, the fraying world needs us to reweave those threads by respecting the integrity of each individual thread while appreciating how woven together, they create something new. Something to hope for.

Spotlight on Betsy Gordon and the Psychoactive Substances Research Collection

STEPHANIE SCHMITZ

THE NAME BETSY GORDON MAY BE FAMILIAR, BUT MANY PEOPLE MAY NOT be aware of the major impact this remarkable woman has made on the psychedelic research landscape. Not one for the limelight, Gordon's involvement in the field of psychedelic psychiatry has been largely behind the scenes, though her support has been instrumental in the development and preservation of psychedelic research. As an early supporter of the Heffter Research Institute,[1] she funded studies that laid the groundwork for the reemergence of psychedelic research, enabling the field to evolve into what it is today.

Betsy Gordon.

EARLY LIFE AND CAREER

Elizabeth (Betsy) Douglas Gordon was born on December 24, 1948, and grew up in rural northwestern New Jersey, the second of three children. She spent the 1960s at an all-girls boarding school largely sheltered from the burgeoning countercultural movement. After a brief stint at Winthrop College in Stock Hill, North Carolina, and later the University of Strasbourg in Germany, she lived, worked, and travelled around Europe for several years.

Upon returning to the United States, she embarked on volunteer work in New York, eventually obtaining a position assisting children with special needs at an elementary school in Queens. Gordon describes this experience as transformative in her process of personal growth. In a circuitous way, she discovered Holotropic Breathwork and in so doing met Stanislav Grof in Mill Valley in the late 1980s. She received continuous training and multiple certifications as a Holotropic Breathwork facilitator[2] and provided assistance to those experiencing a profound and altered state of consciousness through a process of accelerated breath, evocative music, and bodywork in a supported set and setting. In doing so she became close with the small yet impactful community of practitioners involved in this work, assisting Grof in many of his residential workshops hosted in the US and around the world. Conversations about psychedelics and altered states of consciousness arose naturally in this environment, and Gordon made it a personal goal to have an impactful, nonordinary experience by the age of 40.

THE PSYCHOACTIVE SUBSTANCES RESEARCH COLLECTION

Over the years, her alliance and friendships with breathworkers, meditators, and healers blossomed. She formed close working friendships with many founders in the community of psychedelic research, particularly from her involvement with the Gathering of the Elders conference at the Fetzer Institute in the late 1990s. As she observed the reemergence of psychedelic research gaining traction, she recognized that many contributors in the field were an "invaluable resource as an irreplaceable knowledge and hard-won wisdom." Thus, she envisioned a psychedelic research archive to preserve these contributions to the field.

In 2006, she established the Psychoactive Substances Research Collection at the Purdue University Archives. This repository proactively gathers

MDMA conference materials, 1986, from the David E. Nichols papers, MSF 468, Purdue University Archives & Special Collections.

DMT synthesis materials, 1990s, from the David E. Nichols papers, MSF 468, Purdue University Archives & Special Collections.

Rare books and a piece of lab ware from the Psychoactive Substances Research Collection at the Purdue University Archives & Special Collections.

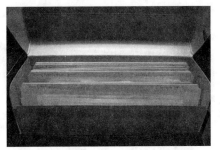

Box of documents from the Psychoactive Substances Research Collection at the Purdue University Archives & Special Collections.

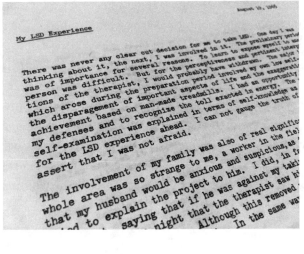

Experience report, 1965, from the Stanislav Grof papers, MSP 1, Purdue University Archives & Special Collections.

and makes accessible primary source materials that illustrate the complex history of psychedelic research and illuminates the many stories and characters behind it. Incidentally, recordings from the historic Gathering of the Elders conference are available on the Psychoactive Substances Research Collection website.[3] Her inspiration came not only from seeing the personal papers of her close friends lost in natural disasters or forgotten, but also because she witnessed how impactful these approaches to healing were—in her own life, in the lives of others, and as illustrated in rigorous scientific studies. As she saw the revival of psychedelic research unfolding, she knew how important it was to use the past as a reference point, to not unnecessarily reinvent the wheel.

The Betsy Gordon Psychoactive Substances Research Collection includes the personal papers of psychedelic research luminaries such as Stanislav Grof, Bill Richards, Sanford Unger, David Nichols, Dennis McKenna, Marlene Dobkin de Rios,[4] and many more. These letters, photographs, clippings, interviews, teaching materials, research notes, personal notes, mementos, and other archival ephemera illustrate how psychedelic psychiatry was administered, patients' responses to these treatments, and the effects of policy and culture on the field.

Individuals from around the world, among them scholars, students, media producers, and the independently curious, can access materials in the Psychoactive Collection for their work on theses, dissertations, articles, clinical applications, scholarly publications, popular books, courses, films, streaming series, radio stories, art installations, or simply personal research. These unique and valuable resources are available for exploration in the archive's reading room. Some collections have been scanned in their entirety and are available virtually.

For decades, Betsy Gordon has played a critical role in moving this research area forward. Her role in creating the Psychoactive Substances Research Collection ensures that the lessons of the past are worthy of examination and can further inform current and future research. It is our hope that she will one day donate her own papers to the archive, so that her achievements and contributions to the field will be recognized, as scholars will invariably mine these resources to piece together the history of this complex and multifaceted field of research.

Coming of Age in the Psychedelic Sixties

DIANA NEGRÍN WITH YVONNE NEGRÍN

If you can just get your mind together
Then come on across to me
We'll hold hands an' then we'll watch the sun rise from the
bottom of the sea.
But first,
Are you experienced?
Have you ever been experienced?
Well, I have.

"Are You Experienced?" Jimi Hendrix (1967)

THE 1960S HAVE BEEN CHARACTERIZED AS A PERIOD THAT CREATED A CULtural and sociopolitical convergence of such magnitude that young people from various households of the postwar period took the leap forward and explored new ways of co-living, making art, and thinking about political life. Psychedelics were an important part of this courageous generational leap just at a moment when United States hegemony struck at precepts of human rights abroad and used every weapon to oppress justice and dissent domestically. The stranglehold of white supremacy, patriarchy, and permanent war was weakened by the new spaces for social life where sometimes psychedelics played an assisting, if not catalyzing, role. My mother, Yvonne Negrín, née da Silva, was one of countless young women who found herself looking through the mirror of this cultural moment, aided by the singularity of the era and two remarkable geographies: New York and California.

Born in 1947 in White Plains—north of New York City—Yvonne was raised by what could be called the prototype parents of the post–World War II era. Her father, Alexander da Silva, was born in Brooklyn to Luso-Brazilian immigrants and was one of tens of thousands of men who went to war in the early 1940s and found their battlefield in German prison camps. Alex returned from war and became a postal worker and continued occasional tree pruning alongside part-time television and garage door repair. Yvonne's mother, Martha McGuire, was from rural Ohio and moved to Stanford, Connecticut, during the war years. There, she and her sisters went to work at PerkinElmer, where they produced precision optics. Once married, Alex and Martha would soon move further upstate New York to Ossining where they would raise Yvonne and her three younger brothers. Yvonne describes her household as a very typical middle-class family for the era, with ample freedom to run around as fathers labored at work and mothers toiled at home in the standard nuclear family format.

While her parents were always progressive in politics, she and her brothers all eventually questioned their conservative Catholic upbringing. For Yvonne, the first elements to unsettle the still unnamable cultural moment came through her connection to music in her early teens:

> I think I just became aware of the reality of things. I got into folk music; I think Bob Dylan was a huge inspiration, and Joan Baez. The songs that they wrote or sang, the issues that they brought up about injustices—there was a lot of food for thought. It was a pretty segregated situation growing up. I don't remember if we even had an African American student in the Catholic school that I went to; there were a lot of Italians and Irish Catholics.
>
> And then also when I was about 15, I met Sonny Sharrock, who was a guitarist; he worked in the record store down on Spring Street in Ossining and used to sell me my 45 RPM records. A lot of it was Motown, but he was the one who turned me on to jazz and introduced me to people that I started hanging out with. By the time I was 18, I moved out of my parents' house and into an apartment, and I remember that Sonny turned me on to John Coltrane and I started going to Manhattan with a friend of his that was also from Ossining . . . we went to lofts where jazz musicians gathered to jam and that was my introduction to jazz and Black culture, and I formed some very close and very good friendships.
>
> So between the folk music scene and the jazz scene, it all really opened up my mind. I think the first time I smoked grass

was listening to John Coltrane's *Ascension*. That was a mind opener! Then I moved to Manhattan, to the Lower East Side, where there was a lot going on during those years. I met a lot of people, among them Abbie Hoffman, who was very interesting, and Frank Zappa.

It was in this way that Yvonne moved from listening to Mary Wells and Marvin Gaye to trying out her own skills playing folk guitar, each time drawn further in by the musical experimentation and political commentary that emerging artists were pushing in the heart of New York City.

We are talking the United States of 1965—a year that began with the swearing in of President Lyndon B. Johnson and the assassination of Malcolm X; it continued with the deployment of US Marine ground troops in Vietnam and the Alabama State Trooper attack in Selma, known as "Bloody Sunday." The year's top musical albums included *Rubber Soul* by the Beatles, *Highway 61 Revisited* by Bob Dylan, *Farewell, Angelina* by Joan Baez, and *A Love Supreme* by John Coltrane. Yvonne was one of many brave young women who moved to the Big Apple. In her case, she landed a job at *Look* magazine and ventured into the be-ins at Central Park, the epic Fillmore concerts, and the small jazz clubs where she continued to be cued into the heart and soul of the "Psychedelic Sixties." It was no small feat for a young woman from a Catholic household to make this countercultural shift and truly believe and come of age within it.

Certainly marijuana had already become deeply criminalized and portrayed as the antithesis to the white, nuclear, hard-working family where new canned food recipes and afternoon cocktails and cigarettes were the permitted stimulants. During the following three years, Yvonne lived in the Lower East Side and navigated spaces where various stimulants, from uppers like methamphetamines and downers like heroin, were taken alongside the increasingly popular use of psychedelics like LSD, STP,[1] and DMT.[2] She recalls how it was the children of the middle and upper-class white families who she remembers using psychedelics. Most of her friends in jazz circles seldom touched psychedelics—this includes her recollections of Sun Ra, who lived across the street and who she recalls being a "natural space cadet" who probably did not need the stimulation of psychedelics to arrive at his creations and political formulations. Without doubt, Yvonne emphasized that "there was a lot of experimentation in general whether it was with or without psychedelics, people were experimenting; the people you were around were being creative."

As a young and independent woman, set and setting were quickly established as important factors:

> My first LSD trip was on Sandoz's acid and it was given to me by this guy that I had met. His interest was seducing me, which didn't work. I got very upset. I was interested in trying LSD; I had heard a lot about it, but I did not know this guy's intentions. And so halfway through the trip, I split his apartment; I left and went walking home totally stoned, walking through the Lower East Side. And on my way home I stopped in The Annex, which was a bar that was near my house. I wanted to get something to drink, a glass of water. I was thirsty and an acquaintance hits on me and it was like a nightmare. Eventually I got home, and once I was in my own space, I was fine. Later I felt LSD was useful for reflection, inner reflection. I remember deciding on that first trip that I was really not turned on by the idea of makeup. I remember at one point looking in the mirror and it seemed like my mascara was really amplified. I stopped wearing makeup after that. It was the idea of peeling away the layers of a façade and getting down to my essence, who I really was.

This was the beginning of Yvonne's intuitive and very personal work with psychedelics.

Young people experimented in park gatherings, in concert halls, and in their city apartments—many of these youth participated in the continuous public protests against the war and ongoing racial segregation. Yvonne fondly recalls counterculture figure and activist Abbie Hoffman's group, the Yippies, and the gatherings she did and did not attend that marked the beginning of a more radical wave of social movements and the US government's ensuing clamp down on activist leaders.

Experimental use of drugs ran parallel to mainstream society and politics, while the excitement of new philosophical doors opening began to close as many people started using larger doses of psychedelics and experienced infamous "bad trips" and lingering flashbacks:

STP then hit the scene, and it was interesting because people were having very heavy trips on STP. It was like a psychedelic trip amplified; not only were they having heavy trips but they were having uncontrolled flashbacks. I was very curious about STP and the only time I took STP was in New York City while I had my last apartment there. I wanted to try it, but being the conservative girl I was, I decided "well, I'm only going to try some of this," so I broke the tablet in four pieces and I took a quarter of a dose, and I had an absolutely wonderful experience. A great trip! And many, many, years later I was talking to Sasha Shulgin, and I asked him why so many people were having such horrible trips on STP and [told him] that I had a wonderful trip once, but I told him that I'd only taken a quarter of a tablet. He said, "well, you actually took what everybody should have been taking!" People were overdosing on STP! And that was the problem, you know, even with LSD; it went from being tablets of 125 micrograms to 250 mics to 500 mics. They were splitable tabs, but people would take the whole 500 and blow their minds wide open.

Further, Yvonne recalls the way speed and heroin created "lost souls" and how New York "deteriorated" with violence and a generally cold social atmosphere. In contrast, sunny and free-loving California was on many peoples' minds, and in 1968 Yvonne journeyed west, landing her first apartment in Lagunitas with blues singer Kathy McDonald who often sang with Big Brother and the Holding Company.

I mean, San Francisco was a really happening place in the music scene, which extended to the psychedelic scene, because psychedelics were really happening in the Bay Area. I really loved music, and I was interested in potentially being a sound engineer, and I would sit with Dan Healy, who is the one who did all the mixing of early Grateful Dead, Steve Miller, and Van Morrison albums. I would sit in the sound room and I got to watch a lot of albums actually be recorded in the studio.

In the Bay Area, Yvonne met her future husband, Juan Negrín (b.

Yvonne starts a new chapter in Berkeley, California, Spring 1968. Courtesy of Yvonne Negrín

Mexico City 1945–d. Oakland 2015), who shared an interest in the political and cultural revolution that appeared to be underway. Juan had also come from the jazz clubs of New York and was optimistic about the potential LSD could have for helping people find a deeper political and spiritual awareness. During that time, Yvonne became a friend of psychedelic chemist Alexander (Sasha) Shulgin. Sasha was active on the UC Berkeley campus at the time and was well into his explorations of psychedelic compounds. Yvonne would often provide Sasha with samples of the substances that people were trading and selling on the streets. He would in turn test them in his personal lab in Lafayette and report back on whether they were pure or doctored substances, and thus worthy of consuming or not. She lovingly remembers Sasha as a mentor and although she never tripped with him, they shared stories about their respective adventures in altered states. On one occasion, Yvonne acquired ibogaine, a plant medicine that she had read about. She provided Sasha with the sample without disclosing what it was and to his own surprise he called her and exclaimed: "Where did you get this?! This is ibogaine!"

And yet, California by 1970 was a changing landscape. On the west coast, social movements had been attacked and degraded while the world of culture and drugs shifted into a darker future. In 1970, president Richard Nixon continued to escalate the Vietnam War. In the United States, there was the Kent State shooting, the Weathermen bombing, and an escalating counterintelligence hunt against the Black Panther Party. In the world of music, the Beatles broke up, and some of the top albums of the year were *Morrison Hotel* by the Doors, Black Sabbath's debut album, the Grateful Dead's *Workingman's Dead*, and *Bitches Brew* by Miles Davis. For Yvonne, the world of drugs and psychedelics emulated the darkness of the moment. On the other hand, policing in the years that led to the formal declaration of the War on Drugs also created a deteriorating and unsafe scene for psychedelics. Many friends and acquaintances were persecuted, in many cases on conspiracy charges. One dear friend died mysteriously after an encounter with a narcotics agent.

Yvonne laments how many people produced psychedelics for pure profit, while only a few had the skilled knowledge and ethical commitment to create pure substances. Others she identifies as "bad actors," who she feels used the rising popularity of drugs as a ticket for fast money. One such breaking point was a man she caught cutting LSD with speed to then sell as mescaline. Sasha would often tell her that one never knew the contents of the pills that were circulating.

It was in 1970 when Juan took Yvonne to meet his father in Guadalajara, Mexico, and there, they came across Wixárika artwork. Could it be that the deep spiritual and philosophical answers they had been searching for had led them to their next journey? Over the following years, Yvonne became closely connected to Wixárika communities and participated in culturally mediated uses of another psychedelic, the peyote cactus. Over the following decades, she and her husband founded a series of nonprofits to support the art and territorial autonomy of the Wixárika. In the 1990s, when she returned to live in the Bay Area, Yvonne continued to connect with the Shulgins and many other local psychonauts to sustain critical discussions on the potential of psychedelics, legislative change, and the delicate balance that it all entailed.

New York was the bedrock that nurtured Yvonne's curiosity; it led her to the nodes of artistic production in Manhattan and then to the San Francisco

Bay Area where she met her lifelong companion, Juan, and continued the experience of linking altered states with deepening commitments to art. This Bay Area then became the springboard to the Western Sierra Madre and the lowlands of Nayarit, a geography that cemented Yvonne's following 50 years of work knitting together culture and ecology. To date, she continues to direct the Wixárika Research Center's archival and grassroots work.

SECTION THREE

Limits of Feminism

Marlene Dobkin de Rios: A Case for Complex Histories of Women in Psychedelics

TAYLOR DYSART

"THE QUESTION ABOUT WOMEN'S ROLE IN THE HISTORY OF PLANT-psychedelic use in society is a fascinating topic."

Thus remarked Marlene Dobkin de Rios in her autobiography, a vivid account that traced her decades of experience as a medical anthropologist and transcultural psychotherapist. Over the course of her career, Dobkin de Rios explored a range of topics: fortune telling cards and the Rorschach; witchcraft and psychosomatic illness; visual arts, music, and drug use. Most of her work, however, focused on the healing practices and therapeutics of Peruvian *curanderos*—local healthcare practitioners—that often braided together a range of techniques.

Ayahuasca's place in Mestizo and Indigenous Peruvian healing practices featured extensively in Dobkin de Rios's work, and the world of popular psychedelics has often referred to her as the "mother of ayahuasca."[1] Her story in the history of hallucinogenic plants is indeed a fascinating and complex one. It demonstrates why we need to go beyond "recovering" women in the history of psychedelics to instead explore the often tense and tender relationships that characterized such psychedelic research, especially in Latin America.

ENTER ANTHROPOLOGY

Marlene Dobkin was born in New York in 1939. Upon finishing high school at the age of 15, she embarked on her post-secondary studies at Queen's College at the City University of New York, where she majored in psychology. After college, she began graduate school at New York University, with the intention to pursue a career in social work. However, she was drawn to anthropology and graduated with an MA in the discipline in 1963. She obtained a teaching position at the University of Massachusetts and considered various topics for her PhD research. A serendipitous meeting in Montreal ushered the young scholar into the world of hallucinogenic research.

While visiting friends in Montreal, she met Oscar Ríos (no relation), a Peruvian psychiatrist working at McGill University's Transcultural Psychiatry Division. Ríos had grown up in Iquitos, an Amazonian city in northeastern Peru that had long captured the imagination of intrepid travelers and is today revered by many as the "ayahuasca capital."[2] In 1962, Ríos completed his medical degree at San Marcos University in Lima and set out to expand his research on the psychiatric potentials of psychoactive chemicals and plants. His colleagues insisted that he include an anthropologist on his research team. With the Peruvian psychiatrist requiring the expertise of an anthropologist and the US anthropologist still seeking a dissertation, the two began a fruitful, transnational collaboration.

PERUVIAN RESEARCH AND RELATIONS

Following her meeting with Ríos, in 1967, Dobkin began an enduring relationship with the Institute of Social Psychiatry in Lima. Under the guidance of the Peruvian psychiatrist Carlos Alberto Seguín, she conducted a study on the ritual healing of the "mescaline cactus" in the northwestern region of Salas, the "capital of witchcraft." Following this project, Dobkin returned to Lima and conducted ethnographic work with Ríos in his northeastern hometown of Iquitos. They examined patients that traveled to ayahuasca healing ceremonies to observe which types of therapeutics local healers used. She remarked that nearly everyone she spoke with in Iquitos had taken ayahuasca at least once for health reasons. While Dobkin and Ríos eventually drifted apart in their research activities and interests, her time in Iquitos shaped much of her future research.

Early on in her research, Dobkin became fascinated with *naipes*—fortune-telling cards that were popular amongst both curanderos in Iquitos and those in metropolitan Lima's middle class. In Iquitos, Dobkin began to read the fortunes of her informants. After encouragement from Ari Kiev, a renowned psychiatrist she had met while in New York in 1968, Dobkin began requesting modest compensation for reading fortunes. She described herself as a "full-fledged *curiosa*, a specialist who could divine the future."

As a demand for her services grew, she opened a consultation office where two of her friends in Iquitos would send her new clients, who "practically lined up to have their fortunes read." Dobkin embraced her new label in the city as the "gringa [female outsider] who knew things."

While she was conducting her fieldwork, Dobkin met her husband, Yando Hildebrando de Rios, an artist who would contribute several illustrations for her work over the years. Her husband had grown up witnessing and experiencing ayahuasca healing practices as his father, don Hildebrando de Rios, was a local healer and *vidente*, or seer, in Pucallpa in eastern Peru. For her research in Peru, newly married Dobkin de Rios received her PhD in anthropology from the University of California Riverside and began teaching at California State University at Fullerton. In the late 1970s, she returned to Peru with her husband and daughter to conduct a formal ethnographic study of her father-in-law and his patients.

Dobkin de Rios described don Hilde, as he was known by his patients, as a "master herbalist and drug healer who uses the psychoactive plant, ayahuasca." He, too, read *naipes* with his clients. The anthropologist observed that don Hilde would see as many as 25 patients a day, most of whom were women, and over half young children. Dobkin de Rios remarked that the patients came with a range of ailments, ranging from bodily complaints to concerns about bewitchment. Often, his patients would see biomedical physicians for their ailments as well.

As with many folk practitioners who included ayahuasca in their therapeutic repertoire, don Hilde communicated with entities and spirits "that come to him in his visions to instruct him about healing plants." Dobkin de Rios recounted his practices, which relied on ayahuasca and toé (or white angel's trumpet [*brugmansia suaveolens*]), another hallucinogenic plant: "He began to mix toé with ayahuasca to have special kinds of visions, first taking the ayahuasca then the toé, and looking carefully at each patient assembled in the main room [of his clinic] to see to the very depths of their intestines . . . When it is a natural illness, don Hilde feels different impressions of his own body, and experiences the person's pain subjectively. In this way he is able to identify where the patient's illness is located."

Dobkin de Rios, as the daughter-in-law of don Hilde, occupied a special position in the clinic. For example, she "acted in the capacity of a nurse" despite not having any formal training in the field. At the same time, she used her position at the clinic to analyze the experiences of nearly a hundred of don Hilde's patients. "Don Hilde," she writes, "would not see his patients unless the person sat with me first and responded to my questionnaire." This questionnaire included 25 questions about their education, social class, professional occupation, reasons for visiting don Hilde, and previous experiences with ayahuasca.

As the anthropologist and Indigenous Science, Technology, and Society (STS) scholar Kim TallBear has written: "Ethnography and physical anthropology are translation. In that is power." TallBear remarks that the writings of anthropologists "cannot be viewed simply as studied or distanced and unproblematic representations of the cultural practices and beliefs of the others they study, but must be read as a cultural-political act in and of itself, as a literary act." Dobkin de Rios's account with her father-in-law and his patients demonstrates the intertwined and uneven relationships that formed much anthropological research in settler-colonial contexts. As historians of science such as Rosanna Dent, Joanna Radin, and Warwick Anderson have shown, colonial and postcolonial relations shaped human and biological sciences research throughout the 20th century.

Despite the power she often held when conducting her fieldwork, Dobkin de Rios's position as a woman in the male-dominated fields of anthropology and ethnobotany in the 1960s and 1970s was marred by personal and professional challenges. For example, she recounted being told by a "gossipy colleague" that her department at Cal State Fullerton had experienced pressure to hire more women. Dobkin de Rios learned that, despite having published a book and several articles prior to completing her PhD, "there was some question" about whether she was a "serious" researcher. One of the anthropologist's interviewers at Cal State claimed: "Oh no, she looks like a model, and I don't think we have to worry about serious scholarship!" She would go on to work there for nearly 30 years.

COMPLEX LEGACIES

Marlene Dobkin de Rios's story in "the history of plant-psychedelic use" is, indeed, a fascinating one. It demonstrates the complexities and fraught nature of conducting psychedelic research, especially for those who have been, and continue to be, marginalized or excluded.

On the one hand, she was certainly what many would call a pioneer in the field of psychedelic studies. Wade Davis, an esteemed anthropologist and ethnobotanist who studied under Richard Evans Schultes at Harvard, wrote that he was enchanted by her accounts and that her work guided his path in ethnobotany. And as one of the few women in this field at the time, she experienced a range of challenges and endured sexist attacks that often sought to undermine her expertise.

On the other hand, when conducting her ethnographic research in Peru in the 1960s and 1970s, it is clear that Dobkin de Rios, through her expertise and family relations, wielded a certain power. To establish her reputation as a fortune-teller, she charged her interlocutors for her services; she acquired ethnographic data from her father-in-law's patients, who were unable to receive treatment from don Hilde until they'd spoken with the "gringa" anthropologist.

It is crucial that we recover the experiences, narratives, and accomplishments of those women who have been marginalized, or omitted, from the historical psychedelic record. However, we must go beyond merely recovery to reconstructing these histories in all their messiness and intricacy. Attending to the colonial and transnational histories that have shaped—and continue to inform—psychedelic sciences, demonstrates the tense and uneven ways through which this knowledge has been produced. The case of Marlene Dobkin de Rios is illustrative of the complexity of these histories.

Sexual Assault and Gender Politics in Ayahuasca Traditions: A View from Brazil

GRETEL ECHAZÚ AND PIETRO BENEDITO

IN AUGUST 2018, A BOMB EXPLODED IN THE WORLD OF NEW AGE PRACTI-
tioners: the Brazilian guru, Prem Baba, a charismatic religious leader who
propelled a New Age movement with a worldwide following, was accused
of sexual abuse by two women who for years had been a part of his closest circle of adepts. Janderson Fernandes (Prem Baba's birth name) was
exposed by his victims to a major Brazilian news source, the *Época* magazine, as having used his charismatic leadership to rope them into a series
of sexual activities, which he called a special kind of "tantric treatment,"
performed throughout by him and each woman "consensually."[1]

One of the women opened up after finding herself experiencing serious
panic attacks. After the news bomb hit, Prem Baba publicly recognized his
"mistakes," minimizing them as "part of his learning path," and charac-
terizing the denunciation as a kind of "dark force growing in the hearts of
his people." The women's accusations were depicted on a YouTube post by
Janderson[2] as a flaw of their spirituality, rooted in inexplicable greed and
pain. Afterward, many of his closest followers publicly rejected his version
of events and stood up for the two women, sparking a massive exodus from
his movement.

AYAHUASCA CIRCLES IN BRAZIL

In Brazil, legal regulations determine that one can engage in an ayahuasca
experience only in religious settings, of which there are three main ones:
Indigenous traditions, the "ayahuasca religions" (Santo Daime, União do Vegetal [UDV], and Barquinha), and the increasingly popular neo-ayahuasquero
centers. Most people drink ayahuasca within the religious ayahuasca groups.

The ayahuasca churches have been present in Brazil since the 1930s.
They combine diverse cultural influences, such as Indigenous, European,

and African-Brazilian through the framework of popular Latin American Christianity. Neo-ayahuasquero centers are characterized by the more fluid and less institutionalized use of ayahuasca and New Age religiosity. Janderson Fernandes began his career as a spiritual leader in one of these nuclei when, as a psychotherapist, he started sharing ayahuasca with his followers.

These non-Indigenous ayahuasca circles in Brazil are demographically predominantly middle-class, white people of often surprisingly conservative views. In an elitist and conservative exception to the popular paradigm of the psychedelic revolution, the religious and therapeutic experience of ayahuasca in urban contexts is available mainly for those who can afford or have access to it.

An example of this is the alignment of some UDV leaders with the reactionary campaign of Jair Bolsonaro, who harbors extreme right-wing views. In September 2018, the ex-general leader of UDV in Brazil, Raimundo Monteiro de Souza, recorded a WhatsApp audio calling for followers to support the fascist candidate and stop a supposed "moral crisis" pervading the country.[3] This did not come as a surprise, as the UDV had in the past expressed reactionary views on multiple fronts. One clear example is an internal UDV statement, which was later leaked on the internet,[4] describing how the family is the unit of society and homosexuals were out of the correct order of things. Also, it is important to remember that, within this group, women cannot reach the top of the hierarchy as masters, a position restricted to men; the rule has been rarely defied.

ALARM SIGNALS

As ayahuasca grew more widely popular in Brazil, cases of sexual assault and misconduct toward female participants in ritual settings began to emerge. The exact number of cases is unknown, since many of them don't come to light. Fortunately, this issue is increasingly illuminated by participants, academics, and activists in a growing international movement that denounces practices previously silenced within ayahuasca circles.

In this article, we want to bring out the strategic relevance of a gendered perspective on religious groups in contemporary contexts, making visible the scenarios that make possible abuses of all kinds, especially those of a sexual nature.

TOOLS FOR ANALYSIS

The complexity of abuse and, specifically, of sexual assault in religious circles has been studied under a number of perspectives,[5,6] but is certainly more complex in cases where a psychoactive substance is included at the core of the religious practice. Such is the case in the evaluation of sexual assault cases in the ayahuasca religious context. What is to blame for the violations: the psychoactive plants or the sexist hierarchies prevalent in those contexts?

Sexual abuse in ayahuasca circles is a very delicate matter that involves, first, a critical reflection about consent and autonomy in the context of hierarchical relationships and, second, thoughts about the influence of ayahuasca in this dynamic. There is a tension between the human rights of collectives, such as the ayahuasca religious groups, and the human rights of individual subjects, particularly those of women, LGBT people, disabled people, and others in situations of social vulnerability respective to their perpetrator.

Our proposal is that, in Brazil, some religious groups are based in a hierarchical and sexist structure in which women are seen as "essentially" different from men. This affects women and LGBT people in different ways. There are some ayahuasca religious institutions and neo-ayahuasquero groups in Brazil that tend to perpetuate this difference regarding their choice of leaders, the configuration of rituals, and the establishment of genealogies of their divine masters.

Following cosmologies and specific liturgies, it is common among some ayahuasca religious institutions to find a strong sense of hierarchy that empowers commanders. (Of course, there is much variation between different churches and organizations and we are using generalizations here for the sake of our argument.)

By presenting their leadership as destined to a spiritual mission, religious authorities often make it difficult for their words and actions to be questioned by followers. Also, the divisions between men and women are strongly based on traditional Brazilian gender roles. Often, men are defined as active rulers and women are portrayed as docile and natural followers.

In some neo-ayahuasquero groups, even though they generally seek to differentiate themselves from institutionalized religions and embrace a more fluid structure, a good number of leaders also tend to assume hierarchical positions.

This situation inside these religious communities risks growing more rigid in the face of the rising political wave of fascism, as epitomized in the recent election of far-right candidate Jair Bolsonaro to the Brazilian presidency. Between this rigid internal sexist hierarchy and an increasingly conservative and hostile political environment, we anticipate the growth of sexual assault and other abuses within ayahuasca groups in Brazil.

The Brazilian state favors freedom of expression and inner organization within the ayahuasca religions. But, like any organization subject to legal scrutiny, its principles should not compromise human dignity; and, despite the importance of thinking about the human rights of collectivities, the dimension of the individual remains fundamental.

Human dignity and human autonomy are values that should be translated into dignity and autonomy for every subject. No religion should impose a perspective obliterating the fundamental human rights of its participants. In the case of women, LGBTs, and other groups in similar situations of vulnerability, this attention should be redoubled.

PROPOSALS

To recognize, reflect about, and change this reality, we propose a few actions toward the politicization of ayahuasca circles in Brazil. First, we support questioning the cultural autonomy of practices that take place in ayahuasca religious rituals, intertwining those experiences with gender, race, ethnicity, class, and other concepts that are sensitive to social differences within settings. In this sense, we argue that abuse is not linked to a unique practice, but to many. For instance, racism and classism might manifest alongside the expression of sexual abuse at times.

On a more concrete basis, we call for the production of materials discussing assault and consent to ayahuasca groups worldwide, highlighting what is and is not a healing practice in a pre-post-ritual context. We support the production and sharing of such resources between heterosexual women and bisexual, gay, and trans people attending ayahuasca rituals in religious contexts as a means to prevention. We also recommend the creation of a headquarters for receiving complaints, offering a space to listen and to assess experiences of abuse in these contexts as a means of treatment, as well as multiplying platforms for complaint and redress that are accessible to civil society.

And last but not least, we wish to highlight the importance of linking ayahuasca's role as a companion plant to social and community development in local, integral, holistic ways to our unfolding story as species who met, built together practices with a purpose, and helped remake society in this era of the Anthropocene.

Gurus Behaving Badly: Anaïs Nin's Diary and the Value of Gossip

ALEXIS TURNER

THIS IS A STORY ABOUT ANGELA ANAÏS JUANA ANTOLINA ROSA EDELMIRA Nin y Culmell, who wanted us to know that she did not care for Timothy Leary. As far as she was concerned, Leary wasn't in or of the world and so he had no feel for people. When her dear friend Virginia Denison's husband was in Europe, Virginia's lover André came over and found her in bed with Leary. André proceeded to beat the yogini, breaking mirrors and chairs and pottery, screaming wildly. He threw a bottle through a window. Slapped her. Proposed to her. Stormed out in a huff. The episode was troubling enough that the writer set it down in her diary multiple times, trying to get it just right. There's one detail that always stays the same, though. It's how you know it was the point. The point, for Angela Anaïs Juana Antolina Rosa Edelmira Nin y Culmell—or Anaïs Nin, for simplicity's sake—was Leary. He'd taken his hearing aids out the night before and he slept through the whole thing. The point was that he was a shitty lover, walled off from others. Oblivious. She could tell as soon as she met him. The Denison affair just cemented what Anaïs already knew with that uncanny writerly insight she liked to brag so much about. But this story is not about Timothy Leary. It is about the role of expertise and truth in American politics.

Anaïs first met Tim Leary and Richard Alpert at a party at Virginia's house overlooking Hollywood Lake on December 2, 1962. Everyone who was anyone in the L.A. LSD scene in the late '50s and early '60s partied at Virginia's. Anaïs joined after a friend suggested she be a test subject for Dr. Oscar Janiger's LSD research experiments several years earlier. Janiger was a regular guest. So were Aldous and Laura Huxley, Christopher Isherwood, and Alan Watts. Disciples would sit meditatively at Watts's feet in silence, usually hungover. On this evening, Leary and Alpert had arrived fresh from their first summer at the Zihuatanejo Project in Mexico, inviting Anaïs for the second season. She was flattered. "I want them to see your films," she wrote to her husband Hugo a few days later. "Invitations are rare and special."

She was not the only one taken with the visitors. Virginia promptly shacked up with Tim for the next several months until he returned to his commune in Mexico. There were problems with the arrangement. André was one, although taking additional lovers had never stopped any of them before. Even Anaïs, troubled as she was by André and Virginia's relationship, wasn't troubled because it was an illicit affair. Hell, she was married to two men at once—filmmaker Ian Hugo for when she was in New York and the actor Rupert Pole for her time in L.A.

What bothered Anaïs was the fact that André was a clumsy lout and Leary was a cold fish. She was bothered by the contradiction that the willowy yogini who taught her and her husband to breathe deep breaths thrived on abuse and drama. But most of all, if I have read her concerns correctly, she was bothered that Leary seemed so . . . *deaf.* Frigidity, for Nin, was a direct consequence of being closed to the world, a pathology American culture cultivated by forbidding imagination, sensuality, and pleasure in the aesthetic realness of the world. Tim sleeping through Virginia's beating wasn't simply physical deafness. For Nin, it was a clear sign of *emotional* deafness.

There was also the problem of Tim's job. He was supposed to be teaching classes at Harvard that spring. But Timothy Leary was not in Cambridge during the spring of 1963. He was in Virginia Denison's bed 3,000 miles away, and Anaïs's diaries make it clear that he was there for months. Leary may have publicly announced he'd been fired for experimenting with LSD, but Harvard, in a rare moment, was telling the truth when they said they fired him for not teaching his classes.

Given the state of the world, I could forgive the reader for wondering whether a historian of science could spend their time in better ways than digging up tawdry gossip. In the grand scheme of things, it likely doesn't matter that Virginia Denison's affair helps settle the longstanding question of why Timothy Leary was fired from Harvard in 1963. What's a bit of truth here and there when we have bigger things to worry about?

If I wish to defend the value of gossip, it's because I suspect our usual way of conducting business is broken because we can't be fussed with small matters. We turn to experts and books or to leaders and big ideas when we want guidance. But small money, small ideas, small people? We revile the powerless. And we ignore gossip. It's seen as too petty, too unimportant, too unvirtuous, too mundane. To put it another way, gossip is overlooked because it's seen as too *womanly*. But it's precisely this invisibility that makes it an excellent device for considering the roles that hero-worship, truth, and "importance" play in American politics. And it's an excellent source for fact-finding. People are more likely to spill secrets to strangers with little influence over their lives. Those with nothing to lose find it easier to speak truth to power. And something jotted in a diary that will never see the light of day is a lot more likely to be honest.

Work written for public consumption is a different matter. The first time I learned to be careful as a historian was reading Leary's description of his 1970 jailbreak. The sensuous, concrete details Nin accused him of not paying attention to were exhilarating. Historians don't get that kind of detail often. But then it hit me. The detail I'd fallen most in love with: the nerdy professor stooping to retrieve his glasses after he jumped the fence, then pushing them back up his nose before running into the night? I've never seen a picture of Timothy Leary wearing glasses. He made it up.

Propaganda is more mundane than nefarious. It's the simple willingness to sacrifice truth in the name of a bigger goal. "All revolutionaries lie,"

Kathleen Cleaver once said. She should know. She was the Black Panther Party's first Communications Secretary. Her husband, Eldridge, their Minister of Information.

Revolutionaries lie. And politicians. Public figures. Gurus. Anyone who believes their goals outweigh the need for truth. Yet we let this immediately self-evident and banal fact surprise us again and again. Should we really be surprised that Timothy Leary, a man who hired a personal archivist to follow him around while still living, was concerned with a carefully curated public persona? Should we have been surprised when we learned tobacco companies buried scientific research on the link between cancer and smoking for decades? Should we trust a person who says giving everyone psychedelics will solve political strife when that person can't even maintain peace in their own bedroom? What about someone who *does* lead a peaceful life, when we see how some other people who take psychedelics behave? If that person is a scientist? A writer? Could we take a shortcut, like Anaïs, and assume that if a person's methods and approach to the world are like ours, they can be trusted?

If I make much of the little things—of gossip and women's stories and emotions and quibbly things like personal motivation and exceptions to the rules—it's because smoothing the bits that don't fit in order to make a tidy story is false. It's false when we do it with history. It's false when we do it with politics. And it's false when we do it with science. And when we do it enough, should we really expect others to continue to have faith in us? How many scientists have to overstate their claims or hide the more ethically dubious parts of their research for the public to lose faith in the endeavor entirely? When does a guru cease being a guru?

I said that diaries are a special treat for the historian because they weren't meant to see the light of day, making them especially reliable. That's usually true. But, again, shortcuts are dangerous. Anaïs was a special case. Fiercely independent, vain, proud, and stifled by the Puritanism she felt in America, she hated having to be dependent on her husbands for her livelihood. Her escape? To sell her diaries. They were never meant to be private. It doesn't mean we should throw them out as sources, but it does mean we have to take care with them.

Anaïs didn't rewrite her entries on Timothy and Virginia to grapple with her friend's shitty love life. She prided herself on seeing people. She wanted her diaries to reflect that she saw it coming. And so "June 1961" is scribbled atop at least one of the drafts where she works over the story of meeting Leary and Alpert, despite the fact she didn't meet them until December 1962. Other versions share substantial portions of the same text, making it clear they were drafts of the same story. But one character stands out, helping date the drafts. She describes an exchange Leary had, one that softened her position towards the man she'd elsewhere described as a cult leader. In it, he was open, relaxed, responsive. Newfound traits, she was at pains to note, so unlike the Leary she'd remembered from those early meetings.

And Leary's interlocutor?

Eldridge Cleaver. Whom he didn't debate until 1971.

The devil's in the details. Anyone who tells you otherwise is selling something.

The events in this essay have been reconstructed from the Anaïs Nin Papers (Collection 2066), Department of Special Collections, Charles E. Young Research Library, UCLA.

A Homosexual Marriage Experience in Santo Daime

LIGIA PLATERO AND KLARISSA PLATERO

FIVE YEARS AGO, WE GOT MARRIED IN RIO DE JANEIRO IN A SANTO DAIME religious ritual. Recently, Shelby Hartman published an article in Chacruna about homophobia in ayahuasca circles.[1] We also went through situations of symbolic violence, inside and outside the rituals. We have much to thank the church adepts for who helped us in organizing the ceremony. However, we cannot fail to mention situations that we consider today as homophobic.

It was May 3, 2014. The place: a house in the middle of Tijuca Forest, in Alto da Boa Vista, Rio de Janeiro, Brazil. At 10 a.m., we went downstairs to the table where the notary judge was. She would fulfill the bureaucratic function of making us legally married. We acquired similar civil rights to those of heterosexual couples. In 2011, in a historic decision, Brazil's Supreme Court had ruled that homosexual couples also have the right to marry legally, with the same rights and duties as heterosexual marriage.

After the civil marriage, the adapted Santo Daime religious wedding ritual took place. Our marriage did not take place in the break at a festival ritual at the hall of the church, as happens in the heterosexual marriages of this religion in Brazil.

We kept three hymns (considered to be sacred songs) of Padrinho Sebastião's that are sung in heterosexual marriages, but we changed the texts read by the officiant. We selected the biblical passage Corinthians 13, which talks about love, replacing a conventional text of this church, Ephesians 5:23, according to which "the husband is the head of the wife."

Each of the betrothed entered the ceremonial space with their respective members of the bridal party, while the guests sang the hymn "The Symbol of Truth." All the people present sang 14 hymns from Santo Daime, selected by us. Guests wishing to drink ayahuasca could go to the altar to receive it. Along with us, several other people, mostly Santo Daime adepts, drank a small dose of the tea.

Years later, we remember the steps taken within the Santo Daime churches that led us to this wedding ritual. Between 2010 and 2012, I, Lígia, lived in Mexico City. There, I went through a process of religious conversion and became a *fardada* (adept) of Santo Daime (Igreja do Culto Eclético da Fluente Luz Universal Patrono Sebastião Mota de Melo—Church of Eclectic Worship of the Flowing Universal Light [ICEFLU]—Sebastião Mota de Melo, Patron).

From the beginning, I was accepted as homosexual in this church. I agree with Clancy Cavnar[2] that the ritual context (the setting) is very important in regard to inclusion or exclusion in the group, and the issue of feeling well received and accepted, or not, by leaders and by other members, as homosexual is something that changes the experience.

This congregation was a small group of urban youth whose social values were very different from those of more traditional Brazilian padrinhos; there was already a homosexual couple in the group. I felt the acceptance of homosexuality; but, paradoxically and simultaneously, I felt the presence of Mexican patriarchy.

The Santo Daime churches, in general, are organized in a patriarchal and hierarchical manner. Women are driven to perform gender roles related to motherhood and discouraged from leadership positions. There is a predominant conservative heterosexual family ideal.

The padrinho of the Mexican church accepted my homosexual orientation, but there was an effort on his part to make me appear to be heterosexual, with a clear female gender identity and normative behavior. There was acceptance of homosexuals, but on the condition that they fit with established hegemonic cisgender norms.

The Mexican church has received Brazilian padrinhos and madrinhas related to ICEFLU. Once, I asked a madrinha about her understanding of homosexuality. For her, it was a "social disease," created due to imbalances between masculine and feminine. Another madrinha suggested to me to seek motherhood through a heterosexual relationship. In other words, she advised me to fit into heteronormative standards. I perceived that, for her, homosexuality was a kind of taboo, a behavior to be fixed. On the other hand, when I participated in rituals at the Mexican church, the plant spirits never prompted me to seek that correction. Then, I realized that the intention to fit homosexuals into heteronormative patterns came from the moralities of the leaders, and not from teachings of the plant spirits.

On one occasion, I participated with this group in a peyote ritual conducted by a Huichol Indian. At the end of the night, the face of a young woman, who I didn't know then, appeared in my mind. After a few months, on a trip to Rio de Janeiro in 2010, I believed I recognized the young woman from the spiritual vision. Subsequently that woman became my girlfriend and, four years later, my wife. At the end of 2011, Klarissa visited me in Mexico City and became an adept of Santo Daime.

In December 2012, we lived together in Rio de Janeiro. At that time, we regularly attended one of the oldest churches of Santo Daime outside Acre State. In the Santo Daime rituals, we began to have spiritual visions and intuitions about our wedding ceremony. As a result, we decided to talk with the leaders of the church about the realization of the ceremony.

We talked at first with the madrinha, who did not oppose our union, despite her clear embarrassment. She emphasized that the ceremony could not take place in the church hall, because "that kind of ceremony doesn't belong to the tradition of Mestre Irineu [the founder of Santo Daime] and Padrinho Sebastião [founder of the ICEFLU branch of Santo Daime]." She gave us permission, but expressed the need to address this with the padrinho of the church.

So, that was what we did. At the end of a ritual, we told him our story and he told us that he would have to ask permission from Madrinha Rita, Padrinho Sebastião's widow and the most important leader in the religion in his understanding. He would give us a definitive answer after this conversation. We agreed to the condition. We requested daime (ayahuasca) for the ceremony, and he initially did not oppose this. We commenced with the legal proceedings of the marriage. We made the invitations and gave them to church members, about 80 people in all.

We could feel, inside and outside the rituals, the opposition to our marriage from some church members. As an example, days before the ritual, an elder from the church, with whom we had a good relationship, called us, saying that, during a different ritual, Padrinho Sebastião's spirit told her that our marriage could not happen. However, in that same ritual, we had experiences with the plant spirit that led us to believe that our spiritual guides, including Padrinho Sebastião, agreed with our union. Weeks after the marriage, this woman left the church.

That episode was not the most discordant one. Days before our ceremony, the padrinho from the church scheduled a ritual for men on the same day as our wedding. This act was shocking to us because our male guests were expected to be present at that ritual, which would start at the same time as our ceremony.

When we went to talk to the padrinho, he claimed that we hadn't confirmed the date with him. However, we had given the invitation to his family with the date on it. The madrinha was aware. Yet, in this conversation, the padrinho claimed that we had transformed the ceremony into a bigger event than he had imagined.

He suggested that we should have a small, more discreet ritual, where we would drink ayahuasca at a break from some ceremony, in the church itself, in a space called the "little house of the daime," only in the presence of the officiant and two groomsmen and two bridesmaids. In other words, away from everyone's eyes and "in the closet." He even suggested that we change the wedding date.

Here, his conservative morals prevailed, and this attitude led him to try to prevent us from having a ceremony attended by church members. That situation was one of the greatest points of tension and conflict that involved the organization of our marriage. On the other hand, the madrinha of the church confirmed the authorization of Madrinha Rita: "Yes, my daughter, you are authorized. Better to marry than to jump from branch to branch."

Despite this, the padrinho in Rio declined to provide the ayahuasca drink he once consented to supply to consecrate our union. We looked for another supplier and got the ayahuasca at the very place where the wedding ceremony would happen, which was the ritual space of another shamanic line linked to local Indigenous peoples (Guardiões Huni Kuin, also known as Tradições Xamânicas da América Indígena [Huni Kuin Guardians or Shamanic Traditions of Indigenous America]).

After the wedding ritual and lunch, the number of male participants at the celebration diminished, as the men left to attend the ritual announced by the padrinho from the church. However, the party continued until dusk, with the presence of women fardadas from the church, children, family, and friends; an unforgettable moment for us.

After a few weeks, an old member of Santo Daime told us that our marriage had softened rumors and gossip about homosexuality among church members. We understood that making our relationship public had exposed the taboo of homosexuality.

At the time, there were other queer members from Santo Daime who chose to continue hiding this aspect of their lives from fellow members. We knew about some of them because of the gossip or because they felt comfortable opening with us because we are also gay.

Despite all the conflicts and symbolic violence we endured, we did get married in an adapted ritual, and were respected as a couple by the other adepts. We believe that, due to the marriage ceremony, there was a relative social change regarding the acceptance of homosexual couples in this church. On the other hand, there continued to be a conservative and heteronormative hegemonic morality. In our experience, we have seen a lesbian couple and a gay male couple who are Santo Daime Church leaders from Padrinho Sebastião's line; however, some of these leaders present publicly as heterosexuals in order to avoid conflicts related to homophobia.

We believe that socio-anthropological research should be encouraged in order to determine whether homosexual-led churches offer a more welcoming environment for homosexuals and transgender people. This is because we have experienced for ourselves how important a welcoming setting is for LGBTIQI+ adepts engaging in personal healing and self-knowledge processes.

Treasures of the Forest:
Jarawara Women and the Plants They Carry

FABIANA MAIZZA

FOR THE JARAWARA, IF SNUFF IS AN ISSUE TO BE THOUGHT ABOUT, A CON-
ceptual question, it is so because it is something that women care for. Snuff
belongs to women: they are its main connoisseurs; they are the ones who
devote themselves to making, having, and "taking" (as the Jarawara say in
Portuguese) this little "treasure" from the village's daily life that is snuff—
here called *sinã*.

This text is based on my ethnography of the Jarawara people, whom
I first met in 2004, at the Casa Nova village, near the middle course of the
Purus River in the southwestern Amazon, and we have been in dialogue
since then.

*This is a map of
the Amazon River
drainage basin with
the Purus River
highlighted. Kmusser,
September 8, 2008,
Wikimedia Commons*

If I could describe, translate in a certain way, the world in which the Jarawara people live, I certainly would have to begin with the ideas of taking (*towaka*), going (*toka*), returning (*kama*), seeking (*waka*), bringing (*kaki*), carrying (*weye*), catching (*wata*), and holding (*tama*). As in other Amerindian societies, all these verbs of movement denote fundamental concepts of a system of action that daily—and often slowly—mark people's lives and activities. Everything, or almost everything, is carried, or rather, must be carried from one place to another. It is as if for the Jarawara, things—just because they are things—must be in constant motion: many species of plants are cultivated close to the houses and then transplanted into the gardens; the plants cultivated in the gardens, such as manioc, cassava, yams, and bananas, are carried back to the houses to be consumed; the prey (*bani*), the hunted animals, are carried dead to the village, to be cooked, as well as the fish, caught in inlets and lakes; small children are carried in slings during walks; firewood is brought from the forest to make fire near the houses; the cassava flour, produced in the ovens, is taken back to the houses. So great an amount of things are carried and taken that it would be exhausting to list them all here, but just remembering some last ones: the engine, the boat, the generator, the gas cylinder, the stove itself, the keyboard for the party, the firewood, clay, etc. . . . and so on, infinitely, people's daily lives are woven by the comings and goings of things.

In these displacements, carrying and taking are central. Perhaps the *paneiro* (*isiri*)—a basket of vine *titica* (*tama*), braided in different sizes, carried on the back, with the main support given by a band of *envira* plant that rests on the forehead—is the most important object on these comings and goings. The *paneiro* allows things, all kinds of things, of all sizes and weights, to be taken, carried.

The ideas of going, returning, taking, carrying, are informed by another existential idea which is "wanting," "having the desire to," and "liking" (*nofa*). We know that the "will" (to do things, for example) is an idea emphasized by many Amerindian groups. A person has to have the will to do something, anything, and when she or he needs help—such as to make cassava flour (an activity that requires at least the work of two or three people)—they need, in an almost contagious way, "to convince," "to seduce," "to give others the will" in order to get other people to accompany them.

Snuff seems to make a connection with this world of taking, going, coming, being taken, being carried, but also with the world of liking, of having pleasure. Snuff is linked to a state I have called *wandering*, acting perhaps as a conductor, a conductor of wills. In this way of understanding, snuff would activate a "takeable" agency in people, and as it is Jarawara women who predominantly consume tobacco, they would be particularly affected by the conductive effects of snuff. Additionally, there would be a certain ability in women to be "takeable" (*towakama*), "carryable" (*weyena*), something I have called "takeable agency."[1]

The concept of takeable feminine agency took shape in my work shortly after I participated in a specific event in the life of a young Jarawara girl. The event was the *mariná*, something that in anthropology is usually called the "female initiation ritual," a passage to adulthood. The event took place in 2014, and after spending the *mariná* very close to Dyimamirira, the young initiate, I realized that during the entire party, which lasted three nights and four days, she had no chance to sleep. By day, she was always in the company of women, and at night, she was in the company of many people in dances and shamanic chants—which closed a cycle of tiredness that had started more than three months before, when she had her first menstruation and began a long seclusion in a little house made especially for her, called *wawasa*.

Everything indicates that during the *mariná* festivities, the young initiate experiences a state of constant drowsiness, which is the effect of sleep deprivation. As if the lack of sleep would make it possible for her to dream at any moment. As if she would be in a state of drowsiness (*nokobisa*) and tiredness (*amaha*) that would put her in a oneiric disposition. Her sleepiness would work almost like numbing that would make her "dream" and would make her "light." Light not as an antonym of heavy but rather as "carryable," a disposition that would make it possible to "be taken" (*towakama*), "to be carried" (*weyena*), "to be led" (*kaki*).

I believe that "being takeable," "carryable," is a quality revealed to Jarawara women during their initiation festivities, their *mariná*. In this sense, the *mariná* has the effect of bringing awareness to the "soul," demonstrating the soul's capacities: showing that souls can be taken (*towaka*), "brought" (*kaki*), "carried" (*weye*), "held" (*tama*).

This description rests on two central concepts in the Amerindian worlds that differ significantly from how these same concepts are conceived by

Westerners: the ideas of "soul" and "dream." We can say that, in most Amerindian worlds, the soul would be a double of the body, and the idea of duplicity has existential implications that I will not be able to discuss here.[2] But in a simple way, we can say that the soul is able to detach itself from the body and live "experiences," meet other types of beings. For those who are not shamans this is involuntary, and it happens above all in dreams and in illness. These experiences are dangerous and unwanted as they denote a lack of control. On the other hand, dreaming is a form of shamanic knowledge. As Yanomami shaman Davi Kopenawa tells us: "We Yanomami, when we want to know things, we make an effort to see them dreaming."[3] It would be as if life here (of the body) and life in dreams (the life of souls) were parallel worlds that could be aligned at certain times, the oneiric experience being a powerful way for this kind of passage from one reality to another, from one perspective to another.[4]

The Jarawara women's "takeable" agency (*towakama*) seems to be analogous to the shamans' knowledge and complex networks of cosmopolitical relations. Jarawara shamans, *inawa*, like other Indigenous shamans, have the difficult task of forging and caring for relations with non-human beings.

Shamanic activity among the Jarawara is always mediated by snuff: the shaman first needs to inhale *sinã* so then he can call his "auxiliary spirits." These are souls of the plants that the shaman cultivates in the gardens, his plant-children,[5] souls with human appearance: the soul of peach palm, tingui, banana, tobacco, among others. These plant-children, when called, descend to communicate with the *inawa*, but they can also carry the inawa on their backs, to distant places, where the shaman establishes relations and alliances with different beings. The Jarawara *inawa* travel by being "carried" on the back (*weye*) of plant beings. Besides the women, only the shamans make *sinã*.

It would be fruitful to think about a proximity between women and shamans, something that would also be connected to the proximity of both to snuff itself, and with a certain "takeable agency"—a female shamanic agency or a shamanic female agency. Maybe, it would be this agency that allows them to be carried by the *sinã*—as if snuff was a kind of conductor of communication and movement that makes things move, so to speak, even if those things are thoughts and words. As if the *sinã* extracted from people the will that would make it possible to be taken.

However, by this I do not want to say that the use of snuff by women and shamans should be associated with the "transcendental." If we reduced the theme to a performative opposition between the sacred and the profane, there would be nothing more profane, immanent, and daily in Jarawara's life than inhaling *sina*. Snuff is taken in the morning, after a meal; in the afternoon, when people visit each other; before taking a bath; and, above all, before going to sleep. Finally, the Jarawara "take" snuff at many times of the day that may even go unnoticed. People take *sina* when they have the will to, or when they're together. Or both. Snuff has, above all, and in many ways, a central role in people's thought; it is what gives courage (*oko badyi*), or will, so that they enjoy the moment.

Sinā is also associated with heat (*hiwene*), with giving heat, making the person warm (*hiwe*); that's why people inhale before bathing in the stream, and before going to sleep. Many people, especially men, "take" snuff only at these two times of the day. This is because many of the tasks assigned to men require strength, and for strength *sina* is not recommended. For example, to carry a basket of cassava or anything else that is heavy, *sina* should not be inhaled—I was even told that too much snuff makes men "lazy" (*lefo ha*).

In the evenings in the Jarawara villages, people visit each other's houses after dinner to talk and "take" snuff. These moments are marked by intense conversation, where everyone shares what they did that day or week, gossip around, remember old stories (myths), and communicate in a very lively and relaxed way—*sina* motivating the whole.

The care taken with the tobacco plants is impressive for anyone who lives with Jarawara women, and it extends throughout the entire process of making *sina*. The love/affection/willingness (*nofa*) that women feel for snuff is also reflected in the special care they take of the tobacco plant throughout its process of growth: in the place where it is sown, so that it does not get too much sun when it is still small; when it blooms; when it is growing, fast or slow; in the way the leaves are removed, as far down as possible from the stem; in the number of leaves removed from each plant, as few as possible; in the time of day it must be done, when it is hot; in the way the leaves are taken to the village, symmetrically stacked and transported in a small basket made specially for them; in the way they slowly remove the midrib and once again stack them neatly and attractively; in the way they are left to dry, tied to small branches, one for each leaf, around a small fire, or on an aluminum plate above the fire, where they are arranged next to each other some distance apart; in the patience required so that they reach the right consistency to be duly pounded, which in the rainy season can take a few days; in the long process of crushing and filtering so that the tobacco dust is homogeneous and with a consistency pleasant to the nostrils, always taking great care not to waste or lose anything when changing the powder to containers during manufacture; in the way that they go out to distant regions of the forest to search for cocoa tree bark, to then reduce them to ash and add them to the crushed tobacco, aiming for smoothness and taste in the mixture. It is also women who provide snuff to those who want to "take it." They leave the pots of *sinã* inside small cases and cloth bags together with the inhaler (*firi*). When someone wants to "take" snuff, they should ask a woman.

This proximity of women and tobacco plants can make us think of tobacco through its coevolution with women, pointing to the idea that women's care for the plants and the care of the plants for the women would be co-constitutive or simply that women and tobacco would be co-constitutive.[6] As it has been said, transcendence is not a fruitful concept to think of these relations. Maybe, it would be more interesting to rethink the concept of care,[7] reaching out to the idea of a politics of everyday life. The care that women take with gardens, with tobacco plants, with *sinã*, with people, with rearing animals, can be seen as a way of creating relations with countless types of beings and with the forest itself. What we see here can be called the "female politics of life," which is marked by the central role of care as a way of acting and perpetuating the world. In this acting, the takeable agency shows that the ability to be taken is part of the vast and complex relations of care, and it would be closer to political action than to a supposed female domestic passivity.

A version of this article is available as Chapter 2 of O uso de plantas psicoativas nas Américas (The Use of Psychoactive Plants in the Americas) *(Maizza 2019). This piece was translated from Portuguese by John Milton.*

Creating Awareness on Sexual Abuse in Ayahuasca Communities: A Review of Chacruna's Guidelines

DANIELA PELUSO, EMILY SINCLAIR,

BEATRIZ C. LABATE, AND CLANCY CAVNAR

THE CREATION OF THE CHACRUNA INSTITUTE FOR PSYCHEDELIC PLANT Medicines' Ayahuasca Community Guide for the Awareness of Sexual Abuse[1] aims to assist individuals within the psychedelic community to understand the common scenarios that can lead to abuse during ayahuasca consumption. Codes of conduct are typically and rightfully held up to scrutiny; the process of collaboratively crafting these guidelines for the awareness of sexual abuse in ayahuasca contexts has been no exception.

Ayahuasca has moved from the Amazonian forests to the global stage. In what was once a localized practice, ayahuasca is now part of a growing tourism market, and is being commodified[2,3] in a process that has sparked an "entrepreneurial industry."[4] Whether it is talked about on *The Late Show with Stephen Colbert*,[5] included in mainstream films, consumed at the sporadic rave, debated at global academic conferences, featured in the writings of psychonauts, or appearing as a key interest of the broader psychedelic community, ayahuasca has been in the spotlight. Part of this enormous growth in popularity has also led to problems: increased abuses of power, intercultural misunderstandings, the proliferation of inexperienced shamans, and vast power differentials that have fueled the unacceptable reality that ayahuasca ceremonies can become spaces where sexual abuse can occur.[6,7] As ayahuasca's popularity is increasing, alarmingly so are incidents of the sexual abuse of women. Nonetheless, many participants seeking ayahuasca healing remain unaware of this potential risk and can unwittingly find themselves in a vulnerable situation.

The Chacruna Guidelines consist of an introduction outlining the problem and provide a set of pointers regarding the most common scenarios in which abuse occurs. Here, Chacruna aims to educate individuals about what might be expected during typical ceremonial practices, so they can be aware of any behaviors that could potentially lead to sexual transgressions. In this way, the guidelines aim to support individuals as they pursue interests in and experiences of ayahuasca, providing key information to enable smart choices. Our hope is that with greater knowledge and awareness of past incidents and the contexts that give rise to potential sexual abuse, individuals and groups can better begin to combat such occurrences in the present and the future.

The guidelines focus on women because the majority of such cases involve the abuse of female participants by male shamans. Nonetheless, the guidelines do address issues applicable across genders and are of value to all. Attempting to cover diverse social and cultural settings where ayahuasca healing takes place, they were created through a collaborative process with experienced individuals in a wide range of ayahuasca settings across different cultural contexts and continents. This shared process—which compiled data from various intensive feedback stages—has included Indigenous as well as Western victims and survivors of abuse, ayahuasca healers and ceremonial facilitators, and social scientists who, like ourselves, have conducted long-term fieldwork in lowland South America and have long-standing experience among diverse ayahuasca communities. The guidelines also aim to be relevant across the wide spectrum of potential abuse that can occur in ayahuasca settings, including verbal persuasion, invasive touching, "consensual" sex between healer and participant, and rape.

Sexual abuse of women in the ayahuasca community occurs across and within specific cultures and communities. Yet, research and experience indicate that the current increase in ayahuasca's globalization further exacerbates the potential for abuse,[8] whereby many Western people now attend ayahuasca ceremonies in South American contexts, and with South American healers traveling to the Global North.[9] Mutual cross-cultural misunderstandings and misconceptions between healers and participants can create confusion at least, and can be brutally manipulated at worst. The Guidelines equip individuals with information about these culturally unfamiliar contexts where ayahuasca ceremonies often take place as a form of empowerment.

While the Guidelines may appear overly directive, risking the allegation that they tell individuals what to do with their own bodies, it would be disingenuous *not* to advise individuals who will be placing themselves in unfamiliar settings and inherently vulnerable context of what the typical basic ground rules are and what some of the high-risk factors might be. With knowledge of the Guidelines in advance of ayahuasca events, individuals can be aware of common manipulative techniques that sexual abuse perpetrators typically employ.

Mutual consent is a complex and critical issue that the Guidelines strive to raise as a significant point of consideration. Research, interviews, and personally related accounts suggest that some incidents of abuse occur in contexts that are described in precarious "consensual" terms. Consent, how it is understood and negotiated, is the basis for all respectful interactions. For consent to be effective, at minimum individuals need to engage in communication that is mutually intelligible so that meanings are shared and intentions are clarified, with an understanding that consent always occurs within specific socio-cultural-political contexts.[10] Indeed, consent and the policies surrounding consent are only as effective as peoples' understanding and use of them.[11]

For these reasons, it can happen that at the time that one might grant "consent," all things might appear to be equal; yet, retrospectively one may come to understand that the reality of such equality had been difficult to ascertain at the time that it was taking place. Furthermore, the healer is in a position of power and responsibility that creates an imbalance between the parties. While some healers may just take this for granted as a given inequality, some abuse these uneven power relations to manipulate women into having sex with them.

In some shamanic ayahuasca practices, there are techniques specifically employed to induce feelings of sexual attraction; these techniques are collapsed together with local cultural concepts of "hunting" as a compatible form of seduction.[12] For instance, many women have reported that they were manipulated into sexual acts through the use of a variety "charm spells."[13] While such claims address intangible aspects of shamanic practices, they remain a unique feature compared to non-shamanic contexts of sexual assault, and are cited in numerous instances of reported sexual abuse among ayahuasca and shamanic healing circles. In such cases where ayahuasca participants are actively seduced or targeted by a healer or facilitator, they are often unaware that they are being manipulated or influenced by the power dynamics of the context in which they are situated, thus making the grounds for mutual consent shaky.

Another common scenario in reported attempts or instances of sexual abuse is that some healers might suggest to a participant that having sex with them is a form of healing, or a way to gain spiritual power. They can also attempt to substantiate this by purporting that these extramarital relations are morally approved by their own wives or partners. In cases where women might agree to relations with shamans, they might be given a special position in an ayahuasca ceremonial space in an attempt to make them feel special or gifted, thus encouraging them to continue to engage in sexual relations. When sexual abuse happens along these lines, following such incidents, women are often confused and ashamed and feel unable to speak up, often believing that they are limited in their ability to accuse or confront the shamans, religious leaders, and other perpetrators of abuse with whom the accountability actually lies. The Guidelines are aimed at empowering participants by describing the features of such deceptive scenarios so that they can make informed decisions and feel encouraged to speak out in cases where they might be doubtful whether an interaction was appropriate.

It is the healer or facilitator's responsibility to resist entering into relationships with ceremonial participants within the healing space, even if women might approach them with this intention. This is an aspect that many shamans frequently have a hard time understanding, and in the future, we would like to find ways to better create and foster these intercultural conversations. The Guidelines do not deny that loving and sexual relationships can develop between ceremonial facilitators and participants in ayahuasca circles. However, as with doctors or therapists and patients, it is widely agreed that this is a harmful transgression in healing contexts, particularly when it occurs between two people not known to each other prior to taking ayahuasca together. However, unlike the health profession, there are no codes of ethics, commonplace rules, or generally accepted guidance as to how long parties should wait after the healing context if they are considering initiating a relationship; indeed, this topic generates contentious disagreements within the ayahuasca community. Chacruna's purpose with the Guidelines is to create a healthy conversation around these delicate issues, and to raise awareness about the complexities of "consensual" sex, so that individuals can be better informed and thus empowered by such knowledge, enabling them to make the best choices for themselves.

Additionally, and of increased importance, is the question of whether consent, either willfully given or acted upon, can be properly granted under any circumstances in any ayahuasca setting. This question is open to much debate and raises broader contemplation about the validity of consent and the use of psychedelics at large. While renowned psychonauts such as Timothy Leary hailed such a combination, as did ayahuasca pioneer Terence McKenna—who referred to the bringing together of sex and psychedelics as "the Mount Everest of the experience"[14]—the variable legal status of psychedelics means that consent is never legally grantable in any context in which an individual is affected by a classified drug. In this sense, it is important to note that the classification and status of ayahuasca as an illegal drug varies across jurisdictions, adding to the complexity of legal issues of consent.

Nonetheless, broader questions of whether consent can ever be granted in any circumstances in which one or more individuals are in an altered state of consciousness, regardless of a substance's legality, need to be considered. Conventionally, following current parameters, sex and psychedelics are legally meant to remain separate. Clearly, the issue of consent regarding sex with the use of psychedelics needs a greater nuance of understanding and increased and ongoing discussions across ayahuasca and psychedelic circles.

The Guidelines are currently available in 14 languages and are downloadable without charge on Chacruna's website.[15] To complement the Guidelines, Chacruna has also researched and developed a Legal Resources Companion to the Guidelines for the Awareness of Sexual Abuse.[16] The Legal Resources Companion, also available online free of charge, provides information about policies and laws in relation to sexual abuse on a country-by-country basis. It provides contacts and places where one can promptly seek information and support from trustworthy organizations should an incident of abuse occur. Importantly, the Guidelines encourage people to not be bystanders. The dissemination of the guidelines is also already exerting influence in local settings whereby shamans, facilitators, and participants are reading about sexual abuse in their own languages and thus making strides to better comprehend the experiences of tourists while also being encouraged to speak out against abuse. This seems especially important in countries where patriarchy and stereotypical gender roles often naturalize women's behavior as being submissive to men. Such important incremental long-term changes are cumulative and will hopefully eliminate the need for the Legal Resource Companion as sexual abuse becomes viewed as more of a community responsibility rather than just an individual one. Until that day, the Guidelines will provide insights about potential signs and contexts for sexual abuse, and in doing so will equip newcomers and veterans alike, to be as informed as possible.

Of course, sexual abuse affects people beyond ayahuasca healing contexts. In fact, the abuse that transpires in ayahuasca circles is part of a global epidemic of violence against women and vulnerable others. Estimated worldwide figures state that 35 percent of women have experienced physical or sexual violence; national estimates are in some cases as high as 70 percent.[17] It is therefore vital to find ways to transform social norms to protect everyone against all forms of violence. The Guidelines, with their own humble yet focused approach, in communicating locally and internationally across borders, cultures, and languages, aim to provide individuals with knowledge while also building allies to unite against the abhorrent problem of sexual violence.

The authors wish to thank the Journal of Psychedelic Studies *for permission to reprint excerpts of "Reflections on Crafting an Ayahuasca Community Guide for the Awareness of Sexual Abuse" by Daniela M. Peluso, Emily Sinclair, Beatriz C. Labate, and Clancy Cavnar (March 2020, vol 4., 24–33, http:// dx.doi.org/10.1556/2054.2020.00124).*

Lola "La Chata": The First Important Drug Trafficker in Mexico City (1934–1959)

NIDIA OLVERA-HERNÁNDEZ

MARÍA DOLORES ESTÉVEZ ZULUETA, ALIAS LOLA "LA CHATA" ("SHORTY" OR "Snub-nose"), was born in 1908 in Mexico City, the daughter of Dionisio and Luisa. She grew up in the neighborhood of La Merced, where she became a trader, selling pork scratchings and vegetables at a stall with her mother; but from an early age she realized that there was a business that was every day becoming more profitable: illicit drugs. In time, Lola came to specialize in trafficking a calming, analgesic, and sedative substance: *diacetylmorphine*, better known as heroin.

In 1898, just 10 years before Dolores was born, Bayer Pharmaceuticals had begun marketing heroin for cough relief and as an analgesic substitute for morphine, as diacetylmorphine was thought to be an opioid with great medical potential and less addictive than morphine.[1] But, less than five years later, various doctors noticed that morphine and other substances could produce dependency, causing what was then called "drug addiction." As a result, in January 1912 authorities of various countries signed the Hague Convention, marking an international move to restrict certain drugs, in particular suppressing opium, cocaine, morphine, and heroin.[2]

The Mexican government approved similar international treaties for repressing drugs and in 1920 promulgated "Provisions on the Cultivation and Trade of Products That Degenerate the Race," which prohibited marijuana, cocaine, opium, morphine, and heroin in the country.[3] By 1929 the production, sale, and consumption of drugs were included among "crimes against public health" in Mexico's penal code, increasing police persecution and imposing punishments such as forced rehabilitation, financial penalties, or imprisonment.[4]

Prohibition did not end drug use; by the 1930s marijuana and heroin were the most consumed illegal psychoactive substances in Mexico City. Consequently, a number of entrepreneurs like Lola realized that, despite the risks, the sale of plants and illicit substances was becoming a profitable business.

This article recounts the criminal history of María Dolores Estévez Zulueta, by analyzing criminal records from the Federal District Penitentiary, presently held in the Historical Archive of Mexico City. Together with other documents from Mexico's General Archive of the Nation, newspaper reports, and scholarly studies, I draw a criminal portrait of the most famous heroin trafficker of the first half of the 20th century: Lola "La Chata."[5]

LA CHATA'S FIRST ARRESTS, 1934–1937

Lola's first recorded arrest was in 1934 when she was accused of "crimes against public health" at the age of 26. Due to lack of evidence she was released after 48 hours.[6] Three years later "Lola La Chata" had become more popular; an operation was carried out in her house on Pradera Street, in La Merced. The agents of the Federal Judicial Police arrested Lola, her brother, and two "addicts," from whom they seized only two small pieces of heroin, a little marijuana, a bottle cap, a spoon, two droppers, and a syringe, all objects used in the administration of morphine hydrochloride.

La Chata denied the charges and blamed her brother's guests for bringing the drugs into her house. She claimed that there had been a mistake as near her house there lived a well-known drug dealer called Rosa, who had repeatedly denounced her because Rosa thought La Chata had denounced her the last time she was imprisoned. La Chata also stated that the agent who arrested her "resented her because she does not want to report anyone else."[7] Most of the detainees went to the Federal Hospital for Drug Addicts,[8] with the exception of La Chata, who, according to the reports, was instead taken to the Lecumberri Penitentiary. However, she was released after nine days by the 3rd District Judge in Criminal Matters due to lack of proof.[9]

DRUGS AND CORRUPTION IN THE CAMPAIGN AGAINST DRUG ADDICTION, 1937–1938

In April 1938, Luis Huesca de la Fuente, who until then had served as chief of the Narcotics Police of the Department of Public Health,[10] was imprisoned in Lecumberri and accused of abuse of authority, perjury, and crimes against public health.[11] Ultimately, he was accused of protecting Lola La Chata, who was alleged to have shared her earnings with him.

Leopoldo Salazar Viniegra, who was in charge of the National Campaign against Alcoholism and Drug Addiction, intervened. Salazar was an eminent psychiatrist from Durango, who conducted studies on marijuana, heroin, opium, benzedrine, alcohol, and other substances; he opted for a drug policy in which consumers were treated from a health perspective and were not criminalized. However, although the doctor saw drug addicts capable of rehabilitation, he did not think the same of traffickers.[12]

When Leopoldo Salazar heard about Luis Huesca's arrest and his ties to Lola, he published a letter in the *El Universal* newspaper directed to Lola, warning her that he was the new official prosecuting drug smugglers. Salazar praised her success with drug addicts, her talent "to know how to maintain her position, simply gaining the compliance of all the police," and her business acumen. The psychiatrist did not hide his displeasure and a certain "class prejudice" towards Lola, when he wrote that "she had not been born under the invocation of Venus" and reviled "the roundness of her body," which he attributed to the sale of tacos, the trafficking of drugs, and police persecution. Salazar added that since the area of La Merced was her territory, most of her clients must come from "the lower town," referring to this commercial and popular neighborhood very close to downtown. In addition, he stated that Mexican society was undergoing a social transformation to get rid of "seditious traffickers" and that he wanted to discuss these topics with her soon.[13] Lola ignored him, and her earnings increased.

Meanwhile, the press announced that the former official "Captain Huesca is in the penitentiary":[14] "Chief of the Narcotics Police arrested. He stole a large amount of cocaine. This drug was collected from a woman, and he exchanged it for bicarbonate."[15] Huesca responded to the article calling it "slander and intrigues." He found some agents "were biting" and he disagreed with Salazar Viniegra, saying: "The doctor had a grudge against me, and this is the result."[16] Luis de la Huesca spent a few days in Lecumberri before an expert chemical report indicated that "the consigned drug is not a drug" and that in reality it was "a chlorinated antiseptic substance"; he was released on bail for the crimes of abuse of authority and perjury.[17]

THE NUMBER ONE ENEMY OF MEXICO—
THE EMERGENCY LAWS OF 1945

Under the pretext of World War II, the government of Manuel Ávila Camacho promulgated an "emergency law." Purportedly due to an increasing number of individuals dedicated to "immoral trafficking," legal rights were suspended for any person who violated the drug laws.[18] Apparently, the first person to whom this rule was applied was precisely Dolores Estévez, La Chata, who was at that time considered public enemy number one by Mexican authorities.

At the beginning of July 1945, La Chata was apprehended outside her house in La Merced and sent to Islas Marías prison, on an island located off the country's west coast. In response, Lola sent a telegram to President Ávila Camacho and his wife, Soledad Orozco de Ávila, denying the charges against her.

She instead argued that the police authorities had tried to influence the presidential couple based on rumors, since she "luckily won the lottery and multiplied money with sacrifices and honest business." She claimed that these profits helped people in her neighborhood by giving them clothes, food, candies, and toys. Moreover she was "innocent of the charges against her"; "evil people" had abused her name. Her first husband Juan Morales had been arrested for drug trafficking, but he had died 10 years earlier. She had nothing to do with contraband goods and the police had persecuted her unjustly.[19] The presidential office never responded and Lola remained in prison until March 1946.

EL MESÓN DEL PARAÍSO, 1947

Nestled in the heart of the Tepito neighborhood was a drug injection site: the famous Mesón del Paraíso (Paradise Inn). Although in operation for over a decade, the police carried out periodic raids, making apprehensions of substance users and seizing drugs.

On January 31, 1947, five Federal Judicial Police agents reported that they had located marijuana, heroin, and hypodermic needles, and arrested several "addicts." The detainees in turn accused La Chata of being one of the main drug distributors in Mexico City. An arrest order was issued for Lola "La Chata," Antonio García Rojas alias "El Venado" ("The Stag"), and "El

Confrontation between General Armando Valderraín and Dolores Estevés, 1957. Photographic archive formerly of the La Prensa newspaper, private collection

Sargento" ("The Sergeant"), as well as for Señora Jova Orozco and Petra García Rojas, wife and sister respectively of "El Venado."

This was nothing new for Lola. In response to the claims made by the Mesón del Paraíso detainees, her lawyer, Señor Pacho Herrera, countered that the accusations were false. He insisted that her rights had been violated because she was targeted for arrest without proof of possession, consumption, supply, or trafficking of seeds, plants, or illicit substances. But since La Chata had a criminal record, she remained imprisoned for two months until she was released on $10,000 bail.[20]

DUEL IN THE UNDERWORLD! FINAL ARREST AND DEATH, 1957–1959

By the 1950s, police called Lola the "Drug Empress." Her fame was such that she was already known beyond the Mexico's borders; she was on the sights of Harry Anslinger, and the American Beat writer William Burroughs called her the "Aztec goddess." The press marveled at her abilities. Her vast network of narcotics distributors throughout the city revealed her brazen and corrupt dealings with high-ranking officials.

Lola La Chata moved again, this time to the south of the city in the neighborhood of Prado Churubusco. In 1957 Commander Armando Valderraín arrested La Chata along with 30 people, her supposed gang of "poisoners." The newspapers headlines declared, "Poor little Lola. The fingers of the well-manicured hands are covered with ostentatious and extremely

Dolores Estévez, alias Lola La Chata, drug trafficker, 1957. Photographic archive that belonged to the newspaper La Prensa, *private collection*

valuable jewels,"[21] "The well-known trafficker of 'artificial dreams' tries to pass herself off as a drug addict,"[22] and "a large amount of money, weapons and drug bottles were seized from her."[23]

Lola La Chata received a 15-year sentence in the Lecumberri Penitentiary, where she died in 1957.[24] Dolores Estévez Zulueta presided over the drug market in the Mexican capital for almost 30 years. As a woman she shattered gendered expectations and subverted masculine schemes by becoming a leading figure in drug trafficking.[25] Although the "Empress of the Underworld" died in prison and her empire came to an end, drug trafficking in Mexico City expanded during the following decades.

SECTION FOUR

Set and Setting

Decolonizing Psychedelics and Embodied Social Change with Camille Barton

SEAN LAWLOR

WHEN ATTEMPTING TO WRITE ABOUT CAMILLE BARTON, IT MIGHT BE easier to begin by listing what they *don't* do, as opposed to what they do. Camille's involvement in a huge array of projects and organizations makes for a somewhat paradoxical challenge in the interview: with so many projects, where does the interviewer begin?

Fortunately, Camille has a way of communicating their vast experience and broad perspective with remarkable clarity. Throughout this interview, they lucidly share their viewpoint on drawbacks to prevailing models of psychedelic therapy, shadow elements of psychedelic use related to extremism, and the myriad ways that dance can connect people with their ancestry and heal trauma through deepening connection with the body.

And that's a core feature of Camille's work: the body. As stated on their website, "The harms that come from racism, sexism, ableism, and other forms of discrimination, are carried in our bodies, often manifesting as physical pain, anxiety, hypervigilance, and other symptoms."

In their work as a somatic educator and embodiment researcher, Camille helps people reconnect with the forgotten wisdom of their bodies. In this interview, conducted in 2021, Camille explains in rich detail how embodied healing is necessary for dismantling the effects of systems of oppression that continue harming people every day and the role that psychedelics can play in that transformation.

Sean Lawlor: You do so many different things. What are you most occupied with at this moment?

Camille Barton: I'm developing a master's program at Sandberg Instituut, an art university in Amsterdam. The course is called Ecologies of Transformation. It's researching how art making and embodiment practices can be used to facilitate social change. It's a very dreamy research area for me because I've always felt that using symbols and beauty are powerful ways to create change and to connect with people.

Being involved in different kinds of activism throughout my life, I've found that there's often a lack of attention on weaving in things that might be humorous, pleasurable, or beautiful. I think there's a lot of scope to develop processes that, in the words of Toni Cade Bambara, "make the revolution irresistible." That program is going to begin in September of this year, and it's a two-year program. Applications are open until April 1.

I will also be running a grief retreat in June of this year, which is called Weaving Grief, the Body, and Transformative Justice. That's in collaboration with an environmental nonprofit called Global Environments Network. The aim is to hold space to explore embodied grief practices and rituals that can support communities to work more cohesively with each other, given the ongoing need to address coloniality and racism within environmental organizing.

Beyond learning about theory in history, we need space to grieve, and we need space to be able to support others in their grief and the multifaceted ways we are holding onto different kinds of pain. That is a deep, deep area of interest of mine.

This year, I will also be leading a training with Embodied Yoga on somatic practices for psychedelic-assisted therapies—exploring the importance of having a regulated nervous system when holding space as a therapist or provider during a psychedelic-assisted therapy session. The training will also incorporate content about embodied social justice and the importance of understanding how our bodies reproduce systems of power in our nonverbal, daily interactions with others.

SL: I hear a theme of *embodiment* in your work. We can intellectually have these discourses all we want, but to make space for the body to process grief and trauma is often missed. Can you talk about how the body carries forth systems of oppression and intergenerational trauma and how embodiment practice can help us heal?

CB: I think the first thing to say about the body is that it's really quite recent in the Western context to have the separation of mind and body, and this rise of Cartesian dualism, or mind-over-matter rationalism, that's taken place in the last few centuries in the West. In many parts of the world, before that revolution of ideas, the body was really seen as a site of wisdom, a space of knowledge, where we are in relationship to our ancestors, to embodied forms of knowing in relation to the land and our ecology.

As much as embodiment is trending and might seem quite new to people in a Western context, I think that what's happening is actually a remembering, a returning to ways of being that were much more commonplace throughout different parts of the world in human history. With that space of remembering, I'm excited to see people expand the conversations around things like racism and power—not just intellectualizing these issues but being able to understand that systems of oppression—racism, ableism, transphobia—may take root in our thoughts, but are also enacted through our bodies.

A lot of this is nonverbal. Our bodies are always giving signals about who we see as safe, who we see as dangerous, who's welcome, who's not welcome. Because our economic system has created a collective situation where we're so disembodied, and mostly valued on what we produce, we are often disconnected from noticing the subtle body language and cues we're giving off at all times.

Dr. Albert Mehrabian, who did a lot of research on nonverbal communication in the 1970s, found that over 55 percent of the way humans communicate is body language alone. Thirty-eight percent is tone of voice and 7 percent is the words we actually say. So much is being communicated through the body regardless of the words we say, so it's worth taking a more holistic approach to social change that goes beyond whether we're reading the right books, newspapers, or voting for a progressive political party. It's more about: How are we showing up in our bodies? How are we treating other bodies? Are we dominating others or are we giving space? Are our actions rooted in care?

Questions around interrelatedness become a lot clearer when we bring in the body. When it's theoretical, I don't think it helps us parse out how we need to *practically* act in order to create new ways of being that move us beyond systems of oppression and allow us to heal and exist in our full humanity and honor the life force within all beings, including the Earth.

SL: Dance is a big part of your life. Can you speak about dance in the context of embodied healing practice?

CB: Dance is one of the great joys in my life. It has been a bridge towards bringing me out of dissociation, because I have experienced a lot of dissociation in my life. It was a bridge to feeling more, to sensing more, to being able to link my emotions to sensations and make sense of them.

In mainstream culture, I rarely see people exploring how we can move emotions through the body as a means to relieve grief and tension. Dance was the catalyst for me to start exploring this and finding pathways to cultivate wellbeing in my body-mind. Before I knew what somatics was, dance was a space in which I could create ritual containers—starting in the context of raves when I was a teenager—and listen to the language of my body, to move what needed to move.

As I've researched more about dance as a ritual tool, it's been a catalyst to learning about my ancestors. I have mixed heritage, and my mother was born in Nigeria—so, it was wonderful to find out that my Indigenous Yoruba ancestors used dance and music in a ritual context to connect with spirit and community to celebrate and grieve. My connection to dance has made more sense the more I've learned about the role of dance in the context of my ancestry, because I think it is a *remembering* that is happening in my body, a returning to ways of being commonplace to my people not so long ago.

There's a book called *Dancing Wisdom* by Yvonne Daniel that was another gateway into the role of dance in many Afro diaspora communities and how ritual dance practices were preserved during the human trafficking that took place during the transatlantic slave trade. Today there are still many religions, such as Candomble in Brazil or Vodou in Haiti or Cuban Yoruba, where dance is still an important ritual tool. I am so grateful for the medicine of dance in my life.

SL: Do you see dance as having any possible role in this psychedelic therapy movement?

CB: Definitely. Sometimes when I'm dreaming with friends, we talk about the current protocols, particularly in MDMA. Granted, it will likely change after Expanded Access and approval, but right now, I don't think that the current protocol will be as effective as it could be for bodies who have an epigenetic legacy or intergenerational memory of healing alongside dance. I have a strong sense that many African heritage folks, for example, would benefit from being given permission to move their bodies and express using dance during psychedelic therapy sessions, which is currently not possible with the MDMA protocol.

It is an important practice of cultural humility to understand that what may work in one context for certain communities may not be what's most beneficial for all communities. I hope that as psychedelic-assisted therapies develop, there is more space to weave in dance and different movement practices and not to medicalize and sanitize all approaches to the point that we're just using a Western psychotherapeutic model where someone has to lie still and be quiet, processing thoughts and emotions without necessarily locating those emotions and moving them through the body. As these therapies are legalized, I hope there's room for a multiplicity of approaches. I sense that dance will have a crucial role in the future.

SL: I hadn't fully considered that this structured, lying-still approach to psychedelic therapy normalizes healing in that context and occludes so many healing practices. I've seen a theme in your work of pointing out trends of white supremacy and colonialism that perpetuate in these easy-to-miss ways into the psychedelic renaissance.

CB: Expecting things to be universal and normalizing one pathway is definitely a legacy of colonization. In the European context, this was really condensed in the Roman Empire. Before, there were many different kinds of Indigenous communities in Europe with different processes and rituals. With the arrival of Christianity and its implementation through Rome, there was a real move toward seeing universalism as *good* and something to strive for.

Some people say, "We shouldn't talk about difference too much, because these divisions just make everything worse." I think this is pointing back to this normalized assumption that universalism is inherently good, that it inherently leads to social cohesion. Really, there may be an argument to suggest that celebrating and honoring humans in our different ways of doing things, our different ways of honoring our dead or being in ritual or working with entheogens, actually will create a lot *more* compassion, care, and understanding, instead of needing a dogmatic, one-size-fits-all approach that will not serve everyone and generally excludes and harms some communities.

In terms of healing from this dogmatic approach, I wonder what it would look like to build a psychedelic therapy space that allows for culturally informed approaches that support different communities to incorporate their ancestral or pleasure-based practices?

In order to imagine that within the medical model, a lot of trust building and repair is needed. I think this process would have to begin with truth and reconciliation processes to name and account for the colonial harms embedded in and perpetuated by the medical system and scientific research. An example text that references some of these atrocities against Black bodies is *Medical Apartheid* by Harriet Washington. *NeuroTribes* by Steve Silberman documents the history of autism, including an overview of the deep violence against neurodivergent and disabled people due to the eugenics movement that was dominant within the sciences. We need to collectively acknowledge and repair what the medical-industrial complex has done, and continues to do, to disabled bodies, Black bodies, queer and trans bodies, and Indigenous bodies. To women's bodies. I don't think we can have inclusive, accessible health care until this traumatic history is addressed and repaired.

One of the ways we can pivot from these past harms is to understand that one group of people is unlikely to know what is right for everyone. With our platforms, with our power, it's beneficial for the collective to share, redistribute, and allow things to iterate and evolve that are led by the communities they are intended to serve. Particularly in regards to those who have been harmed by these same systems, now setting the parameters for how psychedelic-assisted therapies will be designed and rolled out. Within the movement, one of the ways we could pivot from centuries of dominance and universalism is to advocate for the right for different approaches, led by the communities they are intended to benefit.

SL: That gets me wondering about the decriminalization movement. I'm curious if you see that movement as opening things in that direction of more possible expressions in the space of psychedelic healing or if it perpetuates the same trends of colonialism in a different form.

CB: I have complex feelings about that. On the one hand, I was really excited to see what happened in Oregon with the election. At the same time, I have concerns that decrim has arrived in Oregon, which has ongoing, deep issues with racism and police brutality, and I wonder whether or not we're gonna see continued forms of harm against Black, Indigenous, and people of color while the mainstream turns away and says, "Oh, that doesn't exist anymore, because we've decriminalized."

I think we're already seeing this happen in a number of different situations, especially in the context of women of color who are pregnant. Many are going for doctors' appointments and checkups in a state where cannabis is decriminalized or legalized, but when marijuana is showing up in their bodies, these women or pregnant people are sometimes having to deal with child protective services due to using a substance that is legal or decriminalized in their state. We have to work to ensure that public health catches up with decrim and legalization so these grey areas are not used to harm the same communities that have been targeted by the War on Drugs.

As a movement, we have to be much more nuanced in understanding what decriminalization means and how it helps, or doesn't fully benefit, different groups of people. We have to be in solidarity with those who are still being oppressed as a result of drugs, even if decriminalization makes the situation look slightly different than it did before. We have to look at these things that still need to be changed if decriminalization is really going to be equitable and mean the same thing for everyone, to look at the domino effect of what this means in terms of public health, employment, education, immigration status, and what it affects outside the narrow view of drug policy and entheogenic use.

What do these policies mean for people if they start to use these substances, thinking they're safe in all areas of life? What does it mean for undocumented folks? I think these are the questions we have to ask, because it is already affecting people negatively, and they are the same people who have been most harmed by the War on Drugs and state violence.

SL: You've written and spoken about a common perception in psychedelic activism of a kind of "unity consciousness" belief that "we are all one" and a complementary perspective of "if people take psychedelics, people will love each other, and problems will be solved!" I wonder if you might touch on that in relation to spiritual bypassing in psychedelic conversations.

CB: This is something coming up for me a lot right now, given the insurrection or attempted coup that took place at the Capitol and the images all over the Internet of this "QAnon Shaman," who goes to Burning Man, takes psychedelics, and was active in wellness communities. He is a prime example that psychedelics do not necessarily make you left wing and cooperative! Despite many, such as Robin Carhart-Harris, suggesting this for a long time in their research.

It's not that entheogens can't create more openness, but I think it's a dangerous bypass to believe that because someone works with plant medicines, they're going to be left wing/progressive and won't have racist views or dominating behavior. All the allegations that have come up around sexual abuse and violence in psychedelic spaces is another testament to the fact that you may be someone who can hold space and you may have a lot of wisdom to share around plant medicines, but that doesn't mean you're immune from violating others and from causing harm. As humans, we are all capable of causing harm and I think it's important to acknowledge that and build accountability mechanisms into all our movements.

I really hope that we can learn from this moment. I hope that people laugh if they need to laugh—because there was a ridiculousness to what happened at the Capitol—but once that laughter has been processed, I hope that they actually sit with the severity of what this means and the amount of bypassing that is happening by people dismissing these folks because there was a certain amount of ineptness and foolishness. We have to come back to the realization that these people were still willing to kill because of white supremacist ideals, still willing to harm bodies. Some of them use plant medicine. If anything, hopefully this event can paint a broader picture of the spectrum of views among people who work with plant medicines.

It's confronting but necessary for people in the psychedelic movement to have a truth and reconciliation moment, to look back at history and reacquaint themselves with the fact that the Nazi party—and many other far-right groups—were users of entheogens. We need to reframe our thinking around what these medicines do, to see them as things that have great healing potential, but in and of themselves are *neutral* and maybe even have a way of entrenching our existing viewpoints.

I've seen a few people in my circles on social media refer to the QAnon Shaman as someone who had "unintegrated psychedelic experiences." I've responded, "I don't think these are unintegrated! If anything, I think these are *integrated*, because psychedelics have further entrenched his views and further expanded his ego and ability to hold that confidence to express, 'This is who I am.'"

That is something that psychedelics can do. Rather than shy away from that, we need to ask more strategic questions, like, "What would it look like to use psychedelic-assisted therapies in a way that could *undo* the legacies of colonization, or *repattern* legacies of rape culture and gender-based violence?" There may be other structures, models, or protocols we need to create that facilitate that, because it's very clear in this moment, and historically, that entheogens alone will not do that. We need to have specific containers for different processes if social change is an aim. And people may have to think about power dynamics to explore where they are in relation to certain issues.

How do we create architectures of care that sustain life and humanize all people, and how can we do that with psychedelic-assisted therapies? I think that's something we really need to sit with in this moment and not laugh it off and bypass by saying these are just ridiculous people who are outliers rather than reflective of a trend within the psychedelic community. The ridiculousness is a facade, a way to distract from intent. We need to focus on intent as well as action.

SL: And we need to see someone like that as indicative of the shadow of psychedelics. We're so willing to instantly say, "Well, that's just *that guy*, and that's not *psychedelics*." That perspective bypasses a shadow we'd rather not look at. That's a whole different conversation I would love to have with you at a future date.

To wrap things around: your earliest psychedelic publication I found was your article for the MAPS *Bulletin* in 2017. Was that your entry point into being a voice in this psychedelic world?

CB: Yes.

SL: So, that's several years now, and you've been consistently involved in bringing important and nuanced perspectives to the movement since. Could you point to any areas where you have seen shifts in those years, and areas where you have not?

CB: I am very pleased to see that conversations about access and inclusion are now on the table. There's a lot of work to do, but it's in the field now, whereas even a year or two ago I would have said that it's not really a mainstream consideration. At this stage, we have named symptoms, but now is the time to start visioning and building what we wish to grow. We need to create new tools and processes.

I am excited by Journey Colab and Sage Institute. I'm excited to see new models of what clinics can look like that are based in reciprocity, care, cultural humility, and access. I'm excited about the ways that MAPS is incorporating new information, learning and developing as they grow.

What I would like to see more of is cross-pollination between the psychedelic-assisted therapy space and public health systems more broadly. How can we build bridges to support each other and have holistic policies that address multiple-issue areas? How can we ensure that Indigenous people have access to land in which to cultivate their medicines? How do we create regenerative business models that invest in and support Black folks and other communities most harmed by the War on Drugs?

And integration. With the mainstreaming of psychedelics, a lot of the information and harm reduction materials available are not culturally relevant for Black communities and others impacted by police violence and the War on Drugs. We're seeing a particular perspective espoused in documentaries on Netflix, such as *Have a Good Trip*, that mostly relates to affluent, middle-to-upper-class, Western, white, housing-secure people. This content bypasses the risks of drug use for certain communities due to the War on Drugs or poverty and portrays psychedelics as a magic pill that will guarantee fun or healing. These films do not mention harm reduction practices or the importance of integration.

If you don't have a support structure to integrate, if you don't have a community around you who know what you're doing and can support you through the big shifts psychedelics can catalyze, the fallout may be dangerous for some with less access to support. Brilliant advocates such as Yarelix Estrada and organizations such as Liberation Training are offering psychedelic integration circles for BIPOC in order to address this need for culturally relevant support spaces.

Instead of simply thinking about psychedelics as a magic pill and about how people access the medicine, true access involves considering the other components that will allow psychedelic-assisted therapies to be helpful to all people. We have to think about housing, childcare, and public health systems more broadly. How do we build architectures of care that ensure healing is no longer a luxury for the privileged few?

In this vein, I would like to see more cross-pollination between different fields and less psychedelic exceptionalism. These medicines are powerful, but they're not the only piece of the puzzle. We need to think about mending the ruptures and gaps in support that systems of inequity have left, so that more people can benefit from psychedelic-assisted therapies.

SL: Are there any final points that you feel drawn to touch on?

CB: I will talk a little bit about liberation psychology, which was established in the South American context in the 1970s. It is a therapeutic approach that accounts for the ecological conditions of people's lives, including state violence, systemic oppression, and the impact this has on individuals, as well as the collective. It understands that traditional forms of psychotherapy often isolate an individual's symptoms from the collective conditions in which they have been shaped.

I really hope that as psychedelic-assisted therapies develop, we can move away from a hyper-individualized model to thinking more about collective care and collective healing, which is only possible in a sustained way if we repattern systems of harm. An individualized therapy model may not acknowledge that a person's symptoms have emerged due to the social conditions and context in which they live. If a Black, trans woman experiences chronic hypervigilance, and she lives in a heavily policed, heavily surveilled area, being hypervigilant makes sense as a defensive strategy within her body to protect her. However, over time, sustained hypervigilance, without an ability to safely rest and down-regulate, may lead to many other problems in the body-mind. This is simply one example of why it is essential to consider ecological context and acknowledge the lived realities that inform symptoms.

I hope we can weave in lessons from liberation psychology to ensure we also develop strategies to explore collective healing and repair from systemic oppression.

How Music Therapists Helped Build Psychedelic Therapy

STEPHEN LETT

BY THE LATE 1950S, MUSIC'S VITAL CONTRIBUTION[1] TO PSYCHEDELIC THER-
apy was well established. A brief[2] mention[3] of music[4] seems[5] almost[6] obliga-
tory[7] in a central strain of the literature. When discussing their methods in
a 1961 article,[8] however, the team at Hollywood Hospital in New Westmin-
ster, British Columbia, altered the formula. Instead of mentioning music
per se, they write: "We think a group of four [therapists] is best. Generally
this includes the psychiatrist (as therapist), a psychologist (cotherapist), a
psychiatric nurse and a music therapist."

In mentioning music therapy, the Hollywood team recognized the need
for professional expertise regarding music's therapeutic use. Itself in an
early stage of professional development, tensions within the field of music
therapy played out in competing approaches to selecting music in psychedelic therapy: is it music's emotional content or a patient's familiarity with
music that most reliably led to the desired outcome?

Hermina E. Browne in 1939.

In exploring these tensions, this essay traces the contributions of music therapists at three research sites between 1960 and 1975. In particular, I bring to the fore the work of two women in the field, Hermina E. Browne and Helen L. Bonny.

EXPLORING MUSIC'S EFFECTS

Hermina E. Browne[10] (1902–1966) was one of the first music therapists directly involved in psychedelic therapy. An active vocalist throughout her life, Browne's journey to music therapy began in 1943 when she helped[11] survey[12] the use of music in psychiatric institutions in her role as a field worker for the Home Mission Council of North America.[13] After studying with prominent music therapists Harriet Ayer Seymour and Willem van de Wall,[14,15] in 1948 she became director of music therapy at Marlboro State Hospital, New Jersey, where she stayed until joining staff of the New Jersey Neuro-Psychiatric Institute in 1956. There she began developing a method for selecting musical accompaniments during psychedelic sessions for alcoholics.

In the first[16] two studies, Browne's approach was fully exploratory, based on the individual psychedelic therapy procedures carried out in Saskatchewan by Humphry Osmond and Abram Hoffer. Her approach was to play music "continuously for half-hour periods with approximately half-hour rests in between," and she "selected [music] on the basis of emotional content, the patient's age, his cultural background, and his preference." She offers three case studies of music's effects during the therapy. For one subject, the music "did not appear to affect him any more than the mirror or Van Gogh pictures," though later he "state[d] that the music helped him to express himself more freely." A second "had great difficulties in expressing his feelings as he responded to the music because they had been hidden for such a long time," but "he did respond." And a third "automatically responded to the [music's] emotional content."

In the second[17]—carried out in collaboration with Osmond, who had just taken a position at Princeton in 1963—Browne presided over the music selections in a group psychedelic therapy method. As in the previous study, music was again played every other 30 minutes, and, similar to before, she chose music based on "(1) mood projected, (2) quality, (3) familiarity, (4) general suitability, [and] (5) subjects' requests if complying with above criteria." Midway through the study, however, "a more structured presentation of the music was made." She began to play a particular "category" of music for each period of listening in the following order:

1. "relaxing to tense" (for example, "Morning Moods" from Edvard Grieg's *Peer Gynt Suite No.1*)
2. "very tense, disturbed with a purpose" (the third movement of Pyotr Ilyich Tchaikovsky's Symphony No. 6)
3. "solemn, meditative, self-searching, spiritual" ("Asa's Death" from Grieg's *Peer Gynt Suite No. 1*)
4. "relaxing, spiritual" (Franz Schubert's "Ave Maria")
5. "reconciling, restoration of confidence, feeling of hope and faith" (Robert Shaw and Alice Parker's arrangement of Martin Luther's "A Mighty Fortress Is Our God")

She designed the progression of categories of music over the listening intervals "to complement the general pattern of reactions noted in previous experimentation." That is, she chose music based on her previous observations regarding an ideal trajectory of the psychedelic experience.

Unfortunately, Browne never wrote up her 1963 study. Before passing away in 1966,[18] she bequeathed her research notes to E. Thayer Gaston, preeminent professor of music therapy at the University of Kansas, who later passed them on to Charles T. Eagle Jr. to prepare for publication.[19]

Although music's "emotional content" or "mood" was a central factor in how Browne selected the music, Eagle does not offer any explicit observations on the topic. Instead, based on Browne's notes, Eagle observes that "according to the psychiatrist in charge [i.e., Osmond], the most effective music . . . was that music with which the patient was most familiar." Indeed, Eagle draws attention to how "as the study progress[ed], music requested by the patients was presented with greater frequency." He largely ignores Browne's expansive list of considerations for selecting music, focusing almost exclusively on familiarity and patient preference.

INSISTING ON THE FAMILIAR

A few years before he published the report on Browne's work, Eagle, in collaboration with E. Thayer Gaston, carried out his own psychedelic therapy research[20] at the Topeka, Kansas, Veterans Administration Hospital under the supervision of psychiatrist Kenneth E. Godfrey. Whereas Browne's study eventually categorized music primarily by "mood projected," which changed over the course of the session, Gaston and Eagle categorized music based on the patient's familiarity with the music. This approach maintained a condition of *familiar, unfamiliar,* or *miscellaneous* music throughout the session. Sorting patients by these music treatment conditions, they sought "to obtain quantitative data concerning the function of music in LSD therapy" so that psychedelic therapists might make evidence-driven selections instead of choosing music based on "subjective opinion."

Their results were ambiguous, but they did report that familiar music proved most effective. Indeed, they concluded by chastising music therapists who selected music because they find its content "profound." They argued that such aesthetic evaluations are "only an opinion," and insisted that the primary therapeutic value of music resides in its familiarity to each listener.

Although open to considerations of familiarity, Browne's primary concern in selecting music had to do with its emotional content. Gaston and Eagle, however, were solely concerned with the subject's familiarity with the music. In fact, they go so far as to argue that that approaches to music's emotional content were ideological, elitist, and entirely subjective. While establishing a new professional field in the '50s and '60s, Gaston wished to keep such "opinions" at arm's length. As the "father of music therapy,"[21] Gaston avoided emotional content and urged his colleagues to follow suit and, in effect, "man up."

VALIDATING EMOTION

Helen L. Bonny (1921–2010) emerged in the early '70s as perhaps the most influential music therapist associated with psychedelics. Born to a prominent protestant missionary, her own journey to music therapy came out of her personal experience with trauma. Reporting on a breakthrough she experienced while pursuing psychotherapy with Godfrey (of the Topeka

VA), she said: "through hypnosis he helped me to lift a childhood trauma into consciousness. I learned about the power of evoked imagery under his skilled guidance, how it can lead to healing and reintegration." As she writes, this therapeutic experience, combined with a powerful musical conversion experience that she had years earlier, led her, "at the age of 40, [to] appl[y] for study in the field of music therapy." Bonny was convinced by the power of emotional experience as a transformative and healing intervention.

After studying at the University of Kansas with Gaston, who had little interest in Bonny's mystical proclivities, Bonny found home for her research at the Maryland Psychiatric Research Center (MPRC). In 1969, she joined a psychedelics group as a staff music therapist to develop best practices for the selection of music in the sessions. Her article[22] on the topic, coauthored with Walter N. Pahnke, elaborated the practices with music at the MPRC. Her work has come to be a touchstone for approaches to music in therapy today.

Bonny developed several research projects at the MPRC designed to demonstrate that music's emotional content—and *not* the subject's familiarity with the music—was of primary importance. First, she carried out experiments to demonstrate that emotional content is an intersubjectively verifiable (if not an "objective") aspect of the music used. Though never published, her data indicates that it is. Next, her initial plan was to develop one emotionally attuned playlist and one "miscellaneous" playlist that she would use to test her hypothesis that the former would prove more effective.

Like other researchers, however, she abandoned this attempt at controlling psychedelic therapy. Instead, she developed guidelines for the use of music based on the extensive experience of the MPRC staff, referring to their choices as "empirically proven music selections." Though never fully demonstrating the position in her research, Bonny argued that while a person's preferences and history with music were important variables, attention to music's emotional content most reliably leads to a psychedelic experience.

As the psychedelics research was coming to a close at MPRC, Bonny departed around 1975. She continued experimenting with a non-drug music therapy she had innovated as a control for an MRPC study. This therapeutic modality would become Guided Imagery and Music (GIM)—the primary form of receptive music therapy used around the world today.

MUSIC THERAPY AND THE PSYCHEDELIC RENAISSANCE

As psychedelics research was shuttered in the 1970s, some of the prior professional connections were lost. However, with the proliferation of psychedelics research today, we are once again seeing exciting new connections being made. Along with these new connections, we might also consider reconnecting with communities of practice that emerged out of psychedelics research that are still rather isolated from the resurgence of research. In a recent review of the literature on music in psychedelic therapy, Clare O'Callaghan and colleagues write: "Music therapists are well-placed to help with the psychedelic therapy research renaissance."[23] Indeed, as GIM therapist Marilyn Clark[24] has also proposed, now with decades of experience using music to facilitate consciousness exploration, we might reanimate the ideal practices of Bonny's Guided Imagery and Music.[25]

Women's Historical Influence on "Set and Setting"

ZOË DUBUS

IN RELATION TO PSYCHEDELIC DRUG EXPERIENCES, "SET AND SETTING"[1] refers to an individual's mindset and the physical and social environment in which the drug experience takes place. While personalities such as Timothy Leary and Al Hubbard have been recognized for their contributions to the history of "set and setting," pioneering women researchers remain in the shadows.

It is rather striking that the work of Joyce Martin, Margot Cutner, and Betty Eisner is so little known and rarely discussed, in contrast to that of their famous collaborators, Ronald Sandison, Thomas Ling, and Sidney Cohen, respectively. This article highlights their work and their impact on this new emerging therapy in the 1950s and '60s. All three women devised a therapeutic approach with their patients that was comprehensive, benevolent, and nonintrusive, and that broke radically with traditional methods.

"SET AND SETTING": ITS ORIGINS

In the 1950s, some people in the medical community began to reconsider the methodology applied to psychotherapies performed using LSD. The self-experimenting psychiatrists generally recounted very positive experiences, which often took place in their own homes or offices, spaces that were welcoming and comfortable. They were free to come and go, and do as they please, and they had a prior theoretical knowledge of LSD, its effects, and their duration. If the accounts of the self-experimenters gave prominence to the state of euphoria, this was not the case in the experiments carried out on their patients, whether healthy or sick. In these cases, people felt anxiety and even terror. Faced with these results, certain therapists attempted to improve protocols, and in doing so, brought psychiatric practices into question.

In this new framework, which took into account the physical and emotional context, or "set and setting," therapists gave consideration to the patients, their history, and their accounts of the experience. Patients were informed of the effects of the substance, the room where the experiments took place was decorated strategically, and patients were allowed to bring personal items with them into the examination room. Another person stayed with them during the entire session, keeping a watchful eye.

On the other hand, with traditional therapies, the demeanor of the personnel was "disciplined" and distant. The hospital rooms were white, lit by fluorescents, and lacking in any decoration. Some patients were even strapped to the bed. The subjects, often mentally ill, had to submit to the experiments without having received any background information and were subjected to a battery of onerous tests. By the late 1950s, the dominant explanation for the effects of LSD was a "psychotomimetic" concept, which aimed to simulate psychosis, thus confining the understanding of the subjects' reactions to a solely pathological interpretation.

By proposing a new interpretation of the effects of LSD, this time directed towards a therapeutic goal, and by creating a new way of administering the drug, some therapists transformed LSD-assisted psychotherapies.

THE PIONEERING WOMEN IN THE HISTORY OF "SET AND SETTING"

Joyce Martin (1905–1969)

Joyce Martin was a Freudian psychoanalyst. A pioneer in the use of LSD in psychotherapy, she started her research in 1954, both in her private practice and at the Marlborough Day Hospital[2] in London.

In 1964, Martin published an article in which she distinguished her therapeutic method from that of Sandison and Ling; most notably this method brought "direct and active support to the patient of his emotional needs when necessary."[3] She developed a particularly controversial therapeutic method, in which she acted as a mother to the patient. In this scenario, the patient was encouraged to regress to the infant stage, while Martin provided an active and loving presence. Martin insisted that the response to the patient's emotional insufficiency was not artificial. She stated that:

We are not just giving a dummy, but something nearer to the original breast and the beginning of a love relationship. [. . .] This is our aim, therefore: to develop the transference relationship as quickly as possible to enable the ego strengthened and allow the previously unbearable feelings to be accepted and assimilated into the conscious personality, thus relieving the conflict and curing the symptoms and eventually integrating the personality.

With her assistant Pauline McCririck, they developed a system they called "fusional therapy," which consisted of lying beside their patients "holding them in close embrace, as a good mother would do to comfort her child."[4]

Margot Cutner (1905–1987)

Margot Cutner, née Kuttner, was a Jungian psychoanalyst of German origin. Having received a Doctor of Philosophy (PhD) from Hamburg in 1936, she fled Nazi Germany for England, where she anglicized her name. She trained with Elsa Gindler, a pioneer in body therapy and started her own psychoanalyst practice. One of the techniques she developed involved finding the most comfortable position for the patient, free from all tension or stress.[5] In 1955 she joined the Powick Hospital in Worcester, on the team of Ronald Sandison. A special department was built at this hospital to foster LSD research.

In 1959, Cutner presented her therapeutic method. She observed that the research material emerging under the influence of LSD, "far from being chaotic, reveals, on the contrary, a definite relationship to the psychological needs of the patient at the moment of his taking the drug."[6] She emphasized this point: "It is obvious that it would not be safe to give the drug without adequate supervision to anyone who was not on fairly good terms with his own unconscious." Cutner expressed serious reservations about the overly repetitive use of LSD in an attempt to break the psychic resistance of the patient. In her practice, certain patients, under treatment for two years, received only two or three sessions with LSD.

Her special attention to the body and its manifestations made her sensitive to the need for contact by the individual under the influence of LSD:

at a certain level of regression caused by the substance, "it is obvious that the contact by touch, the only thing the patient can understand at such times, revives and represents his first experiences of security in the physical embrace of the mother," Thus "to obtain needed reassurance it is, at times, not even enough for the patient to feel the analyst's hand touching him, but he himself may have to touch the analyst, or his clothes, etc." Cutner, the psychoanalyst, paid attention as well to her own demeanor during the sessions, making sure to act in the most gentle and welcoming manner possible so that the patient might trust her completely. She was especially attentive to her own facial expressions, which were meant to express love and the absence of judgment.

Betty Eisner (1915–2004)

On November 10, 1955, Betty Eisner became Sidney Cohen's[7] first guinea pig. Her second session took place in January 1957. This time, she explored the therapeutic potential of LSD. For her, left alone, the end of the session took on a deeply depressive dimension: "I had an awful experience." She recounted how she eventually decided to contact Cohen, seeking (emotional) support. However, he didn't take her seriously, even when she indicated her risk of suicide, and advised her just to have some rest. "I clearly remember telling him that it wouldn't look good for the research if the psychologist who was the subject committed suicide. He was unimpressed," she recounted.

In two sessions, Eisner had experienced both the frustration of having a battery of tests done and not being able to just let herself go with the substance, and subsequently the terrors that it could produce without adequate support. In the next two sessions, she decided to use only a very low dose, 25 µg, which brought her out of her depression and gave her a "mystical experience." After that, she was convinced to use low doses in her practice, quite the opposite to her American colleagues, who were developing "psychedelic therapy" at high doses. "The beauty of the low-dose LSD was that it enabled a person to let go as much as he or she wanted. Perhaps just a little bit at first, then a little more the next time, and finally they would allow it to happen completely. [. . .] We kept giving them sessions until they did," Eisner recounted.

In addition to requiring that someone stay with patients throughout the session and that doses be low and raised progressively, she was the first to write about the usefulness of playing music during the sessions. Finally, she insisted that two therapists, a man and a woman, be present in order for the patient to see them as parents and project onto the couple their feelings that they were experiencing.

In 1997 she proposed a third concept to add to "set" and "setting": "matrix," representing simultaneously the environment the patient is in at the time of their psychedelic experience as well as their past environment and that into which they will evolve once the treatment is finished.[8]

CONCLUSION

These three women had an important impact on improving the methods of administering LSD. While well known during their careers, Joyce Martin, Margot Cutner, and, to a lesser degree, Betty Eisner were gradually erased from research on the history of "set and setting" and psychedelics. Their work is essential to understanding the major changes brought to LSD-assisted therapy during the period and highlights the role of women and their attention to the bodies and emotions of their patients.

This article was translated by Robert Savery.

Women Who Heal:
Musicians in the Urban Ayahuasca Scene

RAIZZA MARINS

IN THE UNIVERSE OF NEW AGE RELIGIOSITY, THE USES OF AYAHUASCA HAVE been growing along with a global movement of the sacred feminine, which in broad terms refers to the rescue of an appreciation of the feminine through worship, reconnection with nature, its cycles and deities, as well as the search for the re-sacralization and human perception of the feminine. With this particular view of the feminine,[1] we can believe that it "consists of a vigilant vital continuity that ... derives its power from the intimate source of creation." Maternity, maintenance of life, and fertility are intertwined in the relationship of the forest and the feminine. The growing interest in female leadership in the ayahuasca scene, moreover, has also shown that the sacred feminine is not, or at least should not be, only about cycles of nature, menstruation, and biological issues related to women. It needs to be, first and foremost, about race, politics, society, gender disparities, and social class.

MUSIC AND GENDER RELATIONS

Some areas of music scholarship have not yet dealt sufficiently with female musical production in Brazil. Works in musicology, such as those by Susan McClary (1991) and Suzanne Cusick (2001),[2] point to a nonexistence or supposed "irrelevance" of women in the musical composition scene in the Western classical milieu, as well as in the field of musicology, conducting, and music theory. In the popular music scene, women only became prominent as composers in the second half of the 20th century.

Scholar Laila Rosa[3] has come at this topic from a feminist epistemological perspective, looking at new paths that embrace a gendered vision and the role of women in music. Since 2012 she has been coordinating a research project whose aim is to map the production of knowledge about women in music in Brazil in all subareas through the analysis of a database of MA dissertations, PhD theses, periodicals, and proceedings of scientific meetings. These studies foster the representation of diversity so that we can reconsider the historical perspective of traditional and popular music in Brazil and the invisible contributions of both cis and trans women.

In the field of anthropology, works such as that by Maria Ignez Cruz Mello[4] have shown new ways to think about the female trajectory in terms of the implications that gender relations have on music politics and production. In her ethnography of the *Iamurikuma* musical ritual, performed exclusively by Wauja women (Indigenous people from the upper Xingu river in Brazil), she shows how gender issues are inextricably linked to music. The flute house (*kawoká*), common in the upper Xingu, is the men's house, is restricted to the male gender, and the flutes cannot be seen by women, under the penalty of suffering collective rape. In the *Iamurikuma* ritual, the women occupy the center of the village and threaten the men with their songs, intoning provocations and denunciations in poetic-musical forms, taking control of their bodies through music.

The question that we always raise when problematizing the invisibility of studies on gender, body, and music from an intersectional perspective is that, as Rosa has pointed out, before there is music—a sound to be produced—there is a body, and this body is historical and political, crossed by social markers of gender difference, ethnic-racial identity, sexual orientation, social class, nationality, and accessibility or lack thereof, among many other markers.

Among the Indigenous peoples of Brazil, holders of knowledge on ayahuasca, I frequently listen to the narratives of Yawanawa women. In not such remote times, women's participation in spiritual practices was limited to the making of clay vessels for rituals. Research by Cynthia Inés Carrillo Sáenz[5] has shown that the use of *uni* (ayahuasca) was forbidden to women and children: for men, it was a way to protect them because they were weaker, for women, it meant men's desire to keep power for themselves.

The relationship between men and women is central to the social process of these peoples, based on female and male agency in production, distribution, consumption, sex, procreation, and reproduction. Hushahu and Putanny Yawanawa were the first women of their people to be initiated as shamans (spiritual leaders) on the *muká* diet, whereby they were isolated for a year in the forest with an extremely restricted diet. Sáenz quotes Hushahu

Putanny Yawanawa, one of the first female shamans in her community. The Globe.

as saying, "I was happy, I wanted to go, I wasn't afraid of death. I knew that if I died at least I would have died doing something for women's freedom. If we didn't survive, at least everyone would remember that once there were two sisters who had the courage to carry out the diet. . . . But if I go back, I will bring something for women." The learning of ancestral songs is closely linked to dietary processes, and the cultural revitalization of shamanic practices of the Yawanawa people owes much to women, as well as to the rescue of *kenes* (Indigenous graphics) in handicrafts, music, and body painting.

Although women are the majority in various religious contexts, they are often still in a subordinate position in this sphere. Men continue to be representatives of greater prestige, manipulators of the sacred, which leads us to critically assess the conceptions that make sense in the religious symbolic field but which often legitimize inequalities. It is up to women to challenge and deconstruct such stereotypes associated with the male domain that have been naturalized throughout history.

In the universe of ayahuasca, the feminine is of great importance. In a more Andean defining, this happens through devotion to Mother Earth, *Pachamama*, and the awareness of the unity of the whole. The drink is also commonly associated with the Queen of the Forest, a designation given by Santo Daime in reference to the feminine present in ayahuasca and also related to the Virgin Mary. In a 2019 thesis by Camila de Pieri Benedito,[6] whose title follows Suzana Pedalino's hymn, "Maria Who Teaches Me to Be a Woman," she addresses gender relations within the framework of Santo Daime's binary essentialism, the introduction of the sacred feminine into the doctrine, the healing of the injured feminine, and the empowerment given by the Queen of the Forest.

Engaging with this new era, several female archetypes also appear in the neo-ayahuasca scene. One is the figure of the Triple Goddess of the Wiccan tradition, known as the Great Mother, representing the phases of the moon in three faces: the maiden and the crescent moon, portraying purity and innovation; the mother and the full moon, portraying maternal protection; and the old lady and the waning moon, symbolizing wisdom and knowledge.

The hymn "The Flower of Kali," by Jagadananda Saraswati, is part of the Baul trans-religious movement, which consists of translations of songs from eastern religious traditions. In many of these songs, the Hindu goddess Radha is also analogous to the Queen of the Forest, along with the Hindu god Krishna, who is compared to Juramidam, the father and the totality in the Santo Daime tradition, and they represent sweetness in the form of the divine couple.

Among the different symbologies of the feminine that are manifested in these traditions that adapts Asian, Indigenous, African, and European practices through devotion to female deities, there are also archetypes of animals such as the jaguar and *tatanka* (female buffalo), representing female strength, very different to the dualism in which the woman is always seen as sweet and weak. In Brazil, the "mestizo" use of ayahuasca gave rise to the ayahuasca religions in 1930 (Santo Daime, Barquinha, and União do Vegetal), and from the 1990s onwards it went beyond the borders of Indigenous traditions or ayahuasca religions, through the interchange of different traditions alongside the movement of contemporary redefinition. Below is an excerpt from an ayahuasca song from this urban circuit:

> "Female Strength" ("Dan Sonora")
> I came here to salute the female strength
> This strength is delicate, the mother who teaches us
> The jaguar scratched, perfumed the forest
> The same jaguar roared, shook the earth.

When dealing with peoples and cosmovisions that live and think about gender relations so closely enmeshed with music, we are invited to reformulate the social attribution of roles, power, and prestige that are supported by a wide network of cultural practices associated with the feminine and masculine, toward a decolonial and Latin American perspective on music and the body that needs a more profound examination.

WOMEN WHO HEAL: MUSICIANS IN THE NEO-AYAHUASCA SCENE

Forest medicine and the valorization of the feminine seem to enhance artistic abilities, and in the neo-ayahuasca scene, among new ritual arrangements arising from the spread of the drink in Brazil's urban centers, there is a growing movement of female musicians and composers. Focusing on the feminine and fertile symbology of Easter, in 2020 the Portal Yoni Instagram channel promoted the "Feminine Voices at Home Festival," which, according to its directors, took place because of *Pachamama*'s call to bring together art as medicine for the soul, with praying women, singers, and songwriters. There were three days of activities, beginning with Marina Guadalupe, Clan Colibris, Mari Quetzal, and Cris de Holanda; on the second day Andrea Cathala, Kalinne Ribeiro, Tereza Raque, Ayla Schafer, Prem Tarika, and Clarice Nejar; and ending with Luiza Rosa, Suzan Flores, and Ana Muniz.

These women believe that art is an act of service that contributes to feminine and planetary healing, introducing the concept of "medicine women," women who heal and help others to heal. In addition to their original songs, the women brought a theme of sharing and reflection to times of profound transformation, emphasizing the importance of the female voice, singing, and poetry in the daily struggle. The freedom of free curative expression, letting the soul and heart speak, which releases the birth cries of humanity, was one of the central themes of the event, among other issues in the feminine sphere.

The Rezo Brasil Instagram channel, in honor of Mother's Day, launched the "Divine Mother Prayer Festival" in May 2020.[7] It was a whole afternoon of live performances from Vanessa Moutinho, Flávia Muniz, Bruna (Crystal Family), Passarinho Rezador, Carolinne Caramão, Vozes de Raiz, Rô! Barcellos!, Rebecca Durães (Two Suns), Cris de Holanda, Rafaela Schiavinatto,

Khali, Maria Rita Castro, Amanda Leal, Joana Freire, Marcela Chassotar, One Soul Band, and Ana Muniz, singing for different female deities and symbologies.

The expressions "medicine music" and "prayer music," among others, are often used generically to cover the different musicalities of the universe of forest medicine, especially ayahuasca. These collective manifestations, which are sometimes called "movements," are gradually growing and appear to be a crucial contemporary way for women to become important agents of society and break normative standards in order for women to take part in the musical sphere. Below are lyrics from another example of medicine music that deals with these themes:

"Women's Corner (Two Suns)"

I came to sing for the warrior woman
Sorceress woman
I call the strength of all guardians,
Woman of firmness
Woman woman woman
I invoke the strength of women, of Brazilian women
Warrior!
Yemanjá, Oxum, Eparrey Oyá!

With the profusion of chants and songs from the neo-shamanic universe, it can be seen that the increasingly less timid role of women in music has achieved visibility in the neo-ayahuasca scene, an area where so much is said about Mother Earth and environmental disaster but which still suffers from patriarchal oppression. These songs thus portray the times when women were seen as goddesses but also speaks to their being silenced and the violence they have suffered.

"Holy Woman" (Clarice Nejar)

Holy woman, female deity
Your dance brings beauty, and it also brings joy
I will bathe in your crystal clear waters
I will renew myself in your feminine strength

Flowers, fruits and seeds, divine nature
Your love is what supports me and gives light to my life
Hey, ya!

GET TO KNOW THE INDIGENOUS RECIPROCITY INITIATIVE OF THE AMERICAS: SACRED FEMINISM

In the urban ayahuasca scene, predominantly centered on male leaders, cases of sexual harassment and abuse have become more evident, pointing to the vulnerability that can be caused through expanded states of consciousness, as well as to risks that emerge during therapeutic openness and the relations of power and hierarchy which are a potential space for such abuses.

Collectives such as the National Movement to Combat Abuse in the Ayahuasca Environment (MovAya) and organizations such as the Chacruna Institute have set out guidelines on sexism, homophobia, transphobia, racism, and classism in ayahuasca circles, outlining the structures that encourage such practices, proposing educational actions and ways to encourage denunciation and acceptance through the construction of peaceful and safe spaces.

The invisibility of this subject in the ayahuasca environment shows that there is an urgent need for a political position on these themes and on related sacred feminine movements for the silent oppressions that help to bring about abuse. The silencing of victims, encouraged by the impunity of the slow Brazilian justice system, as well as the lack of knowledge of rights, taboos, and spiritual pressure, strengthen these networks of silence. There is no prevention without educational action, without the visibility of cases, and without protection for victims.

A 2018 study by Böschemeier and Benedito[8] emphasized the importance of linking ayahuasca as a "companion plant" for building sustainable and dignified practices that strengthen a perspective of peace and security for all beings. In this sense, I see music as an important ally and those women who sing with their bodies for a conscious feminine in search of their emancipation as the vanguard of a brighter tomorrow. When talking about the ayahuasca universe, it is also common to identify a kind of "ecofeminism," based on environmental issues that relate environmental disaster to patriarchal violence. As Böschemeier and Benedito explain, ecofeminism integrated "nature" and "feminine" into its political agenda, fostering a spiritualist conception of the need to care for nature in order to care for women, and to care for women in order to care for nature.

More than a "sacred female," a "sacred feminism" seems to be what represents the strength of the "National March of Indigenous Women" that took place for the second time in Brazil in September 2021. This movement, the largest female Indigenous mobilization in recent decades, has boosted the political leadership of women in defense of Mother Earth, resisting Brazil's constant civilizational setback engendered by violence against the rights of native peoples and the destruction of Indigenous and environmental policies. The march represents the union of body, territory, and spirit.

Through some of the many examples of women's struggles for a fairer society and a more diverse and tolerant world, we underline here, by way of synthesis, the fundamental importance of looking at women as protagonists in the central struggles of contemporary society, such as the fights for social equity, Indigenous rights, and the protection of nature. These women continue to go against the grain of the mainstream environmental, spiritual, and musical constructs, expropriated and silenced by the white patriarchal hegemonic society.

Let's listen to women! For the sacred that understands the concept of Mother Earth and that does not stay invisible, silenced, and oppressed.

Yaminawa Women and Ayahuasca: Shamanism, Gender, and History in the Peruvian Amazon

LAURA PÉREZ GIL

ONE AFTERNOON IN NOVEMBER 2003, A SURPRISING EVENT TOOK PLACE IN the Yaminawa village of Raya, situated along the Mapuya River in the Peruvian Amazon, where I was conducting research. Suddenly, two young girls were victims of a kind of attack that no one could explain. They screamed in pain, writhing and rolling on the ground. Their stomachs ached, and their displays of suffering left everyone perplexed, but no detailed explanations were forthcoming. Some tablets, as well as compresses and infusions, prepared with herbs that the Yaminawa women cultivate in their yards, were the first attempts at treatment. However, in the face of the obvious lack of effect and the worsening of the screams, the mother of one of the girls began to smoke tobacco and blow the fumes onto her daughter's belly, and then she chewed chili pepper and sucked the sore part of the girl's body.

The woman, Txixëya, repeated this operation several times: after sucking hard, she spat out some mucus. After performing the procedure three or four times, she examined the accumulation of mucus and found that she had drawn blood. She poured water over the saliva, which dissolved and dripped between the cracks in the floor made of pona wood, and continued to smoke, chew chili, and suck on her daughter's belly. When she saw that there were no more traces of blood in the saliva, she terminated the operation. Her daughter Patxuawĩ had by then calmed down.

In addition to these spectacular attacks, one thing caught my attention: the fact it was a woman who performed the operation to draw blood by sucking, which until then I had not witnessed. In all previous accounts I had collected, this ability was attributed to people who were recognized as having shamanic power. This technique, *bëa kuui*, is associated with the treatment of localized pain, swelling, and, especially, the bites of poisonous striped snakes.

The relationship between Yaminawa women and shamanism is far from obvious. It is a primarily male universe though it is not exclusive to men. The most visible and well-known shamanic practice today among the Indigenous Pano peoples, including the Yaminawa, is that which revolves around ayahuasca. Despite this, when I spoke with my female interlocutors about it and asked them if they had ever taken ayahuasca, the most frequent answer was that they had not tried it because they were afraid. For a time, this recurring response made me think that women were simply excluded from shamanic practice, as is the case among other peoples; however, this is a misconception. I argue here that there is a connection between this apparent separation of the shamanic and female universes, and the transformations caused by the establishment of continuous relationships with non-Indigenous people. In this sense, the lack of ayahuasca consumption by Yaminawa women today has to be understood as the result of a certain regional historical process, and, furthermore, this does not imply their exclusion from shamanic practices.

The Yaminawa are an Indigenous people who speak a Pano language who, upon the arrival of colonization in the second half of the 19th century, occupied the region of confluence of headwaters formed by the basins of the Purús, Tarauacá, Envira, and Yuruá rivers. This is currently a border region between the Brazilian state of Acre, the Peruvian state of Ucayali, and the state of Pando in Bolivia. With the arrival of the rubber and seringa extraction fronts, the ancestors of the Yaminawa, like other culturally close neighbors, were captured for their labor, or they spread out to even more inaccessible areas, fleeing violence, slavery, and epidemics. Many Pano peoples established lasting relationships with national societies throughout the second half of the 20th century though there are still today groups that resist this and remain in voluntary isolation.

Several of these peoples share a very close language, as well as similar ways of life, ways of being, and social and cosmopolitical logic. Among the most characteristic and similar aspects are the shamanic practices and cosmologies, in which ayahuasca is one of the main elements. Most of the adult Yaminawa men over 30 years old in the 2000s had, during their youths, undergone a shamanic learning process that combines nutritional and sexual diets, social isolation, intensive consumption of various substances (especially tobacco, ayahuasca, and chili peppers), the *kuxuiti* (curing) songs sung during ayahuasca sessions,[1] and submission to ordeals[2] that involve being stung by certain types of ants and wasps and ingesting organic substances from the boa constrictor.

Through these actions, two closely connected and parallel processes operate. On the one hand, there is a self-management of bodily substances, through the accumulation of certain substances—those which are bitter (*bua*) and/or those that give power (*paë*) to the voice and visions—and the avoidance or expulsion of others, mainly, those classified as "sweet" (*bata*), such as the fermented yucca drink or any non-Indigenous food. Through vomiting, the remains of meat and "dirt" accumulated in the stomach and which interfere with the shamanic agency are also expelled. The shamanic body is light and bitter. After the somatic cleansing, ayahuasca is ingested— the second process I was referring to—and thus comes into contact with the *yuxin* (spirits) and *ihu* (owners) associated with those substances, such as those from the boa or ayahuasca, which are converted into transmitters of knowledge mainly in the form of chants. Thus, if the learning and development of shamanic agency is associated with contact with the *yuxin* and *ihu*, the ultimate sources of this agency, they depend on the preparation of the human body itself and the manipulation of the substances that form it.

Although my female interlocutors claimed not to have taken ayahuasca, they assured me that many of their mothers and grandmothers had. This means that, in the generation of those who were adults when stable relationships were established with broader Peruvian society in the 1960s, it was common for women to consume ayahuasca.[3] According to various accounts, the women took part both in collective ayahuasca ingestion sessions that had no aim other than to interact with the *yuxin*, and in healing rituals, where some women contributed with their *kuxuiti* (song) to restore a patient's health.

But what was the real dimension of women's participation in the shamanic universe? When, on the day after the healing incident described above, I spoke with Txixëya again, she explained to me that she had learned to suck "blood" using chili pepper and tobacco from her father and her mother. Both were *kuxuitia*, a category which refers to those who know the curing songs, typically chanted when taking ayahuasca. Txixëya's mother was taught by her own father when she was young. To do this, he made her diet; get stung by wasps in the mouth and on her chest; take honey to vomit and connect with its "owner"; smoke the pipe which her father had previously smoked; and, certainly, regularly consume shamanic substances such as ayahuasca, tobacco, or chili. The learning and development of shamanic agency operates by the same processes in the case of men and women, but in the case of men it was formerly carried out collectively—several boys undertook the initiation together usually under the direction of two teachers—and with women the initiation took place on an individual basis within the family environment. It was the fathers, mothers, and husbands who encouraged the girls to learn modes of action considered essential to ensure their personal well-being since consuming ayahuasca "fixes" and keeps the body healthy, and also the well-being of the family as it gave them autonomy to take care of their loved ones.

Thus, the ingestion of ayahuasca was part of a much broader framework of practices which included other substances and other techniques, apart from *kuxuiti*. The exercise of shamanism, on the other hand, was not exclusive to specialists, but, with different degrees of effectiveness, was relatively generalized. Certainly, not everyone was given the same credibility, but access to these practices was democratic and basically depended on having among those closest someone willing to teach and on others being determined to face the rigor of learning. Some of my female interlocutors assured me that if they did not learn, it was not due to lack of opportunity but rather because they did not want to face the diets and the painful bites of the insects.

The question that must be asked, then, is why, when they lived apart from Peruvian society, did women participate more actively in shamanism, including the regular consumption of ayahuasca, and when permanent relationships with society were established, why did this consumption decrease?

Shamanism, as a cosmopolitics that is effective through concrete actions, is in constant transformation, and the Yaminawa are always open to incorporating new ideas and techniques. In fact, everything seems to indicate that the use of ayahuasca in this case is relatively recent and differs from previous forms of shamanism, in which tobacco, the jaguar, and hunting, and not ayahuasca, the boa, and the cure, were the main ingredients.[4] This seems to be in line with Peter Gow's hypothesis published in *Shamanism, History, and the State*[5] that the current ayahuasca shamanism was configured in the missions during the colonial era and then expanded towards the headwaters of the rivers, even reaching peoples who had not yet established permanent contact.

The consumption of ayahuasca by Yaminawa women before contact is no exception in the Pano world. Barbara Keifenheim reported[6] a similar situation among the Huni Kuin people, explaining that the fact that women do not currently consume ayahuasca is not due to any prohibition but rather to the sedentarization and transformation of their relationship with the jungle. This consideration converges with observations by other authors, such as Philippe Erikson,[7] who worked with recently contacted peoples and indicates that, before contact and due to a way of life marked by great mobility in the jungle, the border between female and male activities was fluid and blurry. After contact, however, as a consequence of sedentarization and the influence of non-Indigenous ideas, there was a tendency to widen gender differences, as noted by Carlos Fausto.[8]

The evidence that women, prior to contact, exercised shamanic practices and consumed ayahuasca is confirmed in the case of recently contacted groups who are culturally very close to the Yaminawa. In 1995, those known as Txitonawa established stable relationships with Peruvian society. As they had settled in the Yaminawa villages of the Mapuya and Yuruá, I had the opportunity to meet a woman who confirmed to me that she and other relatives of hers had drunk ayahuasca from a very young age and knew *kuxuiti*.

The current decline in the use of ayahuasca among the Yaminawa is not something that affects only women since many men have stopped using it regularly, and it has become a much more sporadic practice than it used to be. However, the truth is that in the case of women there are particular reasons. If it is true, as I mentioned, that a hybrid and mestizo modality focused on the mainly therapeutic use of ayahuasca spread from the missions, the truth is that this modality, when incorporated by various Indigenous and non-Indigenous peoples, took on local characteristics such as female participation. Contemporary Ucayali shamanism, however, has the male ayahuasca healer as its central figure, and as Glenn Shepard has argued,[9] this, together with increasing relations with Peruvian society, helps to distance women from this universe.

Nevertheless, the contemporary shamanic universe of the Peruvian Amazon, highly changeable and in which exchanges between different traditions have multiplied exponentially,[10] opens up new possibilities. As for the Yaminawa, a more intense and frequent interaction with the shamanic ways of the jungle town of Atalaya has led them to appropriate and exercise different shamanic techniques, among which stand out those based on the use of plants or the steamings of the Ashaninka tradition, in order to extract disease from the body. Although the use of ayahuasca is not part of the range of healing techniques that they offer their clients, some of these women, like Txixëya, are successfully entering an urban shamanic field from which, paradoxically, Yaminawa men seem to exclude themselves.

This piece was translated from its original Portuguese by John Milton.

Madrinha Rita:
Brazilian Matriarch of Ayahuasca

GLAUBER LOURES DE ASSIS AND

JACQUELINE ALVES RODRIGUES

THE HISTORY OF RELIGIONS IS OFTEN TOLD AS A STORY OF GREAT MEN; BUT, it has also been built through the struggle, sweat, suffering, and achievements of many women, who, despite their merits, talents, and the incredible stories of their lives, have frequently been silenced and made invisible, including by academic scholars. Talking about religions from a decolonial perspective and being academically rigorous while supporting social justice necessarily involves telling the story of these women and making their roles visible. And this is equally true for the study and understanding of the social evolution of the use of psychedelic plants.

If we want to talk about religions that use plant medicine, then it is essential to highlight women as the protagonists they are. It is with this objective that this article describes the story of a woman who has made a great difference in the religious use of ayahuasca in Brazil and in the expansion of its consumption outside the Santo Daime religion: Madrinha (Godmother) Rita Gregório.

FROM THE DROUGHT IN THE NORTHEAST TO THE SOCIETY OF RUBBER TAPPERS: A RUBBER SOLDIER

Rita Gregório de Melo was born on June 25, 1925, in the rural area of the state of Rio Grande do Norte, in the northeast of Brazil. As with the vast majority of northeasterners at that time, her family had no land of their own, and no livestock, nor property.

Rita and her parents worked as humble fishermen and fisherwomen and subsistence farmers, cultivating crops like beans, corn, watermelons, and carnauba (*Copernicia serifera*) wax. And so they remained until the early 1940s.[1] Before this time, the Brazilian Amazon had been a major producer of rubber, but this economy collapsed due to the illegal smuggling of rubber seeds from the Amazon rainforest in the late 19th century to establish plantations in British colonies, especially Malaysia. These plantations eventually reduced Brazil's share of the rubber market from a virtual monopoly to only 20 percent by 1918.

With the onset of World War II, however, everything changed. The need for rubber increased dramatically and rubber production in Brazil became strategic because of the need to supply the allied troops. For this reason, thousands of people from the Northeast were recruited to go to the Amazon with the promise of better living conditions. This movement became known as the "Battle for Rubber," and the migrants who participated in this process were called "Rubber Soldiers."[2]

In 1944, Madrinha Rita and her family became part of this group, and they went to the Amazon, reaching the wilds of the Juruá Valley, where they settled on a rubber plantation. There, Rita met Sebastião Mota de Melo, later known as Padrinho (Godfather) Sebastião, who was largely responsible for the international expansion of Santo Daime. She married him in the 1940s and gave birth to 11 children.[3] Two of their children, Alfredo and Valdete, are now among the most important worldwide figures in Daime. During the period she lived in the rubber plantations, Madrinha Rita took care of the domestic work; in addition to the upbringing of her children, she was responsible for raising domestic animals, preparing food, and sewing clothes.

Just as in the large urban centers today, in the 21st century, it is absolutely impossible to think about raising families on the plantations and maintaining the productive activity of the rubber economy without the decisive role of women in unpaid domestic work and in sustaining the entire economy. As Sebastião needed to go hunting and fishing in excursions that could last several days, Rita would take care of all the domestic activity and care for the children by herself. And all this without appliances, basic sanitation, government services, electricity, or security against potential invaders. Her circumstances are difficult to imagine compared to the Western standards of today's consumer society.

Due to the difficulty of life on the rubber plantations, in 1957 Rita and Sebastião moved with their family to Rio Branco, the capital of the state of Acre. This was an arduous journey that took many weeks, with precarious transport and involving long hikes lasting several days, in which they carried their children under a scorching sun.[4]

THE ENCOUNTER WITH MESTRE IRINEU AND
THE EXPANSION OF SANTO DAIME

In Rio Branco, Rita and Sebastião started to live in the so-called Colônia Cinco Mil (Five Thousand Colony) that, in the future, would become a hub for the Brazilian expansion of Santo Daime, where they dedicated themselves to farming and raising animals. In 1965, Rita had the opportunity to personally meet Raimundo Irineu Serra, a Black man from Maranhão, grandson of slaves and the founder of Santo Daime. Sebastião received a healing in a ritual led by Mestre (Master) Irineu that motivated Rita to discover ayahuasca through Santo Daime.

Having been brought up in an environment hostile to women's freedom, in the midst of an impoverished family and evangelical religiosity, Rita was shy and was hesitant to approach Mestre Irineu, who was always surrounded by people.[5] In order to get closer to Mestre Irineu, it was necessary for Rita to overcome this shyness (a challenge she repeatedly met in order to be recognized as the great leader she is). And this was how Rita met Mestre Irineu. The encounter transformed her life and defined the course of her existence, community, and spiritual work.

Madrinha Rita.
Source: CEDOC Collection
/santodaime.org, 2015

From then on, Rita, together with her husband, joined the Santo Daime religion and became a leader in the spiritual services performed at Colônia Cinco Mil. Here, they received many people in search of healing and inspiration, including pregnant women looking for help in the delivery of their children, a tradition that has been developed and improved by her and her companions ever since.

After Mestre Irineu's death, Rita and Sebastião took on an important role in the continuity of Irineu's work, and an increasing number of people began to gather around her and her work. From this point on, they became known as "Madrinha" (Godmother) Rita and "Padrinho" (Godfather) Sebastião, an affectionate form of recognition for the dedication they gave to the people who sought them out.

A WOMAN AHEAD OF HER TIME

Right from the beginning, the way that Rita and Sebastião developed their religious experience was marked by their openness to diversity. They welcomed people from different socioeconomic and cultural backgrounds, and they also experimented with psychedelics and incorporated new practices and symbols into their ritual experience. This curiosity was always a characteristic of the couple, who were certainly ahead of their time during a period when Brazil was still living in the shadow of the military dictatorship.

Another hallmark of both was their community experience. This included the production and distribution of food, with the aim of constructing spaces for coexistence and promoting forms of solidarity outside the exploitative economic system of the time. As her followers say, Madrinha Rita has always received and embraced the underprivileged. She has always been very sincere in her demonstration of empathy and love for the rebel, for those who displease, and she has been altruistic in dedicating a large part of her time to the "black sheep" of the community and society.

Another characteristic feature is her unwavering confidence in the causes she embraces and in the spiritual work of expanding Santo Daime.

She radiated calm and tranquility, blessing the expansion of Santo Daime in the large Brazilian cities in a historical period where the social stigma attached to the consumption of psychedelics was much greater than it is today and when there was limited legal support for the use of ayahuasca.

Madrinha Rita. Source: CEDOC Collection

No less interesting was her allowing use of Santa Maria, that is, cannabis, in the religious ceremonies of Santo Daime, and she has been one of the main developers and custodians of the ritualistic character of its use for several decades.

In the early 1980s, Madrinha Rita abandoned the entire structure that she had struggled to assemble in Rio Branco in order to accompany Sebastião in building a community project in the heart of the Amazon Rainforest. This is where Céu do Mapiá was born, a Daime community located in the Purus National Forest, several hours by boat away from the nearest town. With some 1,000 residents, it is today the largest Daime group in the world, considered a kind of Mecca by its followers. In the '80s, together with Sebastião and their children, Rita took on the role of world ambassador for Santo Daime, traveling to different locations to educate people about the Daime culture and liturgy and welcome new followers, called *afilhados* (godchildren).

In 1990, Padrinho Sebastião died, and from then on, it was Rita's task to faithfully follow the Santo Daime doctrine and give support to the entire Daime community and its thousands of adherents around the world. Although her children, Alfredo and Valdete, have now become international leaders (Alfredo is president of the Higher Doctrine Council of ICEFLU—Church of the Eclectic Cult of the Universal Fluent Light—and Valdete is the general administrator), both devote great obedience and pay deference to Madrinha Rita as matriarch of the doctrine.

Her role in social cohesion and the resolution of social, family, and political conflicts in Céu do Mapiá, for example, is of great importance. And it is there, amid the pure air of the forest and the mosquitoes that cause malaria (a disease that has affected Rita dozens of times), Rita lives and continues, at almost 97 years old, to take care of her godchildren.

As she is now very old, Madrinha Rita no longer goes to church or visits people's homes. As she cannot physically reach the church and the community, the church and the community come to her.[6] So, today, the balcony of her house is one of the busiest and most representative spaces of the entire Daime experience in Céu do Mapiá. It is there that Madrinha Rita faithfully performs her daily prayers and distributes blessings to the brotherhood and all visitors. Children are also a constant presence in this environment, which currently also hosts several Santo Daime works (spiritual ceremonies). The presence of Madrinha Rita is also considered something special by the devotees, and this makes the mystical and collective experience deeper and stronger.

Madrinha Rita is never alone but always accompanied by her female companions, which reveals a relationship of sisterhood and a female support network that surrounds her. While these women support Madrinha Rita in her daily needs in terms of health, mobility, company, and work, they are also supported by her in their own personal needs and have themselves become central figures in Santo Daime religious life.

Since the 1980s Madrinha Rita has organized religious ceremonies exclusively for women: "women's works." Historical records even show Madrinha Rita's attempt to institute women-only spiritual meetings every 15 days or monthly.[7] Another historic element is the recognition of the attention, dedication, and affection given by Madrinha Rita to the women who are part of Santo Daime, and her sadness at the injustices that sometimes permeate the relationship between men and women within the religion. It was to a woman—Regina Pereira—that Madrinha Rita gave the house where she had lived with Padrinho Sebastião when she changed residences in Mapiá.

Other striking traits of Madrinha Rita that reveal how she has been ahead of her time are the absence of envy in her relationship with Padrinho Sebastião and her family and her encouragement for her followers to live their lives freely and fully. As Dona Bina, another Santo Daime elder and important chronicler of the religion, says: "Invited by an Argentine group to a ritual with San Pedro (*Echinopsis pachanoi*), I went to consult the godmother. She answered me: 'Go and discover what you don't know. What are you afraid of?'"[8] A very important historic event for all of Santo Daime, especially due to the macho and homophobic attitude of many followers of the religion, was the personal authorization that Madrinha Rita gave to a lesbian couple who were able to marry in the Daime ritual.[9]

AN EXAMPLE OF FEMALE POWER AND AGENCY IN THE UNIVERSE OF SANTO DAIME AND AYAHUASCA

Madrinha Rita has "received" her own *hinario* (hymnal), that is, a group of religious songs believed to be spiritually conferred on one within the scope of Santo Daime. Compiled in an hinario called *"Lua Branca"* (White Moon), her hymns are considered teachings of healing, love, calm, peace, and unity by Daime followers around the world, and have already been translated into English, Dutch, Spanish, Italian, and Japanese. According to Daime mythology, it was a universal goddess, the Queen of the Forest, who delivered the Santo Daime teachings and revealed the mysteries of ayahuasca to Mestre Irineu. More than a mythology that includes women, it is a mythology where female agency and protagonism are decisive and fundamental.

It is very important, therefore, that women's lives in Santo Daime are made visible, and that Daime women are able to tell their stories. Madrinha Rita's life is a marvelous example of the importance of women in Santo Daime social life, of the intimate and beautiful relationship between a plant that teaches and female agency in the ayahuasca universe, and of the power that exists in sharing these stories. May more and more women raise their voices to share their own stories, just as Madrinha Rita raised hers and sang in her hinario:

> I will tell my story
> Since it started
> Santo Daime is my life
> My path, my teacher
> I will now say
> What He taught me

The Religious Uses of Licit and Illicit Psychoactive Substances in a Branch of the Santo Daime Religion

EDWARD MACRAE

IRINEU SERRA WAS A POOR MIGRANT FROM NORTHEASTERN BRAZIL WHO spent many years working in the Amazonian forest. During this time he came across a shaman who gave him ayahuasca to drink, causing him to have many visions among which was one of a woman, initially considered to be a forest spirit and later identified with the Virgin of the Conception.

During many ayahuasca sessions she appeared repeatedly in his visions, teaching him how to use ayahuasca to become a great healer. As part of her instructions, she imparted to him a new religious doctrine based on the ritual taking of ayahuasca. This doctrine continued to be elaborated in visions he kept having for the rest of his life. This then became the basis for his treatment of those who came to him for healing and, after some time, he set up a church in the remote town of Rio Branco in what was then the Brazilian state of Acre.

Among these peoples, psychoactive plants are often called "teacher plants," and it is considered that they allow the user to gain direct access to the spiritual world and to storehouses of wisdom not otherwise available to them. Thus, it is common for shamans to claim that their knowledge of the healing power of plants and of the correct ways of using them was acquired in dreams or visions produced by the ingestion of these entheogens.

One of the most widely used entheogens is ayahuasca. This is a psychoactive brew made from the *Bannisteriopsis caapi* vine and the *Psychotria viridis* leaf, which has been used for many purposes by the native inhabitants of western Amazonia since time immemorial. Its psychoactive properties are due to alkaloids such as harmine, d-leptaflorine, DMT, and harmaline, which appear in varying concentrations in the vine and in the leaf. Conceived of as a means of opening human perception to the spiritual world, this brew has been used mainly by Indian and mestizo shamanic healers for the diagnosis and treatment of ailments, divination, hunting, warfare, and even as an aphrodisiac. Although its use probably originated among the inhabitants of the rainforest, ayahuasca was taken to the Andean highlands where it received the name by which it is best known, which means, in Quechua, "vine of the spirits."

In the last few years, ayahuasca has become the central sacrament of a number of syncretic religions that originated among Amazonian rubber tappers and then spread to the urban middle classes, initially in Brazil, but now reaching several European countries, the US, and even Japan. The oldest of these religions is an eclectic mixture of popular Catholicism, Spiritism, African religiosity, and Indian shamanism known as Santo Daime, after the name given to ayahuasca by its founder, Raimundo Irineu Serra (or Mestre Irineu, as he is known).

The followers of this religion maintain that their sacrament is not a drug, but "the Blood of Christ" or a divine being of great power, even with a will of its own. Thus, it is believed that every time someone takes the brew, she has the opportunity of entering into direct contact with God and, if she is deserving, she might then be able to find solutions for problems she may be facing and even be healed of terminal illnesses, as many followers claim to have been.

Many aspects of the Daimista ritual setting promote order, such as:

1. The dietary and behavioral prescriptions that must be observed during the three days that precede and that follow the taking of the drink, setting the stage for an unusual event that escapes the daily routine.
2. A hierarchical social organization in which a "commander" or "godfather" is recognized as the leader of the session, with the help of a body of "guardians" who are responsible for the maintenance of order and obedience to the commander.
3. The control of the dosage of the drink taken by participants.
4. The ritualized spatial organization, the uniforms generally worn, and the behavioral control of the participants.

All "works" take place around a central table/altar where the double-armed Cross of Caravacca and other religious symbols mark the sacred nature of the event. All those taking part are given a specific place in the room, usually a rectangle drawn on the ground, where they must remain, grouped by sex, age, and sexual status (virgins and non-virgins).

Regular members must usually wear uniforms of a sober cut that serve to stress the unity of the group and help maintain a mood of seriousness. Another important element of control is the music which is sung and played during most of the ceremonies, and which is of great help in harmonizing the group, with rattles marking the rhythms and the voices of the congregation in unison. This ritual use of music harkens back to ancient shamanic customs. Singing and the use of percussion instruments with a strong, repetitive beat are powerful aids in bringing about altered states of consciousness and are thought to act as a way of invoking spirits. The words of the hymns direct the voyages of the participants and help relieve mental or physical ill feelings.

The hymns also help to create connections between the lived experiences and the magical or mythical symbols with which they become invested, and which are of great importance in strengthening the cohesion of the group.

In 1986, the spreading of this and other ayahuasca religions among the middle classes of the large Brazilian cities outside the Amazon region, the publicity involving the conversion of media celebrities to the Santo Daime, and the moral panic over drug use, led the Brazilian Ministry of Health to place the brew in the list of forbidden drugs.

In response, one of the ayahuasca-using religions, the União do Vegetal, petitioned the Federal Narcotics Council to annul the measure. The Council decided to set up two multidisciplinary work groups to report on the matter. These groups included not only lawyers and policemen but also doctors, social scientists, and psychologists. Over a period of two years, they visited several of the religious communities, examined and interviewed their followers, and read news reports.

In their unusually enlightened final reports, the work groups noted that ayahuasca had been used by these religious groups for decades without any untoward social harm. Among the users of the brew, the predominant moral and ethical standards were seen to be similar to those found in mainstream Brazilian society. The rural communities were considered to be well integrated in their environmental settings and as harmoniously integrating individuals of different age groups, social classes, and social backgrounds. In spite of their distance from the Amazon, even the urban communities were found to follow closely the doctrinal practices originating in the rainforest. Although the brew was classified as a hallucinogen and as having other effects apart from those common to this type of substance, such as vomiting and diarrhea, no medical abnormalities were detected and recommendations were made for further and more detailed clinical studies. Following the work group's recommendations, the use of ayahuasca for religious purposes[1] was then endorsed by the Federal Narcotics Council and since then has been considered totally legitimate from a legal point of view, although the religions are still occasionally subject to social prejudice on the part of those who continue to consider adherents to be mere drug addicts.

Keeping within the Santo Daime universe, it is useful to compare the fortunes of the legally accepted ayahuasca with another sacramental substance also worshipped by the followers of one of its branches but which remains illegal: "Santa Maria," or cannabis.

For the members of Colônia 5000 in the mid-1970s, the smoking of marijuana was not an issue, although a few had heard tales about its supposed diabolical nature and its use by outlaws. Their main concern was with alcoholism, endemic in the region and a personal problem for many of the veterans, who considered the Santo Daime to be responsible for their having given up excessive drinking. Tobacco smoking, though discouraged during rituals, was a socially accepted practice and quite widespread.

On the other hand, many of the new young converts had originally been attracted to the religion because of its uses of a psychoactive brew as its main sacrament. Their conversion, although it involved many changes in their value systems, had also led them to view consciousness alteration through substance use not only as socially acceptable, but also as a sure way of acquiring spiritual knowledge and development.

Emphasizing its specific character, this new religious use was to have a different vocabulary from the profane street use so that, like Santo Daime, Santa Maria should never be considered a "drug." Not only was the name commonly used in Brazil, *maconha*, rejected and substituted with "Santa Maria," but all the other terms used in connection with it, like the standard urban Portuguese word for "to smoke," or hippie slang expressions for cigarette papers and the top of the female plant—very prized for being rich in THC—were substituted by other expressions of a more local flavor. Of special significance was the name adopted for those who partook of this sacrament. Leaving aside the Portuguese term *maconheiro* (roughly equivalent to "pot head"), which had strong deviant connotations, the religious users of Santa Maria became known as *marianos*, an expression used in the Roman Catholic Church for the members of certain brotherhoods devoted to the cult of the Virgin Mary.

Dealing with rituals, which are not only social but religious as well, we see how they can be quite effective when allowed to develop in a licit manner, even when dealing with potent substances like ayahuasca. On the other hand, when rituals are banned, it makes it difficult for them to become fully institutionalized, as is the case with Santa Maria; their controlling influence is weakened and it is more difficult to prevent undesired effects. Fortunately, in the case of the Daimista marianos, or devotees of the Virgin Mary, adherence to the doctrine provides them with a structure for their lives.

This article was originally published as "Santo Daime e Santa Maria: Usos religiosos de substâncias psicoativas lícitas e ilícitas" in Beatriz C. Labate and Sandra Lucia Goulart's O Uso Ritual das Plantas de Poder *(Campinas: Mercado de Letras, 2005) on pages 459–485. This version has been translated into English by John Milton.*

A Bridge Between Two Worlds: Ayahuasca and Intercultural Medicine— An Interview with Anja Loizaga-Velder

IBRAHIM GABRIELL

WHEN IT COMES TO STUDYING THE HEALING POTENTIAL OF PSYCHEDELIC plants and substances, it is vital to understand the different approaches to their use, and the powerful Amazonian visionary brew known as ayahuasca is no exception. The psychointegrative[1] qualities found in ayahuasca and other psychedelics are part of a psychopharmacological mechanism by which different neurochemical processes are modulated through the action exerted by certain molecules on serotonergic receptors in the brain. But it is overly reductionist to explain ayahuasca's healing effects without considering the extrapharmacological variables that modulate the experience.

Western medicine has yet to fully embrace methods that incorporate these kinds of features into the healing paradigm. The forms of use to be found among the Indigenous peoples who originally used these psychedelics may be totally alien to the worldview of the modern world and therefore difficult to integrate into contemporary societies.

Such a blending of approaches is intercultural, interdisciplinary (or rather, transdisciplinary), and, above all, ethical. To learn more about this intercultural therapeutic approach, I talked to Dr. Anja Loizaga-Velder, one of the main experts in the therapeutic use of ayahuasca in Mexico. She is a well-known psychologist and psychotherapist who specializes in humanistic and transpersonal psychology. In addition to being a leading international speaker on the subject, Anja is also cofounder and director of Psychotherapy and Research at the Nierika A. C. Intercultural Medicine Institute.

Ibrahim Gabriell: Welcome Anja, can you tell us a little about who you are and why you decided to dedicate your life and research to the field of intercultural medicine?

Anja Loizaga-Velder: It all started when I was 18 years old, while I was taking a gap year. I had the opportunity to live in the Amazon jungle in a Shipibo community, and that was where I first learned about the use of psychedelics in a more structured context. Through ayahuasca I was struck by the potentialities of exploring consciousness, and I became interested in how it could be used to develop therapeutic tools. At that moment I decided to dedicate my life to building a bridge between the knowledge of traditional Indigenous medicine and modern psychology. That's what I do, and there you can see a personal vocation combined with a professional one.

IG: Both you as a researcher and Nierika A. C. have attracted attention for specializing in this intercultural approach to psychedelics and in particular to ayahuasca. Why not dedicate yourself completely to working with either traditional Indigenous usage or to the Western medical-therapeutic approach?

ALV: I think partly because I grew up between two cultures; My mother was Mexican and my father German. From the time I was little, I grew up with the mysticism of ancestral Mexican cultures but also with the scientific precision of the German culture.

My most significant experiences with psychedelics were within traditional medicine, so I consider these people as masters in the use of these technologies; but, on the other hand, I have always had a great professional passion for mental health issues, hence the desire to create a bridge between both types of knowledge. All this is also related to a personal experience I had when I was 16 years old, when a friend went through a suicidal crisis that led him to spend four months in a psychiatric hospital. I was with him every afternoon of those four months, and it was so frustrating to see how conventional psychiatric treatments failed to work, which led me to commit myself to finding paths to more humane and effective therapies.

IG: Considering that psychedelics have long been a taboo subject even within academia and that you were already attracted to the subject, how was your professional training period?

ALV: When I started studying psychology, I found myself deeply frustrated

Anja during her presentation at the Sacred Plants in the Americas Congress. Chacruna Institute, 2018

as I felt that the academic psychology taught in Germany was totally limited and that it failed to take into account the study of consciousness, and was biased in the knowledge that was taught, both from a scientific paradigm and also a practical perspective, where unfortunately it was not always possible to help the patient.

I had made the commitment to bridge both worlds, and this kept me from abandoning my degree, but those moments of frustration made me want to do so. I insisted on writing my master's research on the potential uses of ayahuasca for mental health treatments, but my university told me that this was impossible, that this was not doing science, and they proposed I work on other topics approved by the committee. But I had already made a commitment to myself to work on this topic, so I ended up looking for another university where I would be able to do this type of research, and I lost two semesters in this process. For my PhD everything was very different as, thanks to my master's dissertation, a group of researchers in Heidelberg invited me to collaborate with them, so suddenly I found myself sharing ideas with a group interested in my research.

I later did postdoctoral work at the National Autonomous University of Mexico (Universidade Nacional Autônoma do México—UNAM), but when I finished these studies it was impossible for me to obtain an institutional affiliation at UNAM or another university. I feel that there is still a prejudice against this topic in the Mexican academy as, for example, although they allowed me to teach certain seminars at UNAM, this was unpaid with no contract, and I don't know whether the same thing would have happened if I had been specialized in a more conventional subject.

IG: Can you tell us about the challenges and objections you faced?

ALV: The main challenge at the paradigmatic level was the bias that led the academy to think that what I proposed with my research was not something serious, and this was even stronger when I spoke of integrating Western scientific elements. In the institutes it was thought that these topics corresponded to esotericism or parapsychology, and they invited me to deal with other "truly important" topics.

The other important point is about interdisciplinarity, as psychedelic science studies the phenomenon of consciousness, medical anthropology, and religious studies, and we know that mystical experiences are usually those with the greatest therapeutic value when psychedelics are used. This broader conceptualization does not exist within the status quo of the academy, where only anthropological approaches seem to be accepted and studies merely state that certain Indigenous cultures make use of these plants. In addition, neuroscientific approaches (which are the most feasible in Mexico) analyze the effects of these substances on the brain; but the big question is how we can integrate all this.

At Nierika A. C. we wanted to carry out a study on the therapeutic values of ayahuasca in mental health, integrating the form of traditional Indigenous intervention while also providing participants with psychotherapy before and after the ayahuasca sessions. This project was presented to the National Institute of Psychiatry in Mexico, and they looked at us as if we were proposing something completely out of this world. There is simply no paradigm that allows them to understand how we can use these plants; for them it is easier to work with other substances. Later, we again approached this institute with a proposal on synthetic psilocybin to combat depression, using the American psychotherapeutic context, and this was indeed something they considered scientific, but integrating the elements of traditional Mexican medicine (which have a similar or greater value to the knowledge developed by clinical research with psychedelics in the United States) does not appear to be "scientific" enough to be approved by ethics and research committees. So there are definitely many prejudices, and it seems that in Mexico it is best to import knowledge from the United States or Europe. This makes me absurdly sad as Mexico is one of the countries with the greatest heritage in terms of ancestral knowledge of psychedelic plants and mushrooms.

On the other hand, it is also true that the National Council for Science and Technology (Consejo Nacional de Ciencia y Tecnología—CONACYT) in Mexico has approved a transdisciplinary research project that explores the therapeutic potential of psilocybin-containing mushrooms from a transdisciplinary perspective, and this is very innovative for Mexico as traditional knowledge is being considered as something equivalent to Western knowledge.

IG: According to your research, what are the main contributions made by traditional Indigenous knowledge to modern psychotherapy?

ALV: As I understand the subject, the Western paradigm first extracted the substance, then the active ingredient, then the contexts for its use were created, and when these contexts were created, more and more aspects of traditional use were integrated. This could be seen, for example, in the aesthetic part of the surroundings where these experiences take place, as well as in other elements such as music, the use of The Word as a work tool, or the exploration of different doses according to an intuitive doctor-patient connection and not simply based on body weight.

I think that one of the most important points that we find in traditional Indigenous medicine is the complementary sensitization of the therapist with the patient, as traditional doctors almost always use the psychedelic together with the patient, although they do so only after a very long training, through which they are so familiar with that state that they do not get carried away by the patient's process but rather become aware of what the patient needs and thus accompany them, for example, with the appropriate songs (which are not preassembled playlists, such as in the case of the Western model).

Another point to highlight is the cultural integration that is made of these experiences in Indigenous cultures where, unlike in the West, these practices are not a countercultural phenomenon but are sacred experiences and, therefore, valuable and worthy of respect. All this makes it possible to link the practice to more collective processes, where we see that the patient's family or community can intervene.

IG: Another factor that I think is important to mention has to do with the phenomenon of neoshamanism: nowadays it is common to find people (mainly mestizos), who, perhaps with good intentions, but without knowing in-depth the complexity of the use of these plants, suddenly find themselves offering "ceremonies" with psychedelics. What is your opinion on this whole phenomenon?

ALV: I think there are different types of neoshamanic practices; I wouldn't put them all in the same category. I think there are a few facilitators who do a very ethical and careful job, and they have dedicated themselves to studying consciousness and medicine (under their own terms).

On the other hand, it is also true that there are neoshamans who believe they know how to accompany people in these states; sometimes their ceremonies are very aesthetic, with very beautiful music, but they do not have sufficient preparation to accompany someone who may be experiencing the memory of a trauma, and because there are many of these neoshamanic contexts, there are also people who have had accidents in this type of practice, and this worries me a lot as a mental health professional. It is something that I have seen happen many times, sometimes in the context of the use of *Bufo alvarius*, the secretion of the Colorado River toad, where more charlatans can be found than good practitioners. As ayahuasca has gained popularity, we are also beginning to see more and more ceremonies where the facilitators frequently lack adequate training, but it must be said that this would not happen in an Indigenous culture, where sharing this medicine requires the permission of the elders or wisdom keepers of the community. Unfortunately, many of these "enablers" do not understand the damage they are doing, and this is certainly part of the problem.

IG: Now entering the final part of this interview, in your opinion, what is the future that awaits intercultural medicine?

ALV: I really hope that the field of mental health in Mexico opens up more, that this traditional knowledge is recognized, as has happened in China. I really hope that the guardians of this knowledge are given back their place, and that ideally there may be a "Mexican Institute of Entheogenic Medicine," that is to say, a place where psychiatrists, psychologists, therapists, and traditional doctors collaborate, providing professional training in entheogenic intercultural medicine. A place where there is space for mental health professionals to establish filters, either studying contraindications in terms of medications or developing methods that prepare people to have safe psychedelic experiences, and where the application of sacred plants is in the charge of traditional doctors, supported by an integration service by therapists, so that we really have a dialogue of knowledge.

IG: Do you have any final words that you want to share with the new or future generations of researchers in this field?

ALV: Yes, on the one hand, that they follow their vocation despite the obstacles, and that they realize that this field has a great future in mental health, it is worth continuing to train, and that they choose to integrate Indigenous knowledge and do not limit themselves to Western knowledge, and only in this way can these peoples be revalued. It is also important that when the time comes, they can share the possible economic benefits with the Indigenous communities, in other words, that this is not limited to a dialogue of knowledge but to total reciprocity.

Creating Communities of Healing with Fireside Project Founding Team Member Hanifa Nayo Washington

SEAN LAWLOR

HANIFA NAYO WASHINGTON'S WARM PERSONALITY, STRONG VISION, AND authentic embodiment of her identity quickly become apparent upon meeting her. Even without meeting her, one need not look further than the title she gave herself at Fireside Project to ascertain these qualities: "Cultivator of Beloved Community."

Like the journeys of many who now work in the psychedelic space, Hanifa's journey as a Founding Team Member of Fireside Project, the psychedelic peer support line launched in early 2021, has been unique and unanticipated. Nevertheless, there is a curious way in which her many talents and skills, from being an artist to building spiritual community, filtered directly into her leadership role at Fireside. Currently, Hanifa serves as

Hanifa Nayo Washington.

the Co-lead Investigator of the Psychedelic Health Equity Initiative (PHEI), aiming to identify and encourage philanthropic investments for equitable access to psychedelic-assisted therapies for people from marginalized communities.

In this interview, conducted in 2021, Hanifa reflects on key elements of her background and worldview that led her to Fireside, as well as how her understanding of the importance of community informs not only the nonprofit support line's values, but the organization's very way of being.

Sean Lawlor: How did your interest in working with psychedelics begin?

Hanifa Nayo Washington: My awareness of psychedelics began when I was in college more than 20 years ago. I had my first experiences then, and they were profound. There was no guide, no intention setting, no ceremony. It was purely recreational, and still, I returned to myself and felt alive and playful in ways that I hadn't before.

About 10 years ago, I came into practice of my own transformational healing process, doing work with plant-based medicine that was not psychedelic in nature, and then moving into more psychedelic usage and practice in community. There was a process of preparing and being in the ceremony, then having integration and growth after ceremony.

For me, psychedelics have been primarily a ceremonial experience and a relationship. It is something that I find great refuge in for cleansing and recentering processes that are coupled with a lot of before-care and after-care. The integration of the things that come through or that I release during ceremony has been significant in my ability to be my whole self, to be a leader and a healer. I've been doing healing work for many years now as a Reiki Master Practitioner and holding space for people individually and in small groups.

Through my personal work in ceremony, I wanted more people to have access and realize that this was a path toward healing, particularly around childhood trauma, stress, and the impacts of systems of oppression—which I feel is tied up for me personally with trauma. The thing is, with any medicine or any process of healing, you have to be aware that there's actually harm and pain happening. For a long time, I was unaware of the impacts of the stress from living in a society and world fraught with injustice. What is that doing to how I am thinking and seeing and being in the world, with how I think about and hold myself? How is that impacting my relationships with my family, with my dear ones, with people who I don't know?

During some of my experiences with psychedelics, particularly with ayahuasca and psilocybin, going through a guided process with some support helped me see where I was holding or tensing in my body, where the pain lives, because I've been constantly returning to a society that is sick and broken. It's important for any healing practices, including those with psychedelics, to have an integration process and community, because you can return to spaces and relationships that cause harm. Just because you've had a healing experience doesn't mean that's going to last forever. Learning how to incorporate the learning and to be resilient in a society and in systems that are structured to be dehumanizing and destabilizing has been lifesaving for me, giving me resources and language and the possibility of being able to guide people into a healthy and restorative practice with psychedelics.

So, my experience with psychedelics started as very personal, with my own healing and transformation, quickly learning that they are wildly impactful for undoing and transmuting the harm. Because it's the nature of who I am, I wanted to help more people, particularly Black and brown women, to know the beauty and safety that can be found in ceremony with psychedelics. There's a lot of fear and stigma around psychedelics, so it's been really important for me to create spaces of healing where integration and community are centered.

SL: I'm hearing that community and relationship is a key part of that integration. That's something I don't hear as much in the psychotherapeutic models, where there is a lot of focus on the individual and their relationship with the therapist.

HNW: I'm nothing without community. I grew up in the Baptist Church, in the choir when I was five, doing Sunday school. My grandmother was, and still is, a "mother" of the church, and so I was always there. There was always a sense of people all around the community doing things together, having dinners, supporting each other, so that was baked into me at a very young age. We do things together, share our resources, and share our gifts together. We're stronger together, and we thrive together.

I have learned that when I try to do things on my own, including healing work or starting a project, it often either fails or I'm super stressed out. I can attest to that in my healing process. For years, I was just alone in my therapy. There was a stigma—you didn't tell people you were going to therapy. I think now there is understanding that it's a wonderful thing, but for me, having the support of community is super important. My entire psychedelic experience has been completely attached to community. It's important to have space for one-on-one support and care, but without returning to a community that can also hold you and see you and reflect, there is a lot to be lost. Things are different for all people, but I think that, at the very nature of humanity, we are social beings. We are wired to be together, and I have found that to be delightful in my journey so far.

SL: Your position at Fireside Project is the Cultivator of Beloved Community. I'm curious what that role looks like, and also how you came to be a Founding Team Member of Fireside.

HNW: The Cultivator of Beloved Community is the title that I created and gave myself. I am an artist. I'm a musician and a songwriter/singer. I'm also a creative designer, so I have a lot of skill in graphic design and designing space. I am someone who has upwards of 10 years facilitating healing experiences as well as doing work in DEI [diversity, equity, and inclusion], so I have a background in organizational development. I've started a couple of different nonprofits and community-serving organizations, and I can design and build websites; I have a lot of different skills.

In college, my major was Communications and Russian and Soviet studies: a fun combo. I've always been fascinated with the psychology of how we communicate. Studying media and mass communication was illuminating and fundamental to the development of my worldview. How we gather, why we gather, and how we *are* while gathering are all super important.

With all that said, I can surmise that I'm a community builder and community connector. I'm a cultural activist as well, combining art and justice work to contribute to my community, to my world, to my people. Everything I do is aligned with those things. It's about helping people to gather well together. It's also about creating a space of inclusion, belonging, power sharing, and joy.

Joshua White and I met at Burning Man in 2019—

SL: Cool! I was there in 2018.

HFW: Awesome! It was my first burn. It was wild. Joshua and I met through mutual friends, we shared contact information, and around this time last year, we synced up again. He was sharing this beginning idea around this thing that didn't have a name yet.

One of the practices that I do is being a thought partner. I support people, hold people, and ask the questions that help to propel them forward, that might challenge their assumptions about something. We started to meet every other Sunday or so, and then he invited me to be part of the Advisory Board. Through our meetings, it became obvious we were working together, and there was an invitation for me to be a part of this. I sat down for a minute, I was like, "Yeah, this feels really aligned."

I had this desire, what I felt was an *assignment*, to bring all the things I have done in my life into this emerging psychedelic ecosystem—bringing my understanding of healing work, somatic work, and interpersonal work and combining that with my DEI work to create something new, which I call a Culture of Belonging. It's not necessarily new, but it comes down to how we want to be together in a different way.

How do we build safety within ourselves? How do we build trust? How do we build the skills and the practices of holding difficult conversations and still be in it with each other? How do we not run away when there is a difference and conflict? How do we see each other? How do we understand and relate to each other? How do I get to actually know who you are?

When I think about belonging, there's a piece where you make yourself belong, but the system and the people that you are with also have a responsibility to share the power and the space-making so that you feel like you can show up fully without negating their ability to show up fully. It's very different than a shaming model or a shaming way of being, and what I call the Skittles Game. It's not about the *number*—though I totally understand that representation matters.

So, I felt excited that this was launching, thinking, "How cool is it to bring my passion for justice and for belonging and for access, particularly to support when people are having a psychedelic experience, when they need to be just seen, or things are difficult and they need grounding?" And the integration piece is massive. You've had an experience and you need support unpacking it and understanding it, whether that was last night or five years ago. To know that there's a place for anybody, regardless of whether they can afford a psychedelic integration coach—that there's someone that can pick up a phone and say, "I'm here." That was so inspiring, and so I was like, "Yes, I want to do this." I want to bring my skills as a facilitator and a space holder for the outer container, to ensure that what we are doing is imbued completely with these principles of belonging, wholeness, relationship building, and realness. It goes for everything—how we're making decisions, how we do our outreach, how we train the volunteers. To know that I can contribute to that in a real way, and that that is happening from the ground up and not out of a reactionary place, but this is actually just the way it is. We operate at our core from a Culture of Belonging not because we are seeking to look good or receive validation from our peers in the community, but because it is the way.

My work as the Cultivator of Beloved Community is about ensuring that we have practices that allow us to power-share and hold each other accountable, practices by which we are hearing from all people, and that there is a process to hold conversations when there may be conflict. Also—thinking about how we are engaging the community—networking and coalition building with individuals and organizations that have been traditionally excluded and marginalized by systems of oppression, who should know and have access to this service. Building those bridges, those ways in, and ensuring there is a way for all identities, all lived experiences, to be on the volunteer side of things. And also, those folks will have access on the calling and texting side of things.

That's not something where you just push a button and it's done. It's a long process. I definitely intend to continue to lead and to be an example with my cofounders and volunteers. And it's also everyone's job, which is something I often say.

The other piece is around the inner work. I think the work of the North Star Pledge is really wonderful. I see this piece of the work that I'm doing with Fireside as putting that into action. They talk about commitment to inner work a lot in the North Star Pledge. Often, it's like, "Well, how do you do that?" Who knows that you're doing it? How are you being held accountable? At Fireside Project, we are making space to be together collectively as we do the inner work. We're bringing the inner work into the work.

We hold sessions every other month with volunteers and staff called Culture of Belonging. We go through different exercises and reflective practices together that span across all realms of justice and transformation. We use story sharing as one of the methodologies for how we talk about these things. We do reflective writing. We listen to different speakers and video clips and have discussions. We introduce them to basic vocabulary building, so that when we say "racism," "white privilege," or "the myth of white supremacy," we all understand what those things mean. It's a space of reflective listening.

So much of relationship building is listening, and our society does not teach us how to listen very well. We hear things, and often in our minds we are getting ready to respond, either to outdo someone else or just say something because we feel we need to. There's a lot of practice of mindfulness, of slowing down, of listening to people sharing the impact of experiences they've had due to systems of oppression and violence. In holding this little space, people can keep going deeper and know that it is a safe space where you can have challenging conversations without breaking the relationships and walking away. Cultivating that space inside of the work that we're doing is part of my role as the Cultivator of Beloved Community at Fireside Project.

SL: You've referenced issues around access, which are talked about often in the psychedelic space. What other systems of oppression and harm do you witness playing out in the psychedelic world?

HNW: The ways in which harm is playing out in the psychedelic space are the same ways harm is playing out in the nonpsychedelic space.

A few weeks ago, someone published something about the hundred most influential people in psychedelics. An image came with the title, and it had, I don't even know—12 white men? I didn't click in to even look at the rest of the list, because I was appalled that in some group of people, there had to be a channel of communication and decision making that went into that image and that title being spread throughout social media. That that channel existed to think that was OK and real and acceptable? It took a little bit of air out of my lungs. I know that people have a long way to go for healing and for being equitable and thoughtful. But as a Black woman stepping into the psychedelic space, it was appalling and disturbing. And it represented this larger issue of the *narrative*. Who's controlling the narrative in the psychedelic space? We often use this term "the psychedelic movement." But whose movement is it? Who is a part of that movement? What is it moving toward?

People often say, "There's not enough people of color in the psychedelic space," and I respond, "Because I don't think we're talking about the same things!" When we say "movement," is that relegated to certain psychedelics getting legalized and decriminalized? Is the movement for psychedelics and plant-based medicines and other substances that create altered mind states to be accessible to all people?

When I think of movements, I think about the Civil Rights Movement, for example. To me, a movement shouldn't just last forever, and if the psychedelic movement has been going on since . . . the '60s? The '80s? I'm not sure. But a movement needs to evolve in order to be actualized as a part of society. If a movement lasts forever, it's not doing very well.

Who controls the narrative? Who gets to say who's at the top, what the objectives are? That image was a huge indicator of how alive and well inequality is in the psychedelic space.

And then, it was amazing, because three or four days later, a group of people got together who made their own list and image that was truly representative of all types of different people, including Indigenous people. To me, it felt like, "Yes, that is the psychedelic movement that I'm a part of." This group of people who understand the relics, who have been in the psychedelic movement for a long time, and also see the dangers of the corporate monopoly of psychedelics that's happening. And so, how do we create and keep an ecosystem of holders who have the intention of respecting these medicines and substances, protecting them and ensuring that access is available to them, and ensuring that the narrative around all of it is reflective of all of those people, and all the people to come?

If you look at who has a voice in the space now, it starts to become the same people, usually white males. I think it's important for the space to have an identity-diverse group of folks who are holding the narrative, who are changing the narrative, and that the narrative doesn't center the patriarchy or capitalism, that it doesn't create duality, but that it is emergent and multi-identity. That's the movement I am a part of.

SECTION FIVE

Birth and Dying

Psychedelics and Death: Transitioning from This World with Consciousness

JASMINE VIRDI

WITHIN THE PSYCHEDELIC RESEARCH COMMUNITY, THERE IS A GROWING body of research[1] showing how psychedelics can ease the process of coming to grips with death. However, extending themselves beyond the confines of science, psychedelics have been used to support people through the process of dying for a long time. Working behind the scenes is a niche but growing community of psychedelic death midwives or end-of-life doulas who have trained to help individuals transition with grace.

In many ways, contemporary Western culture is death phobic, and to even broach the topic is considered unlucky or taboo, as though talking about death could somehow invoke it. However, no matter how much we try to steer clear of the dialogue, death is one thing that binds us all. As surely as we were born, the fact that we will one day die presents itself as an inevitability for us all. Even so, the majority of us prefer to distract ourselves from the simple fact, pushing it to the far reaches of our consciousness.

So what exactly is it about death that causes us to avoid it so fervently? Perhaps, one of our biggest fears around death is the fear of the unknown. Even in today's world where science strives to illuminate mystery, we cannot measure, quantify, or make firm conclusions about death.

Instead of being perceived as something natural, modern medicine is expert at keeping us alive; death is now considered the ultimate failure in medicine. But what if we could shift the dialogue around death, and begin to speak about it more openly and honestly? That is where death midwifery and end-of-life doulas come in.

THE UNDERGROUND WORLD OF PSYCHEDELIC DEATH DOULAS

A psychedelic death doula or death midwife is something you're not likely to have heard of, as they largely operate underground. Death doulas work with individuals during their dying process and sometimes even in the moment of transition itself. However, an individual needn't be dying to enlist the support of an end-of-life doula, as a healthy person may also want their support. A death midwife takes care of the logistics and legalities of death, designing funeral services fitting for the individual as well as providing practical and spiritual support for conscious dying, sometimes with the use of psychedelics.

However, one need not work strictly with psychedelics to be an end-of-life doula in the first place. Mangda Sengvanhpheng, practicing death doula and founder of BACII,[2] a platform devoted to reshaping the conversation around death, shared about her experience of what it means to be engaged in this work more generally.

"Being a death doula means providing non-medical, compassionate support and education to those who are facing death, the dying process, or otherwise preparing for the end-of-life," she shares. "Each doula can provide and incorporate their own specific skill sets or areas of expertise. This can include sitting vigil, emotional and/or spiritual care, grief support, preparing or wrapping up affairs, legacy work, end-of-life planning, and so much more."

Whether involving psychedelics or not, death midwifery has to do with reimagining the ways that we live and die. "By bringing awareness and understanding to difficult topics such as loss, grief, and death, we can change the ways we care for ourselves, each other, and how we experience life," shares Sengvanhpheng.

PSYCHEDELICS, DEATH, AND EGO-DISSOLUTION

Psychedelics have long been associated with death and dying, albeit not necessarily the physical kind. Psychedelics induce a mystical-type state which is commonly known as ego death,[3] or ego-dissolution in the scientific literature. In an experience of ego-dissolution, our ordinary, biographical sense of self melts away and dissipates into a larger "cosmic" consciousness.

The experience of ego death can be both blissful and ecstatic, whilst in the same stroke producing feelings of fear and terror. Perhaps paralleling actual death, in this state we may come to the realization that we are much more than our bodies and life experience. Rather, the boundaries of the narrative-self break down into something much greater. This process can be utterly terrifying; however, if we surrender to the unfoldment of it, it can be a healing and transformative experience.

Perhaps it is psychedelics' ability to induce experiences of ego death that make them so beneficial for those with terminal diagnoses, allowing them to confront death prematurely in some way. In fact, a 2016 randomized double blind trial[4] by researchers at Johns Hopkins University linked psilocybin's ability to decrease depression and anxiety in cancer patients with life-threatening diagnoses to the mystical-type experiences by higher doses of the substance. Reflecting on the experience, one study participant shared, "I have the sense that death is not the end but part of a process, a way of moving into a different sphere, a different way of being."

When confronted with death, it is natural that our ego reacts with fear, attempting to cling to the subjective self identity that we have long nurtured and known. However, letting go and accepting ego death within the psychedelic state can help heal some of the fear and anxiety about death itself in that we are graced with the realization that there is something greater beyond, that it is not necessarily an end.

Recognizing the transformative potential of the ego death experience early on, Timothy Leary, Ralph Metzner, and Richard Alpert, later known as Ram Dass, famously coauthored *The Psychedelic Experience*[5] as a user manual created with the purpose of using psychedelics to navigate the cycle of death, the bardo, and rebirth set out by the *Bardo Thödol*, or *The Tibetan Book of the Dead*. In Tibetan Buddhism the bardos are the states of existence that permeate the realm between death and rebirth. Subsequently, *The Tibetan Book of the Dead* places the utmost importance on the state of consciousness at the time of death, making efforts to guide and support the dying person to attain a higher state of awareness.

LAURA HUXLEY, THE FIRST KNOWN PSYCHEDELIC DEATH MIDWIFE

Partially inspired by Leary, Alpert, and Metzner's yet-to-be published manuscript, and having his own longstanding interest in the Bardo, English writer and philosopher Aldous Huxley decided to transition with 200 micrograms of LSD pumping through his blood.

Diagnosed with laryngeal cancer in 1960, Huxley's health deteriorated slowly up until the time he died in 1963. Leading up to the time of his death, he had not taken a psychedelic for over two years, and thought about it often in his last weeks, telling himself that he would explore them once again when he felt better, and according to his wife, Laura Huxley,[6] he was adamant in his belief that he would get better.

However, in his last hours as his condition worsened, he consciously decided that he wanted to ingest LSD. Laura administered two intravenous doses of 100 micrograms to him. Laura wrote an account of Aldous's death, primarily for friends and family; however, she later published it in her memoir of her husband.[7] She wrote, "Aldous died as he lived, doing his best to develop fully in himself one of the essentials he recommended to others: Awareness." Aldous felt that his departure from his body might lessen his awareness and so he prescribed what he referred to as his own "sacrament."

Acting as a death midwife for her husband, Laura perpetually reminded him not to become caught up in visions, which in Tibetan Buddhism are considered to be illusory, as he died, continually guiding him to move towards the pure light. Whispering to him gently, she said, "Willingly and consciously you are going, willingly and consciously, and you are doing this beautifully; you are doing this so beautifully—you are going towards the light—you are going towards the light—you are going towards greater love—you are going forward and up."

It is speculated that Aldous Huxley's decision to use LSD as he was dying was also linked to the work of the little-known clinician Dr. Eric Kast. Kast was actually one of the first researchers[8] to describe the impact of LSD on death and its possible benefits in terminal patients. As early as 1964, Kast published research pointing to LSD as a painkiller, providing support for its analgesic effects. With this realization, Kast experimentally tested LSD on over 300 terminal cancer patients, finding LSD to not only decrease physical pain but simultaneously reduce existential anxiety and distress related to end-of-life diagnoses. Later in 1970, Kast authored an article[9] exploring LSD as a treatment for fear around death.

THE CALL FOR A MORE COMPASSIONATE WAY TO DIE

Despite countless studies[10] that suggest psychedelics, in particular psilocybin, are able to help individuals make peace with death and dying, they are still not legally available to access for this purpose. Recognizing this injustice, there has been an ongoing lawsuit in which terminally ill patients are suing the Drug Enforcement Agency (DEA) for its denial of their application to use psilocybin in end-of-life care.[11]

The ongoing lawsuit is an extension of Seattle-based palliative care doctor Sunil Aggarwal's work. In 2021 Aggarwal took the DEA to court[12] over its denial of an application[13] for terminally ill patients to legally use psilocybin. The fight for expanded access was based on the premise of existing state and federal right-to-try laws which allow patients with life-threatening conditions the ability to try experimental treatments that have yet to be approved by the FDA for general use.

In 2018, President Donald Trump signed a federal Right to Try Act,[14] allowing terminally ill patients across the US to try medicines that have yet to be approved. The DEA's rejection of Aggarwal's application asserted that his petition did not possess the authority to waive the federal Controlled Substances Act, in spite of the Right to Try Act.

Compared with the US, the use of psilocybin as palliative care for terminally ill patients has been permitted on a case-by-case basis in Canada. In August 2020, TheraPsil, a Canadian nonprofit that facilitates access to legal psilocybin-assisted psychotherapy for individuals suffering from end-of-life distress, set a precedent when four Canadians with terminal cancer were granted legal exemptions to use psilocybin with the guidance of a therapist approved by Canada's Ministry of Health.[15] As of March 2021, Health Canada has approved exemptions for over 50 patients for legal psilocybin-assisted psychotherapy.

Given that a single dose of psilocybin has been shown to yield such dramatically promising results for battling with the transition to the other side, it seems altogether unethical to deny terminally ill individuals this kind of relief. Perhaps an extension of the cognitive liberty movement, the idea that humans should have sovereignty over their consciousness, ought to apply to death equally. Everyone has the right to choose how they transition from this world, and for that reason talking about new approaches to death and dying is of increasing importance.

Undoubtedly, a radical shift is in the way we understand and deal with death and dying is critically needed. Pondering the same question whilst providing her account of Aldous Huxley's death, Laura Huxley wrote,

"Now, is his way of dying to remain for us, and only for us, a relief and consolation, or should others also benefit from it? Aren't we all nobly born and entitled to nobly dying?" Death is as individual as the person who lived, and under the influence of a psychedelic or not, having the loving support and gentle guidance of a death doula to aid the process of transition could help many more leave from this world nobly, with the dignity and compassion they deserve.

Ayahuasca and Childbirth in the Santo Daime Tradition: Solidarity Among Women and Psychedelic Cultural Resistance

JACQUELINE ALVES RODRIGUES AND

GLAUBER LOURES DE ASSIS

WE ALL KNOW (OR WE SHOULD KNOW!) THAT IN THE HISTORY OF THE so-called Western civilization, which is so proud of itself, women have systematically suffered countless forms of physical, psychological, economic, sexual, and symbolic violence.

Unfortunately, these forms of violence are still present in contemporary society. The gender pay gap and the limited representation of women in positions of power and leadership compared to men are just two examples.

The marks of patriarchy also extend to the control and surveillance of female bodies. Deprived over the centuries of freedom in relation to themselves, women have often been given the place of spectators of their own lives, with men playing the role of managers and administrators of their bodies and desires.

The impacts of these biopolitics are also felt in the establishment of medical/hospital protocols that remove the autonomy of women from pregnancy to childbirth—in some cases resulting in obstetric violence—and in the stigma of traditional practices of care for the female body. Further, the contribution of women to Western psychedelic culture has been traditionally undervalued both by psychedelic practitioners within the culture and in mainstream coverage of the culture.

For these and other reasons, it is very important that when we discuss psychedelics, we emphasize female agency and the solidarity networks formed by women, which are an important aspect of the relationship between human beings and sacred plants and the formation of cultures, religions, and collective representations associated with their consumption.

Jacqueline and her son Guaracy in a Santo Daime ceremony. Picture by Alice Okawara

In this article, we will discuss the art of midwifery, the relationships of care and support established among women in the Brazilian religion of Santo Daime, and the connection of these practices to sacred plants.

SANTO DAIME AND FEMALE RESISTANCE

Founded in the 1930s, Santo Daime is the oldest of the Brazilian ayahuasca religions. Founded by Mestre (Master) Raimundo Irineu Serra, a Black man from northeastern Brazil who migrated to the Amazon to work in the rubber industry that developed there in the 20th century, this religion has a female entity, the Queen of the Forest, a "Universal Goddess," as its spiritual patron.

Some of the most important leaders of the religion are women, including Madrinha (Godmother) Rita, matriarch of Church of the Eclectic Cult of the Universal Fluent Light (ICEFLU), and Madrinha Peregrina, Mestre Irineu's widow and undisputed leader of the Universal Christian Light Center of Illumination (CICLU) in Alto Santo, Acre.[1]

An aspect still little discussed in the literature on Santo Daime, however, is the female agency within its practices, and the network of support and sisterhood that women have nurtured and kept alive over the decades, despite the difficulties inflicted by a sexist society and the work overload borne by many women in Santo Daime.

This network of solidarity can be seen in an especially heroic way with regard to pregnancy and childbirth. There is an art of midwifery, practiced in the Daime tradition, that remains alive, passed on from generation to generation, and protected by zealous guardians.

It is also important to say that this article deals specifically with Santo Daime. Each ayahuasca tradition has its own culture, and what happens in the Daime context cannot be generalized to the whole ayahuasca field.[2]

In Santo Daime, women have the right to drink ayahuasca throughout their pregnancy and during labor. It is a woman's individual choice, and no one can force her to do so. As in the case of children, pregnant women consume smaller doses (which is often symbolic) than the rest of the group. Pregnant women can also participate normally in the rituals, but are not obligated to do so because they have the freedom to choose.[3]

State and moral entrepreneurs, vocal in sensationalist media, have challenged this freedom over the decades despite the absence of scientific evidence that the consumption of ayahuasca harms pregnant women, fetuses and small children, and families in Daime communities, which is widely documented in the anthropological literature.

A historic event took place in 2010 when the Brazilian government agency responsible for national drug policy, CONAD, made the decision to guarantee pregnant women the autonomy and right to consume ayahuasca in their religious practices.[4]

This decision remains in effect in Brazil and is a landmark in the country's drug policy and an example to the world. In the Brazilian context, it is understood that it is up to the woman to decide whether or not to ingest ayahuasca during her pregnancy, and the family has the power to decide on giving the drink to children.

In this case, therefore, the experiences of families over generations and the principle of religious freedom have taken precedence over social prejudice, infamous War on Drugs policies, and the patriarchal surveillance of women's bodies.

The use of ayahuasca by women during pregnancy and during childbirth can be seen as an act of resistance to colonial and patriarchal violence, as well as a maintenance of traditional care practices and possibilities to cultivate and share wisdom, knowledge, and experiences linked to the world of midwifery.

TRADITIONAL MIDWIVES AND THE SOLIDARITY NETWORK AMONG WOMEN

"It is useless for a woman to say that she is a midwife if there is no trust in the community," says Clarice Andreozzi, a recognized midwife of the ICEFLU Santo Daime community.

The art of midwifery is involved in the transmission of knowledge between women, and is not a solo, individual activity, but part of a network of support and solidarity with ancient roots.

"It is traditional, ancestral knowledge, passed on from generation to generation," recalls Clarice, who adds: "The knowledge of traditional midwives is not only linked to labor itself; often it is also associated with knowledge of herbs. Many midwives are prayer leaders and faith healers and serve as a point of reference in terms of recognizing women in a community. A midwife is a woman that other women trust. She not only takes care of childbirth, but also of women's problems."

One of the main historical midwives in the Daime tradition was Madrinha Cristina Raulino. "From the ninth month onwards, Madrinha Cristina started to accompany the women. From the ninth month, a dessert spoon (of ayahuasca) every night. It helps to relax and relieve pain during childbirth," recalls Vera Fróes, a leading researcher of plants and the female experience in Santo Daime.[5]

Madrinha Cristina mentored and supported many women in the art of midwifery, among them Clarice, who says that she became a midwife to "support women so they don't go through the same difficulties I did. All the obstetric violence. A total lack of information in the postpartum period when I was breastfeeding."

Today, Clarice is part of the *Daime a Luz* ("Daime-That-Births-Light") Network, a project of women linked to ICEFLU, that seeks to strengthen and empower midwives who live in Daime communities in the forest, "and who become teachers of new midwives," especially in the Céu do Mapiá headquarters of the Santo Daime expansionist line in Amazonia, founded by Padrinho (Godfather) Sebastião (who is himself a recognized midwife by the community).

THE ART OF MIDWIFERY AND WOMEN'S FREEDOM OVER THEIR BODIES AND DESIRES

With the expansion of Santo Daime into large urban centers, the makeup of the Daime community has begun to change, and the new socioeconomic profile of its members is more accustomed to the medicalization of the birth experience, distant from the Amazonian cultural roots of the religion. As a result, the delivery performed by traditional midwives with the use of ayahuasca, even in forest communities, has in many cases been passed over in favor of so-called modern methods, and in this way the home/community has given way more and more to the hospital as a place to give birth.

According to Meyer and Meyer,[6] this transition is also related to the average Brazilian's perception that childbirth is an "illness" or "disease," which would help to explain the high rate of deliveries performed by modern medicalized means. On the other hand, they point out that the continuance of traditional home births in remote and isolated forest communities is related to the scarcity of resources and difficulties in accessing hospital services.

It is not a question, here, of necessarily placing modern biomedical knowledge in opposition to traditional knowledge. It can be safely said that most followers of Santo Daime do not see a contradiction but rather a complementarity between modern and traditional care techniques.

What interests us here is not a fallacious opposition between "tradition" and "modernity" but rather an opposition between violence and women's agency over their own lives, bodies, and desires. Here quality information about the possibilities of choice involving pregnancy and childbirth, as well as an appreciation of female expertise in women's care, play an important role.

It is in this sense that Vera Fróes states that "keeping alive the tradition of humanized childbirth is an act of resistance against the monopoly of health practices and the industrial production of medicines, in addition to valuing our cultural heritage, contained in traditional, intuitive, or empirical knowledge and practices in the use of plants."[7]

AYAHUASCA AND THE DAIME CHILDBIRTH RITUAL

We can define living together in a Santo Daime community as a ritualized life experience. There are rituals for all sorts of initiations, from marriage to baptism, and childbirth is no different.

Clarice defines the Daime ritual of childbirth as a "ritual of simplicity, which unites the simplicity of the Daime and the naturalness and simplicity of giving birth." Women's faith and trust in their own process are fundamental elements of this moment:

> First of all, with all those who are present, the spiritual works are opened: the Sign of the Cross is made, and the Lord's Prayer and a Hail Mary are recited. Afterwards, prayers are made, asking Our Lady of Good Birth, Mestre Irineu, Padrinho Sebastião, and our spiritual guides for protection. Soon after we consecrate the Daime [ayahuasca]. Depending on the situation, we may chant other prayers or carry out a hymnal session [a ritual session with singing] until labor starts.
>
> The delivery time varies a lot. That is why we observe the rhythm, the confidence, the presence, the empowerment of women in their process. After a while, we serve a little more Daime, and we can also carry out a smoking or smudging process and provide sitting baths.
>
> When the woman is afraid, we make our prayers and incantations. And we take our spiritual strength to carry out the work. Sometimes the woman wants to meditate. Sometimes she wants to stay in the bathtub. She has the freedom to experience her own process. When the baby is born, we sing the hymn "Sol, Lua, Estrela" [Sun, Moon, and Star], by Mestre Irineu, and the hymn "Sou Luz, Dou Luz" [I'm Light, I Give Light] by Padrinho Sebastião. After the baby is welcomed, we say the Lord's Prayer and a Hail Mary, thank the guides and ancestors who are present, and then we close the spiritual work.
>
> If the placenta takes a long time to come out, there is the prayer of the placenta, for Saint Margarida. In the meantime, we make massages—there are several different techniques, such as steaming the uterus, smoking it with Santa Maria

(*Cannabis sativa*), invoking her sacred presence—and in this way we carry out the needs that arise during childbirth. Each birth is a new experience, a new learning experience.

Doctor Adelise Noal, another important Daime midwife, shares some of the emotion of experiencing childbirth within Santo Daime: "The whole body trembles when receiving a newborn human being from the maternal womb, as if it were in a state of trance. The blooming of a flower, watered with the wine of souls [ayahuasca]!"[8]

As can be seen, the Daime childbirth ritual is deeply related to the faith and values shared by the women who make up this religion, a feeling that is shared by the first author of this article, who drank ayahuasca in a Santo Daime church throughout her pregnancies, and considers that Daime also played an important role in the birth and postpartum processes:

> During the entire period of labor to give birth to my second child I took small doses of Santo Daime, which gave me the necessary confidence in myself, in the baby, in the team that helped us, and in the whole process. Although this birth took place in a hospital environment, we were able to set up a small altar in the room. During the baby's expulsive period, which began to take longer than expected, I drank some Daime, said some prayers, and lit a candle, and from that moment on, the baby was born quickly. On the same day, we moistened the child's mouth with cotton wool containing Santo Daime, and all this contributed to a meaningful experience, which continued during the puerperium and breastfeeding period.

Therefore, linking the experience of childbirth to the consumption of ayahuasca within Santo Daime can give participants confidence and support them through the birthing process. This is illustrated by a statement from Padrinho Sebastião, quoted by Vera Fróes, according to which "a woman who drinks Daime does not die in childbirth."[9]

RESPECT FOR WOMEN'S FREEDOM AND AUTONOMY

Throughout the history of Western civilization, women have lived with all kinds of violence and interference. Female agency has been constantly relegated to the background, in favor of moral and technical discourses made mainly by men. Despite this, women have been resisting, and the example of the art of childbirth in the Santo Daime religion shows the power and luminosity of women united together.

This power has profound subjective and collective implications, which help to keep the social fabric of the community, its rites, and its culture alive and strengthened in the midst of the various attacks against traditional knowledge, lifestyles, and female autonomy.

We hope that this paradigmatic Brazilian case can inspire people to question the War on Drugs, awaken an anthropological sensitivity to observe human cultures in their own terms and worldviews, and fight for women's rights.

And we also hope that more and more women raise their voices and become protagonists of their own lives, with full freedom over their bodies, their desires, their consciences, and their spirituality. It may be possible for humanity to gestate and give birth to the long-awaited utopia of a better world for all.

Abortion, Plants, and Whispered Networks of Botanical Knowledge

NAOMI RENDINA

THE FAMOUS SUPREME COURT OF THE UNITED STATES DECISION ROE V. Wade (1973) is a landmark in abortion rights, that enshrined legal access to elective abortive procedures at the federal level. In 2022 the federal government turned back the clock on this legal measure, putting abortion access once again in peril, with the possibility of compelling women to seek alternatives.

WHISPER NETWORKS

Whether or not abortion is legal, women will terminate pregnancies. As they always have. Before Roe, American women resorted to a variety of self-aborting methods, including, but not limited to, the infamous

40 years of Roe v Wade Event—San Francisco. Photo by Steve Rhodes

coat-hanger method, various herbal remedies, and physically hurting the abdominal region. Historians, such as John Riddle, have shown that even women in antiquity aborted pregnancies by using concoctions made from herbs like pennyroyal and other herbs, which had more of a contraceptive property that helped prevent ovulation or pregnancy. While this plant-based knowledge was widespread, Riddle argued that it fell out of favor with the rise of male-dominated medicine in the 18th and 19th centuries. The fact that women's knowledge of herbal remedies was associated with "witchcraft," and that its practice could result in women being condemned to death, didn't help.

However, while the development of medical science negatively characterized this domain of women's knowledge, it turns out that such knowledge did not merely fall out favor as much as it slipped underground: women healers continued to share valuable information with one another in whisper networks. Publicly, there was coded language in newspapers informing women where to obtain an abortion. Indeed, it may be said that legal access to abortion has meant that much of the plant-based knowledge about contraception and abortion in the United States has been forgotten. It appears that there was no longer a reason to maintain the whisper networks that shared botanic knowledge about women's health.

PLANTS AND ABORTION

One plant-based substance consistent throughout whisper networks of abortion knowledge is ergot. A fungus found on rye, ergot is known for its potential to cause hallucinations and other supranormal perceptual experiences. Ergot alkaloids were foundational to the research that led Albert Hofmann to his discovery of LSD (lysergic acid diethylamide). Ergot has also long been used as an abortifacient to help post-partum hemorrhage, and even induce labor. Given, or unintentionally ingested, too early into pregnancy, ergot can ignite abortion.

In the first decades of the 20th century, ergot was most often given as an intramuscular injection, and determining a safe dosage was a delicate and complicated task. Physicians and pharmacists knew that ergot was a poison. They also knew that while a small dose created uterine contractions, too much ergot administered too quickly could seize the uterus and kill the fetus. The ideal dose was unclear because each woman's tolerance was different. When given too large of a dose, ergot could be deadly, and when given at the wrong time, it could kill a fetus.

Evidence shows that when used during both the early stages and post-partum phase of childbirth, ergot has a variety of side effects, including vision problems, headaches, irritability, and nausea. Obstetricians by the 1920s recognized that ergot's effectiveness in childbirth ranged from use-less to catastrophic. While the evidence is difficult to pinpoint, historians suspect that ergot use contributed to increased maternal mortality rates of the late 1920s and early 1930s. Yet, it is also clear that women have been historically willing to take even grave risks when it comes to abortions.

Medical historian Edward Shorter has argued that ergot, for the purposes of abortion, was not effective prior to about the fourth gestational month, making ergot useless to women wanting to abort early in the first trimester. While there is limited information about how women procured and used ergot, due in large part because its use for abortions was a criminal offense

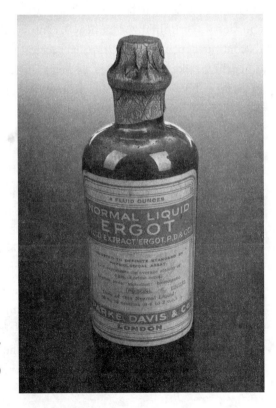

Bottle of ergot extract, London, England, 1891–1950. Science Museum, London. (CC BY 4.0)

in many jurisdictions, it appears that its use (along with other botanics) became part of women's networks of knowledge, often concealed, protected, and quite possibly subject to lots of inconsistent use as desperate women sought solutions that could be kept secret.

Historians Shorter and Riddle both found evidence of ergot poisoning, which included high rates of miscarriages and a decrease in birth rates. The historical efficacy of ergot for early abortion is unclear, but ergot's oxytocic effects are known. It not only produces contractions, but can produce hallucinations, and warrants serious warning when used outside of medical supervision. Ergot, (un)fortunately, is not so easy to get ahold of commercially. It is not made into a tea or sold at apothecaries or mainstream drug stores, meaning that women seeking this substance often must go to great lengths to procure it.

Pennyroyal, an even more popular and well-known herbal abortion method, carries its own warnings and side effects. Ancient Greek physicians understood the power of pennyroyal, so much so that Hippocratic works refer to the herb as birth control. It was used in this medical capacity until abortion was criminalized in the 19th century. This doesn't mean its use was discontinued; pennyroyal tea is easily accessible as a commercial remedy for other things like colds and flus, as well as headaches. It is a fairly mild dose in tea form, but when consumed in quantity, cannot only abort a pregnancy, but can cause liver damage as well.

Even today, you can purchase such teas from mainstream vendors, including on Amazon. There are other herbal plants that can be used for abortion, including queen anne's lace, mugwort, and blue cohosh. While not considered as dangerous as ergot, all of these plant-based medicines have a long history of being used to regulate women's reproduction, while the risks and doses for these purposes are rarely discussed openly, or included on a label. None of them should be used without serious knowledge, or in place of safe, professional medical care.

Although herbal remedies remain available today, the knowledge about their use for contraception or for inducing miscarriages seems to be disappearing even further. Now that abortion is re-criminalized in the US, our problems will only be compounded by the fact that our whisper networks about the common secrets of botanic knowledge for women's health concerns have gone silent. Women's knowledge of plants has long been politicized, not the least of which due to its associations, rightly or wrongly, with contraception and abortion.

Psychedelic plant medicines are beginning to be decriminalized at an auspicious moment in the history of feminism and reproductive health justice in the United States.[1] As we dismantle a War on Drugs, Americans have also turned the clock back on reproductive rights in a move that will leave women seeking alternatives, and resorting to networks of secret knowledge with unintended risks.

Psychedelic Motherhood:
The Altered States of Birth

LANA COOK

> *"It was getting us both very high . . . In fact, everybody in the room looked golden to me. Valerie and Amber and I hung out and kind of melted into each other and fell in love."*
>
> —Amber's birth story, Ina May Gaskin's
> *Spiritual Midwifery* (1975)

PSYCHEDELICS AND CHILDBIRTH. NOT TWO WORDS WE OFTEN PUT together. In the stories of Amber and others like her in the classic 1975 childbirth guide *Spiritual Midwifery* by Ina May Gaskin, one of the foundational figures in modern midwifery, there's a vision for childbirth that is sensual, ecstatic, and *decidedly psychedelic*. A strange juxtaposition to the typical media portrayals of childbirth. Close-up of a woman screaming in agony, swearing obscenities at her partner, and demanding pain-relieving drugs. And then cut to her gazing with pure adoration at the newborn child. Labor and delivery in this version is a story of trauma followed by the bewildering wonder of new motherhood. But, on the Farm in Tennessee, a community shepherded by counterculture hero Stephen Gaskin, the women under the care of Ina May and her midwives describe a rich tapestry of heightened sensation, shifts in the sense of time and space, feelings of expanded consciousness, emotional oneness, and connection with a larger cosmos or collective. In short, they use the language of psychedelics.

This essay feels transgressive to write because bringing together the illicit language of psychedelics with the secretive realm of childbirth collides two realms that women are not supposed to speak about so explicitly.[1] Like the incomplete histories of women and psychedelics, we don't have the full story of childbirth on record, because women's birth stories are passed along in conversation, the oral tradition of sisters and friends, mothers, and daughters. So, how do we make sense of these curiously psychedelic stories told by women like Amber who delivered their babies on the Farm? What made their births so psychedelically attuned? And what would it mean for modern women to harness that psychedelic energy?

If we look at firsthand accounts of childbirth and psychedelic trips, they suggest a closer kinship than our cultural taboos have space for. I am not advocating for the use of psychedelics during pregnancy and labor. Though there is little Western scientific literature on the harm or benefit of psychedelics on pregnancy and fetal health, such use may put mother and baby at risk. Though we might look to the Wixárika or Huichol Indians of Mexico[2] who are known to use peyote, and women of the Amazonian Santo Daime religion[3] who take part in Daime, or ayahuasca, ceremonies during pregnancy, and in some cases, labor, believing it allows the expectant mother "to experience the pregnancy and contact with the baby, to interiorize the experience more profoundly." I bring them together as a thought exercise, to see how we might develop a language for the altered state of childbirth and the transformations enacted in that wondrous bodily process.

Psychedelic states of body and mind offer us a map for navigating one state of self to another: from complacency to awakening; from individual to bonded parent. In childbirth, this altered state is not triggered by external psychoactive agents, but by the emerging baby itself—a hormonal chain reaction set off within the mother's body by the emergence of a new life, propelling the mother into the altered state of labor, birth, and then motherhood itself.

PSYCHEDELIC VAGINA AND BUDDHA BABIES

> "Douglas held up a mirror for me to see my vagina and I was amazed. It looked very psychedelic, like the big pink petals of a flower opening up. It was really beautiful. It surprised me and I felt like I had a new respect for my body. I remembered and told everyone how the story of Buddha says he was born from a lotus blossom. Everybody, every Buddha, is born that way."
>
> —Lyle's Story, *Spiritual Midwifery*

I wanted a natural childbirth. No drugs. No epidural. Just pure awareness for myself and for my child for that moment of entrance into the world. I spent the last half of my pregnancy preparing for this natural birth, working up the endurance for what lay ahead. I did prenatal yoga, stretching the body and meditating to find my center. I read voraciously, finding solace in even the most traumatic of birth stories, because as the cliché goes: knowledge is power. But, I kept asking myself, how would I really prepare? How would I summon and trust my inner strength as the power of labor began to overwhelm? Especially if I were to believe all the media stories: Women unmoored by the pain. Their sense of control set loose. Their grip awash. How would I cope? What would I need? As I was pondering these questions, seven months pregnant, anxiously awaiting the due date, some solace emerged in a strange set of birthing books: *Ina May Gaskin's Guide to Natural Childbirth* and *Spiritual Midwifery*. I stumbled upon these as recommended guides for natural childbirth and was surprised to find some *curiously psychedelic* stories.

As a psychedelic historian, the psychedelic metaphors of the Farm women were a comfort as I anticipated the birth of my own child, not

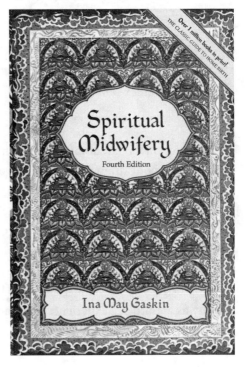

because I thought it would be pure ecstasy or a wondrous body high (psychedelics themselves do not always deliver such one-sided effects). Rather, psychedelic language gave me a useful map of the powerful emotional terrain I would journey through in labor. The gradual, yet distinct, stages of labor (early, active, transition, and pushing) are sequenced like psychedelic experiences: the onset, the peak, the comedown, and the fleeting traces remain as cognitively hazy, yet emotionally vivid, flashbacks in our memory.

Set and setting are essential: a relaxed mindset, safe and comfortable settings, and caring, competent aides can markedly improve outcomes for mother and child. Like shamans and psychedelic therapists, midwives, doulas, and other support persons play a crucial role in creating and facilitating the set and setting for labor and delivery and for guiding a woman through the process. Understanding childbirth as psychedelic gave me a set of tools: preparing a setting that would put my mind at ease; surrounding myself with reassuring guides on the same wavelength who could steer me back when I entered rockier waters; holding onto totems to anchor me to the everyday, pain-free state to which I would eventually return, and to enter the birthing state with curiosity and joy at this immense range of human experience; and, most importantly, to open myself up to be transformed by motherhood.

SEARCHING FOR THE PSYCHEDELIC. FINDING A C-SECTION.

> *mother is a cocoon where*
> *cells spark, limbs form, mother*
> *swells and stretches to protect her*
> *child, mother has one foot in this world*
> *and one foot in the next,*
> *mother, black venus*
>
> —Warsan Shire, "I Have Three Hearts" (2017)

The preparation for parenthood begins with the transformation of the body. The pregnant body dramatically changes over the course of the 40 weeks of gestation. Organs and skeletal structures shift and move to make room for the expanding fetus. An entirely new organ, the placenta, grows to nourish the new life. Externally, there is the emergent bump, with the necessity of a new wardrobe to accommodate the changing form. The pregnant woman becomes an expectant mother over time. With each bodily change, the swelling belly, breasts, hands, and feet, I became aware of my emergent identity as a mother. I experienced my own skin anew, my pregnant body anchoring me to my bodily present. I entered the transformative space of motherhood as I meditated on my baby bump, dreaming of the future child

I had only begun to know. I approached full term, this state intensified as the baby increasingly kicked, hiccupped, and squirmed within me.

During my labor, this intense bodily awareness reached its apex. As the uterus insistently tightened and relaxed, I drew increasingly into myself, acutely aware of my body. In labor, women often feel their bodies and minds taken over, moved by an instinctual force to deliver their babies. Energy coursed, stretched, and ached within me, with cramps insistent, rhythmic, and powerful. In Gaskin's books, contractions are called "surges" or "waves" a language that moves away from metaphors of mechanical pain to a more ecological sense of the body. With each surge, my vision narrowed into a tunnel, the activity edged out. My memories of this time are like flashbulbs: the fiery skyline of sunrise moving to sunset; the smell of food mistakenly ordered; clock time irrelevant; spatial boundaries disappeared; staring out the window like I was high. My vision focused on the distant vistas, drifting into the space of a passing cloud, a darting bird, a pine bough as it shimmied in the wind. I inhabited these forms as I breathed through each contraction. These visions were a place for my mind to temporarily take refuge from my body's push and pull.

Unfortunately, where my experience diverged from the women under Gaskin's care was in the final stage of delivery. On the second day of labor, my son's heartbeat began to drop and, after careful, yet anxious, consideration of our options, we underwent the Cesarean section to get him safely into the world. Amidst my disappointment at this outcome, I remember during the surgery looking up at these big overhead spotlights that had an incandescent rainbow glean to them and thinking "well, this at least is psychedelic," finding a moment to laugh to myself in what otherwise was a peak stressful moment as we waited for him to be brought out in the world, unsure of his condition. First, I heard him. His voice rang out like ripples in a pond. And then I saw him. My universe closed in and expanded all at once. The perimeters blurred, partly with tears, partly with my singular focus on his very presence. His skin seemed to glow, a halo of rosy pink. Locking eyes with him I felt my life, my heart and mind, transform. My being changed in a moment as I became a mother, his mother.

My son's birth was psychedelic. Not in far out visions or swirling Day-Glo colors, but in a greater cosmic sense. Through his birth, I transcended my individual self and connected with something sublime, a kind of psychedelic grace. Was my birth experience psychedelic because I wanted it to be, because I framed it as such? Is it simply then a matter of perspective? Well, yes, perhaps so. So what's enriched in my experience by framing birth as psychedelic? Most simply, it helped me transform into a mother.

THE ALTERED STATES OF MOTHERHOOD

Language shapes our experiences, giving us containers for understanding the sensations and emotions of being in the world. A new language of birth is needed that empowers women's bodies and minds, and one that honors the integrative support that is needed for women before and after they undergo these profound transformations. What I found in Ina May Gaskin's books was that their psychedelic metaphors offered up surprisingly fitting language for the altered states of birth. The language of psychedelics, one of healing and integration, rather than pain and trauma, could help guide women in understanding the profound bodily, hormonal, and emotional transformations that take place in this life-altering experience.

If we treat birth as psychedelic, if we accept that entering motherhood happens through an altered state, we can see motherhood as adaptation. Motherhood, fatherhood, or any parental role for that matter, is a radical change of identity, altering the way we see and experience ourselves, each other, and our world. Yet, we must balance how to remain stably ourselves while we also learn an entirely new persona. Some may choose to sling off this new parental identity, disavowing their responsibilities to child and partners. Could such cases of parental abandonment be the result of a failure to acknowledge and integrate the shifts in self-perception that this altered state of childbirth should have brought?

There can be a painful sense of separation in birth, a physical and psychic disconnection as both mother and baby begin their lives as independent beings. Integrating birth experiences, particularly difficult ones, can help heal such bodily and psychic traumas, to bring together the seemingly contradictory waves of emotion when ecstatic joy collides with postpartum mourning and depression. Psychedelic frameworks can teach new parents about the power of integration as they straddle these two worlds.

My own psychedelic thinking and experiences opened me up to be willingly transformed by pregnancy and birth (despite the C-section). Like the transformation of a psychedelic trip, I trusted that the core of my being would remain. Many new mothers fear their identities will disappear in motherhood. As any new parent can attest, the ratio of self-care gets seriously imbalanced amidst the blur of feedings, diapers, baby smiles, and late nights. It's easy to get caught up in the mythical expectations of self-sacrifice. This is, of course, only a myth, and one thankfully with diminishing currency as women's identities become increasingly expansive. Yet, the fear of self-dissolution remains for many new mothers. Psychedelics teach us that this kind of ego-death can be beneficial, enabling a self-reflective letting go of the past and embracing new shifts of perspective while remaining faithful to a core sense of being. Psychedelics would ask mothers to kneel to that divine altar of motherhood, humbled in its power, but without all the self-sacrifice that patriarchy would have us believe.

"Mother has one foot in this world / and one foot in the next," as Warsan Shire writes in her poem that helped announce online the birth of Beyonce's twins. Like Gaskin's stories, Shire's poem "I Have Three Hearts" is the language of the psychedelic—of spaces in between, of mysterious connection between two worlds, and how to evolve amidst these immense life-altering experiences. Psychedelic language adds to our understanding of the incredible in-between of new parenthood, about how we talk about such extreme states of physical and emotional experience, and how we might use the lessons of psychedelic integration to support new parents through birth into parenthood. The language of psychedelics speaks to the divinity of mothers' bodies, shining a glowing light on the miracle of new birth, and reminding us of the precious fragility and powerful strength of a mother's identity emerging, as if from a cocoon, utterly transformed and ever transforming.

This Is Not Native American History, This Is US History with Belinda Eriacho

MARIA MOCERINO

BELINDA ERIACHO IS A NATIVE AMERICAN HEALER THAT WAS BORN AND raised in the capital of the Navajo nation: Window Rock, Arizona. Although she grew up learning the medicinal traditions of her ancestors, Belinda decided to pursue a life as a healer when her brother fell ill with pancreatic cancer and she was diagnosed with systemic lupus.

Returning to her medicine roots, Belinda dug deep into herself and her trauma in an intensive healing process that included Native American techniques such as lightning medicine, sweat lodges, and sacred plants.

From her perspective, her illness was her teaching and initiated her on the path of the wounded healer. As a result, she started a company called Kaalogii that promotes Native American teachings and education. "'Kaalogii,' in the Navajo language, is 'butterfly,'" Belinda said, "which was born out of my transformation from who I thought I was to who I really am. I wanted to empower others to do the same."

As a Native American woman, *Belinda Eriacho.*
Belinda witnessed and experienced the effects of the intergenerational trauma afflicted by the US government and its policies that remain, to this day, ignored. Currently, for example, Native American women are being kidnapped, raped, and murdered in the US and Canada.

In this interview, conducted in 2020, Belinda Eriacho does not teach us a lesson on "Native American history." In her words, "This is US history that we share." This includes Belinda's own experience growing up on a Navajo reservation, the intergenerational trauma afflicting Native Americans, the inclusion of Native American and Indigenous voices in the psychedelic conversation, and her healing journey using Native American medicine techniques.

Maria Mocerino: How do you introduce yourself to your people?

Belinda Eriacho: When I introduce myself to my people, I acknowledge myself as being from the Hónágháahnii (One-Who-Walks-Around) clan on my mother's side. I was born from the Naasht'ézhi (Zuni). My maternal grandparents are from the Black Sheep clan and my paternal grandparents are from the Zuni.

MM: What is your lineage, and where did you grow up?

BE: On my mother's side, I am Diné. On my father's side, I am Ashiwi. I primarily grew up on the Navajo reservation in a little community called Window Rock, Arizona. It is the capital of the Navajo nation. The Navajo nation, geographically, is approximately the size of West Virginia. It's the largest geographic area for a Native American reservation.

MM: What did you see growing up on the reservation?

BE: As a child, in the summer months, my siblings and I spent our time working and helping at our maternal grandma's home in southern Arizona. She lived in a very rural area, and part of our chores was to herd sheep. It was not uncommon for us to help gather wood and haul water for my grandparents, so I was primarily raised in that way. We had to find our own way of entertaining ourselves because there was no TV, electricity, or running water, so we spent a lot of our time outdoors riding horses and just being out in nature. When I was growing up, I saw a lot of family dysfunction. There was alcoholism in my family and in the Native American community in general, as well as domestic violence and intergenerational trauma. I don't think the adults really recognized what intergenerational trauma was until much later on. School was my escape. I spent a lot of time in my room reading and learning. I was a nerd.

MM: When you were growing up, did you learn about plant medicines? How much of your culture was preserved?

BE: My culture played a significant role. My grandparents were very traditional, which included the use of sweat lodges, traditional plants, and ceremony for healing. My maternal grandmother knew nature. She would pick plants and make medicines from the sap of the tree, which she'd use for her aches and pains. She had arthritis. I learned from her as I grew up, but I forgot about it until I got to college and my oldest brother was diagnosed with pancreatic cancer. I took herbs and nettles, made medicines from the sacred plant medicine (marijuana) to make suppositories, so it got me back into re-membering.

MM: How did the reservation come to be?

BE: You got a week? This is a long story.

MM: I do.

BE: Reservations were created similarly to states, but this issue goes back further than that. Let's talk about a document called the "Doctrine of Discovery."

The Doctrine of Discovery (also known as the "Inter Caetera," issued as a Papal Bull by Pope Alexander VI) was created in Europe in the 1400s. Essentially, the Queen sent out explorers to "discover" new territories that she believed were uninhabited, but they were inhabited: by Native Americans.

There were four basic principles under this Papal Bull:

1. Any land that was not possessed or occupied by a Christian was considered available. This did not consider the Native people that were already occupying the land.

2. The first Christian to discover a piece of land received some kind of sovereignty over that land and its resources. Christopher Columbus was part of that, even though he was also declaring it for the crown. By the way, Christopher Columbus did not discover North America.
3. They had full title, which means that they physically possessed the land. When the Pilgrims landed, they made that land theirs, but Indigenous people were already living there.
4. Added territories were assumed and treated in the same way.

Keeping that in mind, around this time, we were also in a Civil War. The US government knew that much-needed resources, such as metal, existed on our lands. In a roundabout way, the US government wanted to get access to Native American lands, so they created these reservations. We were considered "savages." We needed to be "tamed." We needed to be put on "reservations." A lot of times these "reservations" were just a small piece of land. A lot of these "reservations" were passed by President Andrew Jackson in 1825. So how did that piece of legislation impact me personally?

The Navajo reservation was established in 1868. That was only after the Navajo people were rounded up and marched to Fort Sumner, New Mexico—this is referred to as "The Long Walk" to Bosque Redondo. My maternal grandfather was required to sell his land for 80 cents an acre. My mom's family was put on a reservation.

MM: How was the land distributed on the reservation?

BE: On the reservation, my maternal grandfather was entitled to a plot of land that he and his family could use. All rights to that land—surface rights, mineral and subsurface rights, such as groundwater—were relinquished to the US government. Native people were living on land that they didn't have entitlement to, according to US policy. This plot of land was given to my great-grandfather for the benefit of his family. When the land was initially given to him, there were five family members, but now he has more than 200 family members. People don't usually understand that.

MM: What was the mindset of the US government in creating these reservations?

BE: At that time, the mindset of the government was to "assimilate Native people." They were marched to prisons like Fort Sumner and turned into farmers. However, the land was not fit to grow anything. The winters were brutal. There was disease. Many of my ancestors and relatives died.

MM: What happened when your great-grandmother and her family arrived at Fort Sumner?

BE: As the story goes, my great-grandmother, her father, and their relatives survived Fort Sumner. Her mom had been captured from the Mescalero Apaches, so she primarily grew up with her father and her father's relatives.

MM: What happened to your maternal line at Fort Sumner once the Treaty of Bosque Redondo was signed in 1868 between the Navajo and US government?

BE: My ancestors ended up walking back to what we know as the southern Arizona of the Navajo reservation, where my grandparents lived and where I spent much of my childhood. It is said that it took them two years to walk back. Can you imagine a two-year-old walking in the dead of winter, sometimes without shoes? She ended up living to 102 years old. Her name was Bizh de bah, which, in Navajo, means "The One Who Rides with the Braves," because she would always travel with the men.

MM: "Assimilation policies" seem to be so central to white culture. Any thoughts about that?

BE: The US policies of assimilation were well intended and allowed for westward expansion, but they did a lot of damage to the Native people throughout this country. These impacts still exist today, including intergenerational trauma. I understand what the US government was trying to do, but conquerors only see things from their perspective, and not the perspective of those being conquered.

For instance, the Diné people are a matrilineal society. Who we are as Diné people comes through our mother's lineage, not our father's, which is totally contrary to Western thought. Our religious essence of who we are comes from the women; it has always been that way and it will always be that way.

MM: Can you give an example of something that did a lot of damage to the Native American people?

BE: The arrival of Europeans into this continent.

In the 1500s, white Europeans were trying to get control of the lands that the Native people owned. The Europeans started lacing blankets with smallpox and giving them out. A lot of Native American people died of smallpox as a result.

MM: What about the Native Americans' connection to the land? How did reservations affect that? Who are a people without land?

BE: As a Native American person, you become familiar with everything in your environment. This interconnectedness becomes a part of who you are: your essence. We have been going to sacred places to offer our prayers for eons. When you move a tribe—for instance, the Cherokee people, from the southeast of the US to Oklahoma—there is no way maintain this interconnectedness and the culture. As a result, you lose some of your culture.

MM: Can you talk about intergenerational trauma and how that is affecting Native American people?

BE: People ask me, "Why do you keep bringing up this stuff that was in the past?" A lot of these "things that happened in the past" still carry on today. That's the intergenerational trauma that we have to deal with.

There's a term called "disenfranchised grief." That means that trauma upon trauma upon trauma is compounded because you never have the opportunity to grieve that loss. You have people with anger, guilt, sadness, shame, and feelings of helplessness. That's why we, Native Americans, have such a high rate of suicide—about two and a half times the national average. It's the second leading cause of death for our Native American youth between the ages of 15 and 24.

MM: Besides the high suicide rates, what are the other issues pertaining to the Native American people?

BE: There are very high rates of substance use. A lot of our women have gone missing or murdered. It wasn't until 2020 that President Trump put some legislation in place to try and deal with that.

MM: Speaking of the Native American girls that are being sex trafficked, raped, and murdered: what's the Red Dress Project?

BE: It was a project started in 2011 by a Canadian artist, Jaime Black. She wanted to do this because they are dealing with the same issue in Canada. The Red Dress Project is a community-driven movement to bring awareness to the epidemic levels of murder, sex trafficking, disappearance, and rape among Native American women.

MM: What is happening? What's going on with the authorities and what do you know about who is perpetrating these crimes?

BE: Let me give you a legal framework. From a judicial standpoint, if a Native American woman has a partner who is Anglo, and he beats and murders her, the local jurisdiction on an Indian reservation cannot prosecute him because the laws do not apply to non-Native citizens. The local law enforcement has to go to the FBI in order to prosecute him and, realistically, are they going to go to a reservation for a person that gets killed?

On a federal level, there's a federal database that is maintained for the US to track missing people. If a non-Native Anglo female gets murdered in the city, she is automatically put into this database, so they can figure out where she is. For a Native American woman, that doesn't happen. A lot of times the perpetrators are law enforcement people. The sex trafficking issue is not only here in the United States. This is a worldwide issue.

MM: What about the construction camps in Canada that these Native American girls are being sent to?

BE: In Canada, they are building pipelines. A lot of times, the construction men have to live in camps, in trailers. From my understanding, there are Native American women that are being taken from the reservations and being put into these man camps to perform sexual favors, and not allowed to leave. It's a big issue.

MM: Thank you. Let's go into your healing journey through systemic lupus.

BE: I ended up getting diagnosed with systemic lupus, and I had to get hospitalized. I was losing my hair. You know when you pinch your finger, and have a kind of a blood clot in the skin? I had those all over. I was very fatigued. My body was shutting down. At one point, I was probably taking 68 pills.

MM: Sixty-eight pills!

BE: Yes, I remember sitting at my sisters, trying to pay for my bills, and I couldn't even write. As part of my healing journey, I remember being in church on my knees, crying out: "What is happening to me?" Because up until that point, I always needed someone to help take care of me, because I couldn't do simple things by myself. This was my initiation into the wounded healer path. Experiencing this from a psychological, spiritual, mental, and physical standpoint was my teaching.

I was on my healing journey. I had to dig deep inside myself to figure out where this lupus was coming from. This process immersed me into my Diné traditional teachings, from my mom's lineage. I had to go through many traditional ceremonies that had to do with lightning energy, death, and the Beauty Way.

MM: Wait, what? Lightning medicine?

BE: Yes, "lightning medicine." When a tree is struck by lightning, the plants that grow around them are then energized by that lightning energy.

I learned that the energy that comes through the lightning can impact us physically. I had to go through ceremonies day and night. During these nine days of ceremonies, I had to live out in a rural area without electricity, running water, and just be immersed in nature. Every day, my ceremony began outside at 4 am with prayers, with the medicine of nature, the cosmos, and the elements.

Some ceremonies were outside and involved the recitation of ancient chants and prayers, for example. I prayed and sang, aligning my voice with the frequency of the earth energies in order to come back in balance with who I was as a human being and everything that existed around me. I had to clean my body from these toxins that were inside of me. Part of that was being in a sweat lodge, taking plant medicines, and other rituals, such as sand paintings that held images of sacred deities. I had to sit on top of the sand painting of lightning strikes in the form of snakes, for example. The snake is the representation of the lightning and the rain in a lot of Indigenous cultures.

MM: Wow.

BE: So yeah, I went to the school of hard knocks. (*Laughter.*)

MM: (*Laughter.*) Belinda. I must share a nugget of Native American wisdom that fundamentally changed my life. I don't know if you're aware, but I studied clowning. I learned that the Sacred Clown is found in many Native American cultures.

BE: Every Native American tradition has clowns . . .

MM: I read somewhere that the initiation for a clown is that the individual person—obviously predisposed—realizes that people who love each other can be cruel to one another. This throws the individual into such a state of despair, to the point of death, maybe. But if that person can emerge from that experience, the person can emerge a clown and navigate that razor-sharp edge: laughter. I suppose that's what makes the clown the social critic, or able to respond to "order" or the "hierarchy" that exists.

BE: Yes, we have clowns in the winter ceremonies. The way that I look at it is, we have clowns because they teach us as human beings that sometimes we take ourselves too seriously, and that laughter, too, is healing medicine. That's an essential aspect of who we are as human beings. That is what I have been told.

MM: Now, just to start wrapping up, what about the church that you're working on right now? Practically speaking, what info can we get to people?

BE: I live in the Tempe area, and we have about 40 members. I typically hold sweat lodges at my home every month. I also do talking circles and traditional healing ceremonies with my niece and one of my brothers, a Diné medicine man. We work with doctor Dr. Joe Tafur, who is a Colombian who comes from a Western medical perspective as well. We created a church that we call the Church of the Eagle and Condor.

MM: Please share the prophecy of the eagle and condor.

BE: There are many interpretations for that particular prophecy, but the gist is when the eagle and condor come together, representing North (eagle) and South (condor) America, then humanity can heal. We learned this through the traditional teachings of the Indigenous people that were living in the Americas before the Europeans arrived.

I'll read you something:

> According to the Eagle and Condor Prophecy, the essential feature of this age is extraordinary planetary crisis and upheaval: Tied to the cumulative effects of alienation, separation, and deep amnesia, this crisis increasingly characterizes both humanity and the world. The defining moment of this age is the "re-encounter" of all elements having suffered separation during humanity's prior unfolding. It becomes a time of coming together of peoples, ancestry, and traditions, along with the restoration of harmony between humankind and Mother Nature. It culminates symbolically in the meeting of all races, and their "breaking bread" together at the table of the World Teacher. This event indicates the emergence of humanity from its illusion of separation.
> —Don Oscar Miro Quesada, Pachakuti Mesa Kamasqa Curandero, Alto Misayoq

MM: Can you talk about the language used to name Native Americans?

BE: There are many terms that are used to make reference to us, including American Indians, Native Americans, Natives, and Indians. Some Native people don't like the term "American Indian" because Indian is associated with Columbus, who didn't discover anything. He didn't discover us. We like to call ourselves Americans.

MM: Since Native Americans view themselves as the caretakers of the land, how do you see your own responsibility as an American?

BE: There is a concept called "sacred responsibility." There is also a word in the Andean traditions of South America called "Ayni," which means "sacred reciprocity." Again, this ties back to the Eagle and Condor Prophecy. There's always an exchange with nature; in other words, not only from a human standpoint, but also from an environmental standpoint. If I'm out there harvesting a sacred plant for use as medicine for healing, then I need to give something back in return, because it has given its life for me to heal.

Like I mentioned, many of the tribes in North America are matrilineal societies. That puts a sacred responsibility on us, as Native American women, to care not only for our families and communities but also the environment in which we live. This includes the care of sacred plant medicines and making sure there is enough medicine for future generations. All the decisions that we make are not just for today, they are for tomorrow and the future. We have to think about our grandchildren and our great-grandchildren's children. We cannot be selfish. But that is not the mindset of Western culture.

MM: How does this Western mindset show up in policy making around sacred plants in terms of how Native Americans are being treated right now?

BE: Right now, there is a big effort to "decriminalize nature," which allows people to use these sacred plants. It started in the Oakland [California] area. Native American people were brought into the conversation after the decrim legislation had already gone to the city for approval. And they put peyote on there! As you can imagine, this was very upsetting to many Native American people.

Native Americans fought for the use of peyote all the way up to the Supreme Court in order to use peyote legally as part of the Native American church. The DM resolution was done in a way that reminded me of a colonialist approach. Meaning that "you do what we tell you to do," as opposed to you being a part of a conversation.

MM: What do you say when you go to psychedelic summits and conferences and the like?

BE: It is time now to come together and find something that works for everyone. What if we were to come from a heart place, instead of from the mind place. "What's best for all of us, and how can we get there?" I'm sure that there are many creative ways of doing that, it's just that people have their own personal agendas.

MM: Right now, in terms of your interaction with this psychedelic renaissance world that's emerging... what are Western people not understanding?

BE: People don't understand Native American people or how we view the world. It's part of the problem with the colonial mindset of "I'm going to do this." This time is about pulling yourselves back. Western thought tends to put things into buckets and silos: mathematics, psychology, and medicine, for example. In Native American cultures, they are interrelated and cannot be separated.

MM: What about spirituality? Where is that bucket in Western medicine?

BE: I went to my first psychedelic conference in Arizona with over 200 medical people and researchers there. I got frustrated when they were talking about mental illness.

Finally, I said, "If I may say something—where is spirituality in all of this?"

When we arrive in this physical realm that we know as the Earth, we come in spirit first and foremost. Then, our physical bodies become a part of that. This is what we are taught in Native American cultures. It's missing from the Western medical model. These psychedelic experiences take us into our own inner divinities, yet we don't include them in our healing practices.

Everything that we have—this chair I'm sitting on, this computer I'm on—everything comes from the earth. Even my car, when I travel, I imagine it as a horse. I say, "Thank you for taking me here and there; thank you for watching out for me." I honor it in that way. This is about respect.

MM: What did you tell the people at the Psychedelic Liberty Summit?

BE: Number one, I told them to include all stakeholders, including Indigenous people and those from South America. Number two, how can we ensure protection for the sacred plants? First of all, these are living beings. It's very critical that people understand that, now, at this time. Everybody wants to have these medicines, but no one wants to think about keeping them alive. I also said that professionals doing psychedelic work need to have some cultural understanding of Native American cultures. If you don't understand who the people and individuals are, it's going to be difficult for you to relate to a Native American person.

MM: What is the concept of *hozho*?

BE: In Navajo, *hozho* means "to be in harmony and balance," but it's part of a larger concept. The way we say it is *Sa'ah naaghai bik'eh hozhoon.* "Old age will walk in the trail of beauty."

As a Diné person, that is always my responsibility. I always think about the good things in life that will give me health, a long life, happiness, wisdom, knowledge, harmony, and the experience of working with the Divine. It's part of this whole concept of hozho.

Even though I may have ups and downs with my health, I have to embrace all of it, including what I have learned, so that I can walk into a longer life. That adds something to my "wisdom pouch." My experience with my health gave me, also, knowledge of things that I didn't know, and to walk in that balance of hozho.

MM: The concept of hozho then is also about knowing and not knowing?

BE: We don't have to know everything, yes. I had to go through that nine-day ceremony as part of my healing journey from lupus. I had glimpses of the Diyin Diné, which, in Navajo, means "the Holy Ones." My psychedelic experiences with ayahuasca and MDMA changed my life. And these mystical experiences with the Holy Ones are who I pray to now. I know who I am in my own being.

In our Native American cultures, they say that we are "crystal fire children," meaning that we are from the stars. As an Indigenous person, as a Diné person, I embrace that.

I know who I am.

I am also from the stars as a cosmic being.

Contributor Biographies

Patrick Barber lives in Buena Vista, Saskatchewan, Canada and works full-time as an Indigenous Health Policy Analyst. His book *Psychedelic Revolutionaries* recounts Saskatchewan's psychedelic research in the 1950s and '60s and the related work and theories of Humphry Osmond, Abram Hoffer, and Duncan Blewett.

Amy Bartlett is a curiosity enthusiast, legal professional, NGO geek, and PhD candidate at the University of Ottawa. Her research explores the role of community in psychedelic healing and integration, focusing on harm reduction and diversity and inclusion. She helps coordinate the Ottawa Psychedelic Education Network (OPEN) amongst other projects. Before returning to school, she worked for over 15 years as a social justice advocate in Canada and abroad.

Pietro de Pieri Benedito has a Master's (2013) and PhD (2019) in Sociology from the Brazilian UFSCar (Universidade Federal de São Carlos). His PhD thesis analysed gender and femininity within Santo Daime. Currently, he is part of the Healing Encounters program (CNRS, Paris), conducting fieldwork in Brazilian laboratories that carry out biomedical research with ayahuasca.

Samantha Black (she/they) is a PhD candidate in psychology, a Lecturer in psychology at First Nations University of Canada and the University of Saskatchewan, and Director of ReGeneration Arts research group. She is an artist and a past clinical social worker. Her research centers on community health, 2SLGBTQI+ wellness, creative/psychedelic therapies, and decolonizing strategies.

Lana Cook, PhD, is a cultural scholar writing on the aesthetics of altered states of consciousness. She is writing a book on the history of the women of the psychedelic Sixties. Cook is a strategist and program designer for MIT Open Learning at the Massachusetts Institute of Technology. She received her doctorate from Northeastern University.

Tal Davidson is a PhD student in the Historical, Theoretical, and Critical Studies of Psychology program at York University in Toronto. His current work explores ecopsychology as a framework that combines social and ecological justice with personal healing and psychotherapeutics.

Zoë Dubus is a PhD student in contemporary history in France. She studies the transformations of medical practices and health policies in relation to the use of psychotropics drugs (morphine, cocaine, and LSD), from the 19th century until the present. She seeks to understand the relationship between physicians and consciousness altering products, conceived alternatively as innovative medicines or as poisons.

Taylor E. Dysart is a PhD candidate in the Department of History and Sociology of Science at the University of Pennsylvania, where her research explores the intertwined history of science, plants, race, and place in the Amazon. She holds a BA (Honors) in History and Psychology from McMaster University and a MA in the History of Medicine from McGill University.

Ana Gretel Echazú Böschemeier is an Argentinian-Brazilian feminist, mom of two children, anthropologist, and translator; associate professor in the Anthropology Department (DAN) and the Post-Degree Program of Social Anthropology (PPGAS)—Universidade Federal do Rio Grande do Norte, Brazil. She worked as an advisor at the UNESCO/UNTREF Chair, is a member of the Ethics in Research Committee, and ambassador at the Parent in Science movement.

Chris Elcock is an award-wining independent historian of psychedelics who has recently cofounded the Lyon Psychedelic Society. He is finishing a book on the social history of psychedelics in New York City.

Andrea Ens is a PhD candidate in History at Purdue University. She completed her MA in History at the University of Saskatchewan in 2018. Her research interests broadly include the history of sexuality, psychology, and psychedelics in 20th-century North America. Her dissertation studies the affective experience of conversion therapy in Canada and the United States during this period.

Ivo Gurschler is a theoretically informed psychonaut working on his PhD "On the Genealogy of Mescaline." He has lectured at the Academy of Fine Arts in Vienna, Austria, at the University of Saskatchewan, Canada, and published papers on psychedelics and philosophical books. He collaborated with *nadaproductions* and is a coeditor of *Schriften zur Verkehrswissenschaft* (formerly *TUMULT*). Additionally he is working as a project manager for an educational publishing company.

Andrew Jones is a PhD candidate in the history and philosophy of science program at the University of Toronto. His dissertation examines how psychedelic drugs made their way into American child psychiatry in the 1960s. He traces the stories of three groups of psychiatric researchers who used these substances in radically different ways to help children who were described as "isolated" or "withdrawn" make connections with other people.

Sean Lawlor is the author of *Psychedelic Revival: Toward a New Paradigm of Healing*. With Sounds True, the book's publisher, he also hosted and cocreated the Psychedelic Wisdom Intensive, a three-month online course for which he interviewed many leaders in the field. Lawlor holds a master of arts in clinical mental health counseling from Naropa University, and he has completed additional trainings in ketamine-assisted therapy, MDMA-assisted therapy, and Internal Family Systems. He facilitates ketamine therapy in Fort Collins, Colorado, where he's fortunate to be part of a wonderful team of psychedelic practitioners.

Stephen Lett is a Post-Doctoral Fellow in the History of Medicine at the University of Saskatchewan. His research explores practices with music in psychotherapy.

Edward MacRae was born in São Paulo. He completed a BA in Social Psychology University of Sussex and obtained a Master's degree in Sociology of Latin America at the University of Essex. He is an Associate Professor at the Department of Anthropology and Ethnology and is an Associate Researcher at the Center for Studies and Therapy of Drug Abuse (CETAD), both at the Federal University of Bahia.

Fabiana Maizza is an assistant professor in Anthropology at the University of Pernambuco, Brazil. She obtained a PhD. degree in Social Anthropology from the University of São Paulo, Brazil. Her current research focuses on the relations between humans and cultivated plants, as well as on gender relations among the Jarawara. She has published articles on female agency, feminist politics of life, ecology, and feminism, and human-plant relations.

Mariavittoria Mangini, PhD, FNP, has written extensively on the impact of psychedelic experiences in shaping the lives of her contemporaries and worked closely with many of the most distinguished investigators in this field.

Raizza Marins is a musician, composer, and music educator. She has a bachelor's degree in Opera Singing and an MA in Ethnomusicology from UNIRIO. Her main area of interest is the study of music in the ayahuasca universe and power plants. As a composer, she writes *pontos* from the Umbanda tradition and *musica medicina* from the neo-ayahuasca scene.

Maria Mocerino is an interviewer and writer who has been published in the *Irish Examiner, Rogue Magazine, Reality Sandwich,* and Sun Potion Journal. For the Chacruna Institute, she did the interview series on people of color making a difference in psychedelics. She's working on her first book, *Christmas in Naples Is a Sport*, and splitting her time between Naples and Istanbul.

Diana Negrín is a geographer, writer, and curator based in Berkeley, California and Guadalajara, Mexico. She is the president of the board of directors of the Wixárika Research Center and helps run this nonprofit organization dedicated to the art, culture, and territorial autonomy of the Wixárika people. Negrín also teaches at UC Berkeley and has collaborated with the Chacruna Institute since 2018.

Yvonne Negrín is the director of the nonprofit foundation the Wixárika Research Center, founded in 2001 to promote the study and defense of Wixárika culture and territory. She has 50 years of experience working in Wixárika communities on initiatives that range from art and design, health, and ecology through various productive projects in several localities of the Western Sierra Madre Occidental.

Nidia Olvera-Hernández is a historian and anthropologist who studies psychoactive substances. She has a PhD in modern and contemporary history at the Mora Institute in Mexico City, where she researched the history of drugs.

Geneviève Paiement is a Montreal-born, Toronto-based screenwriter, poet, and former journalist with an MFA in Dramatic Writing from the University of Guelph. Her work has appeared in the *New York Times*, *Vice*, Salon.com, the *Globe and Mail*, the *Guardian* (UK), the *Literary Review of Canada*, and elsewhere. She is a Pushcart nominee, a Tin House Summer Workshop alumna, and a Canada Council for the Arts grant recipient.

Daniela Peluso received her PhD in 2003 from Columbia University and is an Emeritus Fellow in social anthropology at the University of Kent. She has been actively involved in various local efforts on issues relating to health, gender, Indigenous urbanization, and land rights and works in close collaboration with Indigenous and local organizations. Her publications focus mostly on Indigenous ontologies, urbanization, violence, and relatedness.

James Penner is the editor of *Timothy Leary: The Harvard Years* (Inner Traditions, 2014) and the author of *Pinks, Pansies, and Punks: The Rhetoric of Masculinity in American Literary Culture* (University of Indiana Press, 2010). He is a contributor for the *Los Angeles Review of Books* and also writes for *Lucid News*, Chacruna, and Medium.

Laura Pérez Gil is a professor in Anthropology at the Federal University of Paraná (Brazil) and Director of the Archaeology and Ethnology Museum of the same university. Her recent publications concern the transformation of Amazonian Indigenous systems in contemporary context, as well as the connection between shamanism and violence. She also conducts research on ethnographic collections of Amazonian Indigenous peoples in museums.

Klarissa Platero has a PhD in sociology and is professor in the National Security department at the Federal Fluminense University (UFF). She is the coordinator of the center for studies and research on subjects, society, and state (Nepsse). Her research of mixed methods focuses on violent deaths, forensics, and criminal justice in Brazil.

Lígia Platero has an interdisciplinary formation in Anthropology, History, and Latino American studies. She holds a PhD in human sciences with an emphasis in Anthropology at the Federal University of Rio de Janeiro (UFRJ). Her research involves inter-ethnic relationships and ayahuasca.

Naomi Rendina (@NaomiRendina) recently earned her PhD in History from Case Western Reserve University. She is a Lecturer in the Department of Health Sciences at California State University, East Bay, and is the Social Media Coordinator for the American Institute of the History of Pharmacy (@histpharm) and the Points Blog (the blog of the Alcohol and Drugs History Society, @PointsADHS).

Jacqueline Rodrigues has a master's degree in anthropology at the Federal University of Minas Gerais (UFMG). She is cofounder of the Céu da Divina Estrela, a Santo Daime church in Minas Gerais, Brazil. She is an actress and a mother of two children. She is also a member of the ICEFLU Women's Working Group, formed to safeguard women's safety and female participation in Santo Daime. She develops academic research on Santo Daime and ayahuasca.

Isabel Santana de Rose is a Brazilian anthropologist and a researcher in the field of the ayahuasca religions for over 20 years. Her PhD dissertation focuses on the emergence of contemporary shamanic networks in Brazil. Her main research interests encompass anthropology of health, anthropology of religion, shamanism, and traditional knowledge. She is currently a member of the project "Healing Encounters: Reinventing an Indigenous Medicine in the Clinic and Beyond" (CNRS/CERMES3—ERC).

Stacy B. Schaefer is Professor Emerita in the Department of Anthropology, California State University, Chico. She has researched and published on peyote among the Huichol Indians and the Native American Church for more than three decades.

Stephanie Schmitz is the Betsy Gordon Archivist for Psychoactive Substances Research at the Purdue University Archives, working closely with donors in transferring materials to the Archives, facilitating access and use of these materials, and collaborating with educators to incorporate these materials into their teaching.

Emily Sinclair is a social anthropology PhD candidate with Durham University, UK. Her research focuses on the globalization of ayahuasca in the context of the Iquitos region in Peru, where she was based between 2014 and 2018. Emily is a member of Chacruna's Ayahuasca Community Committee and is involved in Chacruna's initiative on preventing sexual abuse.

Osiris Sinuhé González Romero holds a PhD in Meso-American Studies from Leiden University and has been involved in psychedelic research since 2008. He is working on the book *New Essays on History and Philosophy of Psychedelics*. He is part of the Chacruna Chronicles editorial team.

Alexis Turner is a PhD candidate in the History of Science at Harvard University. Alexis's current research is on the early scientific and political history of LSD in the United States.

Jasmine Virdi works as a freelance writer in the psychedelic space. She has written for *Psychedelics Today*, Chacruna Institute for Plant Medicines, and *Lucid News*, to name a few. Additionally, she is pursuing an MSc in Transpersonal Psychology with the aim of working as a psychedelic practitioner. Jasmine's goal as a psychedelic advocate is to help integrate them into our modern-day lives in a culturally sensitive, ethically integral, accessible, and meaningful way.

Monnica T. Williams, PhD, ABPP, is a board-certified clinical psychologist and Associate Professor at the University of Connecticut. She has published over 100 articles on ethnic minority mental health, psychopathology research, and psychedelic therapy. She is part of Chacruna's Racial Equity and Access Committee.

Editor Biographies

Clancy Cavnar has a doctorate in clinical psychology (PsyD) from John F. Kennedy University in Pleasant Hill, California. She currently works in private practice in San Francisco and is cofounder and a member of the Board of Directors of the Chacruna Institute for Psychedelic Plant Medicines. She is also a research associate of the Interdisciplinary Group for Psychoactive Studies (NEIP). She combines an eclectic array of interests and activities as clinical psychologist, artist, and researcher. She has a master of fine arts in painting from the San Francisco Art Institute, a master's in counseling from San Francisco State University, and she completed the Certificate in Psychedelic-Assisted Therapy program at the California Institute of Integral Studies (CIIS). She is author and coauthor of articles in several peer-reviewed journals and coeditor, with Beatriz C. Labate, of 10 books. For more information, see http://www.drclancycavnar.com.

Erika Dyck is a Professor and a Canada Research Chair in the History of Health and Social Justice. She is the author of several books, including: *Psychedelic Psychiatry: LSD from Clinic to Campus* (Johns Hopkins, 2008; University of Manitoba Press, 2011); *Facing Eugenics: Reproduction, Sterilization and the Politics of Choice* (University of Toronto, 2013), which was shortlisted for the Governor General's award for Canadian non-fiction; *Managing Madness: The Weyburn Mental Hospital and the Transformation of Psychiatric Care in Canada* (University of Manitoba Press, 2017), which won the Canadian Historical Association Prize for best book in Prairie History; and with Maureen Lux, *Challenging Choices: Canada's Population control in the 1970s* (McGill-Queens University Press, 2020). She is also the coeditor of *Psychedelic Prophets: The Letters of Aldous Huxley and Humphry Osmond* (2018) and *A Culture's Catalyst: Historical Encounters with Peyote* (2016). Erika is the coeditor of the *Canadian Bulletin for Medical*

History/Bulletin canadien d'histoire de la medicine and the coeditor of a new book series on the global history of alcohol and drugs, called *Intoxicating Histories*. Erika is member of Chacruna's Board of Directors and Associate Director of Chacruna in Canada.

Patrick Farrell is an editor, researcher, and writer based out of Toronto. He has been involved in several projects related to psychedelic history, most notably *Psychedelic Prophets: The Letters of Aldous Huxley and Humphry Osmond* (2018). He is also an instructor in a range of topics in history and philosophy at the University of Toronto's School of Continuing Studies.

Ibrahim Gabriell is a podcaster, editor and researcher. As a former professor in the state of Chiapas, Mexico, he has taught both Communication Studies at the Universidad de los Altos de Chiapas and Transpersonal Psychology at the Universidad Jose Vasconcelos. He is Communications and Editorial Associate of Chacruna Latinoamérica in Mexico. He is also cofounder of Vía Synapsis, an academic society that organizes the University Congress on Psychoactive Substances at the National University of Mexico and a member of the psychonaut collective MindSurf.

Beatriz C. Labate is a queer Brazilian anthropologist based in San Francisco. She has a PhD in social anthropology from the State University of Campinas (UNICAMP), Brazil. Her main areas of interest are the study of plant medicines, drug policy, shamanism, ritual, religion, and social justice. She is Executive Director of the Chacruna Institute for Psychedelic Plant Medicines (https://chacruna.net, https://chacruna-iri.org, https://chacruna-la.org). She serves as Public Education and Culture Specialist at the Multidisciplinary Association for Psychedelic Studies (MAPS), and Adjunct Faculty at the East-West Psychology Program at the California Institute of Integral Studies (CIIS). She is also a member of the Oregon Psilocybin Advisory Board's Research Subcommittee, and Diversity, Culture, and Ethics Advisor at the Synthesis Institute. Additionally, she is a cofounder of the Interdisciplinary Group for Psychoactive Studies (NEIP) in Brazil and editor of its site. She is author, coauthor, and coeditor of 24 books, two special-edition journals, and several peer-reviewed articles. Her website is https://bialabate.net.

Glauber Loures de Assis is a postdoctoral fellow at the Federal University of Minas Gerais (UFMG) in Belo Horizonte, Brazil, where he also earned a PhD in sociology. He is also Research Associate at the Interdisciplinary Group for Psychoactive Studies (NEIP) and cofounder of the Center of Sociology Studies Antônio Augusto Pereira Prates (CESAP). He has developed research on Santo Daime groups from Brazil and Europe and has also studied the sociology of religion from a wider perspective. His main interests include the ayahuasca religions, New Religious Movements (NRMs), the internationalization of the Brazilian religions, and drug use in contemporary society. He is Associate Director of Chacruna Latinoamérica in Brazil.

References

SUSI'S TRAM RIDE: RECOGNIZING THE FIRST WOMAN TO TAKE LSD

1. Albert Hofmann, *Ergot Alkaloids: History, Chemistry, and Therapeutic Uses* (Berkeley, California: Transform Press, 2023).
2. Albert Hofmann, *LSD My Problem Child: Reflections of Sacred Drugs, Mysticism, and Science* (Santa Cruz, California: Multidisciplinary Association for Psychedelic Studies, 2017).
3. Erika Dyck, PhD, "Women in the History of Psychedelic Plant Medicines," Chacruna.net, Women, September 16, 2020, https://chacruna.net /women-history-psychedelic-plant-medicines/.

ESTHER JEAN LANGDON: HALF A CENTURY OF RESEARCH ABOUT SHAMANISM AND AYAHUASCA

1. Jean-Pierre Chaumeil, "Voir, savoir, pouvoir: le chamanisme chez les Yagua du nord-est péruvien [Vision, knowledge, power: shamanism among the Yagua of northeastern Peru]," (Paris: École des Hautes Études en Sciences Sociales, 1983).
2. Esther Jean Langdon, "Medio siglo de investigaciones de campo: reflexión autobiográfica sobre las contribuciones de la perspectiva de género [Half a century of fieldwork: an autobiographical reflector about the contributions of a gender perspective]" *Maguaré* 27, no. 1 (2013), 215–240.
3. Esther Jean Langdon, *Cosmopolitics Among the Siona: Shamanism, Medicine and Family on the Putumayo River* (Popayán, Colombia: Editorial Universidad del Cauca, 2017).
4. Esther Jean Langdon, ed., *Xamanismo No Brasil: Novas Perspectivas [Shamanism in Brazil: New Perspectives]* (Florianópolis, Brazil: Editora da UFSC, 1996).
5. Esther Jean Langdon, "Configuraciones del chamanismo siona: modos de performance en los siglos XX y XXI [Configurations of the Siona shamanism: modes of performance in the 20 and 21st centuries]," *Maguaré* 34, 1 (2020), 17–47.
6. Pedro Musalem, PhD, "Drinking Yagé to Resist Capitalist Violence," Chacruna.net, Culture, September 11, 2017, https://chacruna.net/yage-resist-capitalist-violence/.
7. Esther Jean Langdon, "New Perspectives of Shamanism in Brazil: Shamanisms and Neo-Shamanisms as Dialogical Categories," *Civilisations* 61, 2 (June 2013), 19–35, http://dx.doi.org/10.4000/civilisations.3227.

8. Langdon, "New Perspectives of Shamanism in Brazil."

9. Langdon, "New perspectives of shamanism in Brazil."

10. Esther Jean Langdon and Isabel Santana de Rose, "Contemporary Guarani Shamanisms: 'Traditional Medicine' and Discourses of Native Identity in Brazil," *Health, Culture and Society* 3, issue1 (September 2012), 29–48, http://dx.doi .org/10.5195/hcs.2012.98.

11. Esther Jean Langdon and Isabel Santana de Rose "Medicine Alliance: Contemporary Shamanic Networks in Brazil," *Ayahuasca Shamanism in the Amazon and Beyond*, ed. Beatriz Caiuby Labate and Clancy Cavnar (Oxford and New York: Oxford University Press, 2014), 81–104.

12. Langdon, "New Perspectives of Shamanism in Brazil."

13. Langdon, "Configuraciones del chamanismo siona," 31.

14. Esther Jean Langdon, "The Revitalization of Yajé Shamanism among the Siona: Strategies of Survival in Historical Context," *Anthropology of Consciousness* 27, 2 (September 2016), 180–203, http://dx.doi.org/10.1111/anoc.12058.

15. Langdon, "Configuraciones del chamanismo siona," 41.

16. Langdon, "New Perspectives of Shamanism in Brazil."

17. Esther Jean Langdon, *La negociación de lo oculto: chamanismo, medicina y família entre los Siona del Bajo Putumayo* [*The negotiation of the unseen: shamanism, medicine and family among the Siona on the Lower Putumayo*] (Popayán, Colombia: Editorial Universidad del Cauca, 2014).

MESCALINE SCRIBE

1. All quotations from Simone de Beauvoir, *The Prime of Life* (Penguin Books, 1965).

2. Mike Jay, *Mescaline: A Global History of the First Psychedelic* (New Haven: Yale University Press, 2019).

3. John Gerassi, ed., *Talking with Sartre: Coversations and Debates* (New Haven, Connecticut: Yale University Press, 2009), 193–194.

4. Zoë Dubus PhD, "Women's Historical Influence on 'Set and Setting,'" Chacruna .net, Women, September 30, 2020, https://chacruna.net/women-and-history -of-set-and-setting/.

HEROINES OF MESCALINE

1. Stacy B. Schaefer, PhD, "Peyote: Plant Medicine for the Body, Mind and Soul," Chacruna, Culture, April 18, 2017, https://chacruna.net /peyote-plant-medicine-body-mind-soul/

2. Heffter Research Institute, "About Dr. Heffter," Accessed July 6, 2023, https:// www.heffter.org/about-dr-heffter/.

3. ScienceDirect, "Hallucinogen," Accessed July 6, 2023, https://www.sciencedirect .com/topics/neuroscience/hallucinogen.

MRS. AMADA CARDENAS: KEEPER OF THE PEYOTE GARDENS

1. Stacy. B. Schaefer, *Amada's Blessings from the Peyote Gardens of South Texas* (Albuquerque: University of New Mexico Press, 2015), 90.
2. Schaefer, *Amada's Blessings*, 134–135.
3. Schaefer, *Amada's Blessings*, 233

ANOTHER ASPECT OF REALITY: MARIA NYS HUXLEY'S INFLUENCE ON PSYCHEDELIC HISTORY

1. Cynthia Casson Bisbee et al., *Psychedelic Prophets: The Letters of Aldous Huxley and Humphry Osmond* (Montreal, Canada: McGill-Queen's University Press, 2018).
2. Erika Dyck, PhD, "Historian Explains How Women Have Been Excluded from the Field of Psychedelic Science," Chacruna.net, Women, October 16, 2018, https://chacruna.net/historian-explains-how-women-have-been-excluded-from-the-field-of-psychedelic-science/.

"PLEASE WRITE UP YOUR WORK!": LAURA ARCHERA HUXLEY AS A PSYCHEDELIC PIONEER

1. Andrea Ens, MA, "Another Aspect of Reality: Maria Nys Huxley's Influence on Psychedelic History," Chacruna.net, Women, November 25, 2020, https://chacruna.net/maria-nys-huxleys-influence-on-psychedelic-history/.
2. Maria Popova, "You Are Not the Target: Laura Huxley on Course-Correcting the Paths of Love and Not-Love," *The Marginalian*, June 26, 2017, https://www.themarginalian.org/2017/06/26/you-are-not-the-target-laura-huxley-love-not-love/.

NINA GRABOI, A FORGOTTEN WOMAN IN PSYCHEDELIC LORE

1. Devin R. Lander, "Start Your Own Religion: New York State's Acid Churches," *Nova Religio* Volume 14, Issue 3 (February 2011): 64–80, https://doi.org/10.1525/nr.2011.14.3.64.
2. Chris Elcock, "High New York: The Birth of a Psychedelic Subculture in the American City," PhD thesis, University of Saskatchewan, 2015. http://hdl.handle.net/10388/ETD-2015-10-2295.
3. Erika Dyck, PhD, "Women in the History of Psychedelic Plant Medicines," Chacruna.net, Women, September 16, 2020, https://chacruna.net/women-history-psychedelic-plant-medicines/.
4. David Farber, "Building the Counterculture, Creating Right Livelihoods: The Counterculture at Work," *The Sixties: A Journal of History, Politics and Culture*, Vol. 6, Issue 1 (2013): 1–24. https://doi.org/10.1080/17541328.2013.778706.

WILMA MAHUA CAMPOS, SHIPIBO AYAHUASQUERA

1. Debora Gonzalez et al, "The Shipibo Ceremonial Use of Ayahuasca to Promote Well-Being: An Observational Study." *Frontiers in Pharmacology.* 2021 May 5;12:623923. https://doi.org/10.3389/fphar.2021.623923.
2. Silvia Mesturini, PhD, "Preserving Entangled Ayahuasca," Chacruna.net, Culture, December 7, 2020, https://chacruna.net/preserving-entangled-ayahuasca/.
3. Plant diets are an ancient Indigenous Amazonian practice and are administered by traditional healers. The dieter limits food intake and lives secluded in a natural setting while consuming concentrated doses of plant medicines. Many traditional healers diet in seclusion from two to five years to prepare for their role as a healer.

BETTY EISNER: HEROINE WITH A HITCH?

1. Tal Davidson, "The Past Lives of Betty Eisner: Examining the Spiritual Psyche of Early Psychedelic Therapy through the Story of an Outsider, a Pioneer, and a Villain," MA thesis, York University, 2017. http://hdl.handle.net/10315/34493.
2. Zoë Dubus, PhD, "Women's Historical Influence on 'Set and Setting,'" Chacruna.net, Women, September 30, 2020, https://chacruna.net /women-and-history-of-set-and-setting/.

LAURETTA BENDER: SEMINAL PSYCHIATRIST AND FORGOTTEN PSYCHEDELIC PIONEER

1. Tal Davidson, PhD, "Betty Eisner: Heroine with a Hitch?" Chacruna.net, Women, March 17, 2021, https://chacruna.net/betty-eisner-heroine-with-a-hitch/.
2. Regina Cicci, Katrina de Hirsch, Ralph D. Rabinovitch, Roger Saunders, Rosa A. Hagin, Archie A. Silver, and Alvin E. Grugett, "Remembering Lauretta Bender," *Annals of Dyslexia* 37 (1987): 3–9. http://www.jstor.org/stable/23769272.
3. Leo Kanner, "Autistic Disturbances of Affective Contact," https://mail.neurodiversity.net/library_kanner_1943.pdf.
4. Lauretta Bender, MD, "Children's Reactions to Psychotomimetic Drugs, " https://neurodiversity.net/library_bender_1970.pdf
5. Bruce Bower, "In 1967, LSD was briefly labeled a breaker of chromosomes," ScienceNews, March 23, 2017, https://www.sciencenews.org /article/1967-lsd-was-briefly-labeled-breaker-chromosomes

THE WONDERFUL AND ABSURD ADVENTURES OF ROSEMARY WOODRUFF LEARY: FASHION ICON, FUGITIVE, AND PSYCHEDELIC PIONEER (PART ONE)

1. Rosemary Woodruff Leary, *A Magician's Daughter*, Rosemary Woodruff Leary papers, 1935–2006, OCLC number 968787201, New York Public Library,

https://www.worldcat.org/title/rosemary-woodruff-leary-papers-1935-2006
/oclc/968787201.

2. Rosemary Woodruff Leary, *Psychedelic Refugee: The League for Spiritual Discovery, the 1960s Cultural Revolution, and 23 Years on the Run,* ed. David F. Phillips (Rochester, Vermont: Park Street Press, 2021).

3. Alexis Turner, PhD, "Gurus Behaving Badly: Anaïs Nin's Diary and the Value of Gossip," Chacruna.net, Women, March 10, 2021, https://chacruna.net /anais-nin-diary-and-timothy-leary/.

THE WONDERFUL AND ABSURD LIFE OF ROSEMARY WOODRUFF LEARY: FASHION ICON, FUGITIVE, AND PSYCHEDELIC PIONEER (PART TWO: FREEDOM AND UNFREEDOM)

1. Laird Borrelli-Persson, "Rodebjer: Resort 2020," *Vogue* Runway, July 1, 2019, https://www.vogue.com/fashion-shows/resort-2020/rodebjer.

JANE OSMOND: THE WONDER OF WEYBURN

1. Andrea Ens, MA, "Another Aspect of Reality: Maria Nys Huxley's Influence on Psychedelic History," Chacruna.net, Women, November 25, 2020, https://chacruna.net/maria-nys-huxleys-influence-on-psychedelic-history/.

"A 'DOSE' OF RADICAL CHRISTIANITY": PSYCHEDELIC THERAPY WITH DR. FLORENCE NICHOLS

1. Erika Dyck, *Psychedelic Psychiatry: LSD on the Canadian Prairies* (Winnipeg: University of Manitoba Press, 2012).

2. Ruth Compton Brouwer, *Modern Women Modernizing Men: The Changing Missions of Three Professional Women in Asia and Africa,* 1902–69 (Vancouver: UBC Press, 2002).

3. Erika Dyck, PhD, "Women in the History of Psychedelic Plant Medicines," Chacruna.net, Women, September 16, 2020, https://chacruna.net/ women-history-psychedelic-plant-medicines/.

PSYCHEDELIC SASKATCHEWAN: KAY PARLEY

1. Kay Parley, *Inside the Mental: Silence, Stigma, Psychiatry, and LSD* (Saskatchewan: University of Regina Press, 2016).

2. Erika Dyck, PhD, "Jane Osmond: The Wonder of Weyburn," Chacruna.net, Women, March 24, 2021, https://chacruna.net/jane-osmond-wife-of-humphry-osmond/.

3. Kay Parley, interview by Anna Maria Tremonti, *The Current,* CBC Radio, June 14, 2016, https://www.cbc.ca/radio/thecurrent/the-current-for-june-14-2016 -1.3634082/93-year-old-former-psychiatric-patient-and-nurse-on-lessons-from -lsd-1.3634214.

4. Kay Parley, *The Grass People* (Regina, Saskatchewan: Radiant Press, 2018).
5. A David Napier, "Francis Huxley obituary," *Guardian* (UK), December 20, 2016, https://www.theguardian.com/science/2016/dec/20/francis-huxley-obituary.
6. Dyck, "Jane Osmond."

OF MEDIUMS AND MIND-MANIFESTORS:
EILEEN GARRETT AND PSYCHEDELIC EXPERIENCE

1. Erika Dyck, PhD, "Historian Explains How Women Have been Excluded from the Field of Psychedelic Science," Chacruna.net, Women, October, 16, 2018, https://chacruna.net/historian-explains-how-women-have-been-excluded-from-the-field-of-psychedelic-science/.
2. D. B. Blewett, PhD, and N. Chwelos, MD, "Handbook for the Therapeutic Use of Lysergic Acide Diethlyamide-25 Individual and Group Procedures," originally published 1959, digital edition published online 2014, https://maps.org/research-archive/ritesofpassage/lsdhandbook.pdf.

THE COST OF OMISSION: DR. VALENTINA WASSON
AND GETTING OUR STORIES RIGHT

1. Rick Hire, "Heroines?: Valentina Pavlovna Wasson and Psychedelic Wives," Points: Joint Blog of the Alcohol & Drugs History Society and the American Institute of the History of Pharmacy, September 29, 2020, https://www.pointshistory.com/post/heroines-valentina-pavlovna-wasson-and-psychedelic-wives.
2. Jamilah R. George et al., "The psychedelic renaissance and the limitations of a White-dominant medical framework: A call for indigenous and ethnic minority inclusion," *Journal of Psychedelic Studies* Volume 4: Issue 1 (March 2020): 4–15, https://doi.org/10.1556/2054.2019.015.
3. Ben Feinberg, PhD, "Cute as Children, but Not Handsome as Adults: María Sabina, Life Magazine, and Cold War Propaganda," Chacruna.net, Culture, June 16, 2020, https://chacruna.net/cute-as-children-but-not-handsome-as-adults-maria-sabina-life-magazine-and-cold-war-propaganda/
4. Erika Dyck, PhD, "Historian Explains How Women Have Been Excluded from the Field of Psychedelic Science," Chacruna.net, Women, October 16, 2018, https://chacruna.net/historian-explains-how-women-have-been-excluded-from-the-field-of-psychedelic-science/.

MARÍA SABINA, MUSHROOMS, AND COLONIAL EXTRACTIVISM

1. Antonella Fagetti, "Perplos nocturnos."
2. Virginia R., Gastón G., & Florencia R. "Las especies del género Psilocybe conocidas del Estado de Oaxaca,su distribución y relaciones étnicas." Revista Mexicana

de Micología, no. 23 (2006):27–36. Redalyc, https://www.redalyc.org/articulo.oa?id=88302305.

3. Amy Barlett and Monnica T. Williams, PhD, ABPP, "The Cost of Omission: Dr. Valentina Wasson and Getting Our Stories Right," Chacruna.net, Women, November 11, 2020, https://chacruna.net/dr-valentina-wasson-and-getting-our-stories-right/.

4. Marcelo Leite, PhD, "Researchers Demand Reparations to Mazatecs for Mushroom 'Spirit,'" Chacruna.net, Culture, February 12, 2021, https://chacruna.net/researchers_demand_reparations_mazatecs/.

5. Osiris García Cerqueda, "Hongos psilocybe, memoria y resistencia en la sierra mazateca," Chacruna Latinoamérica, Cultura Español, accessed August 11, 2023, https://chacruna-la.org/osiris_garcia_psilocybe_memoria_resistencia_mazateca/.

6. Diana Negrín, "Rastros coloniales en el 'renacimiento psicodélico'," Chacruna Latinoamérica, Cultura Español, accessed August 11, 2023, https://chacruna-la.org/rastros-coloniales-renacimiento-psicodelico/.

KATHLEEN HARRISON: WISDOM, ENDURANCE, AND HOPE— REFLECTIONS FROM A PSYCHEDELIC WOMAN

1. Botanical Dimensions website, accessed August 11, 2023, http://botanicaldimensions.org/.

SPOTLIGHT ON BETSY GORDON AND THE PSYCHOACTIVE SUBSTANCES RESEARCH COLLECTION

1. Hffter Research Institute website, accessed August 11, 2023, https://www.heffter.org/.

2. "GTT History and Founders," Grof Transpersonal Training, accessed August 11, 2023, http://www.holotropic.com/grof-transpersonal-training/gtt-history-and-founders/.

3. "Interviews & Documentaries," The Betsy Gordon Psychoactive Substances Research Collection, Purdue University Libraries and School of Information Studies, accessed August 11, 2023, http://collections.lib.purdue.edu/psychoactive/media.php.

4. Taylor Dysart, "Marlene Dobkin de Rios: A Case for Complex Histories of Women in Psychedelics," Chacruna.net, Women, February 3, 2021, https://chacruna.net/marlene-dobkin-de-rios-a-case-for-complex-histories-of-women-in-psychedelics/.

COMING OF AGE IN THE PSYCHEDELIC SIXTIES

1. The letters STP stand for Serenity, Tranquility, and Peace; it is a psychedelic compound synthesized by Alexander Shulgin.

2. DMT is a hallucinogen that occurs naturally in plants and animals and can also be chemically synthesized.

MARLENE DOBKIN DE RIOS: A CASE FOR COMPLEX HISTORIES OF WOMEN IN PSYCHEDELICS

1. Xavier Francuki, "A Tribute to the Mother of Ayahuasca Research, Marlene Dobkin de Rios (1939–2012)," Kahpi: The Ayahuasca Hub, June 27, 2019, https://kahpi.net/marlene-dobkin-de-rios-ayahuasca/
2. Emily Sinclair, PhD (C), "The Corona Crisis: A View from the Ayahuasca Capital of Iquitos," Chacruna.net, Inclusion & Diversity, May 11, 2020, https://chacruna.net/the-corona-crisis-a-view-from-the-ayahuasca-capital-of-iquitos/.

SEXUAL ASSAULT AND GENDER POLITICS IN AYAHUASCA TRADITIONS: A VIEW FROM BRAZIL

1. Juliana Dal Piva, "A cirada de sexo, dinheiro e mentiras de Prem Baba," *O Globo*, *Época*, Reportagem de Capa, September 13, 2018, https://oglobo.globo.com/epoca/a-ciranda-de-sexo-dinheiro-mentiras-de-prem-baba-23066393.
2. Suhur. Mash, "PREM BABA, GURU ESPIRITUAL FAZ POSICIONAMENTO SOBRE A ACUSAÇÃO DE ASSÉDIO SEXUAL," posted August 30, 2018, YouTube, https://youtu.be/Lb8npgeSQtQ.
3. Beatriz Labate, "Ex-Mestre Geral da UDV solta áudio apoiando o candidato Jair Bolsonaro a presidente do Brasil," Blog, September 29, 2018, https://www.bialabate.net/news/ex-mestre-geral-da-udv-solta-audio-apoiando-o-candidato-jair-bolsonaro-a-presidente-do-brasil.
4. Vinelight, "did you know UDV uses hoasca to heal homosexuals?" Ayahuasca Forums: The online ayahuasca community, December 21, 2010, 5:34 p.m., http://forums.ayahuasca.com/viewtopic.php?f=46&t=24013.
5. Marie Keenan, *Child Sexual Abuse and the Catholic Church* (New York: Oxford University Press, 2011).
6. Bette L. Bottoms et al., "Religion-Related Child Maltreatment: A Profile of Cases Encountered by Legal and Social Service Agencies," *Behavioral Sciences and the Law* 33:4 (August 2015): 561–579, https://doi.org/10.1002/bsl.2192.

A HOMOSEXUAL MARRIAGE EXPERIENCE IN SANTO DAIME

1. Shelby Hartman, "Why LGBTQI+ Members Are Creating Their Own Ayahuasca Circles," Chacruna.net, Queer, June 3, 2019, https://chacruna.net/why-lgbtqi-members-are-creating-their-own-ayahuasca-circles.
2. Clancy Cavnar, "Ayahuasca's Influence on Gay Identity," in *The Expanding World Ayahuasca Diaspora: Appropriation, Integration and Legislation*, ed. Beatriz Caiuby Labate and Clancy Cavnar (London: Routledge, 2018).

TREASURES OF THE FOREST: JARAWARA WOMEN AND PLANTS THEY CARRY

1. Fabiana Maizza, "As Mulheres Leváveis: Conexões Sobre o Rapé e Agências Femininas Jarawara," in *O uso de plantas psicoativas nas Américas*, edited by Beatriz Caiuby Labate and Sandra Lucia Goulart (Rio de Janeiro: Gramma/NEIP, 2019), 57–71.
2. Tânia Stolze Lima, "O que é um corpo?" *Religião e Sociedade* 22, 1 (2002), 9–20.
3. Davi Kopenawa and Bruce Albert, *La chute du ciel: paroles d'un chaman Yanomami* (Paris: Terre Humaine/Plon, 2010), 502.
4. Tânia Stolze Lima, "O dois e seu múltiplo: reflexões sobre o perspectivismo em uma cosmologia tup," *Mana* 2, no. 2 (1996).
5. Fabiana Maizza, "Persuasive Kinship: Human–Plant Relations in Southwest Amazonia," *Tipití: Journal of the Society for the Anthropology of Lowland South America* 15, no. 2 (2017): 206–220, https://digitalcommons.trinity.edu/tipiti/vol15/iss2/6.
6. Donna Haraway, *Staying with the Trouble. Making Kin in the Chthulucene* (Durham: Duke University Press, 2016).
7. Maria Puig de la Bellacasa, *Matters of Care: Speculative Ethics in More than Human Worlds* (Minneapolis: University of Minnesota Press, 2017).

CREATING AWARENESS ON SEXUAL ABUSE IN AYAHUASCA COMMUNITIES: A REVIEW OF CHACRUNA'S GUIDELINES

1. "Ayahuasca Community Guide for the Awareness of Sexual Abuse," Chacruna Institute for Psychedelic Plant Medicines, Sacred Plants, Ayahuasca Community Committee, accessed August 14, 2023, https://chacruna.net/community/ayahuasca-community-guide-for-the-awareness-of-sexual-abuse/.
2. Daniela M. Peluso, "For Export Only: Ayahuasca Tourism and Hyper-Traditionalism," in *IASTE Working Paper Series: Shifting Landscapes, Selling Tradition*, vol. 183 (2006), ed. Nezar AlSayyad, 482–500, https://iaste.org/2006-working-paper-series/.
3. Christine L. Holman, "Spirituality for Sale: An Analysis of Ayahuasca Tourism" (PhD diss., Arizona State University, 2010), https://www.scribd.com/document/426744151/Spirituality-for-Sale-an-Analysis-of-Ayahuasca-Tourism.
4. Daniela M. Peluso, "Global Ayahuasca: An Entrepreneurial Ecosystem," in *The World Ayahuasca Diaspora: Reinventions and Controversies*, ed. Beatriz Caiuby Labate, Clancy Cavnar, and Alex K. Gearin (London: Routledge, 2017), 203.
5. *The Late Show with Stephen Colbert*, "Chelsea Handler's Ayahuasca Journey," posted February 20, 2016, YouTube, https://youtu.be/EZgvRzRoYJY.
6. Daniela Peluso, PhD, "Sexual Seduction in Ayahuasca Shaman and Participants Interactions," Chacruna.net, Sex & Power, October 5, 2018, https://chacruna.net/sexual-seduction-ayahuasca-shaman-participants-interactions/.

7. Emily Sinclair, PhD, and Beatriz Labate, PhD, "Ayahuasca Community Guide for the Awareness of Sexual Abuse," *MAPS Bulletin* 20, no. 1 (Spring 2019), 34–36, https://maps.org/news/bulletin/ayahuasca-community -guide-for-the-awareness-of-abuse-2019/.

8. Daniela Peluso, "Ayahuasca's Attractions and Distractions: Examining Sexual Seduction in Shaman–Participant Interactions," in *Ayahuasca Shamanism in the Amazon and Beyond*, ed. Beatriz Caiuby Labate and Clancy Cavnar (Oxford, UK: Oxford University Press, 2014), 231–255.

9. Peluso, "Sexual Seduction in Ayahuasca Shaman and Participants Interactions."

10. Miguel N. Alexiades and Daniela M. Peluso, "Prior Informed Consent: The Anthropology and Politics of Cross-Cultural Exchange," in *Biodiversity and Traditional Knowledge: Equitable Partnerships in Practice*, ed. Sarah A. Laird (London: Earthscan, 2002), 221, https://doi.org/10.4324/9781849776080.

11. Angela M. Borges, Victoria L. Banyard, and Mary M. Moynihan, "Clarifying consent: Primary prevention of sexual assault on a college campus," *Journal of Prevention & Intervention in the Community* 36, 1–2 (2008), 75–88, https://doi .org/10.1080/10852350802022324.

12. Peluso, "Ayahuasca's Attractions and Distractions."

13. This is a translation of *pusangas*, a set of pan-Amazonian practices, mostly involving plants that are believed to affect one's will or motivation in ways that the maker of the concoction intends (Peluso 2003). They are popular enough to be experiences as culture-bound syndromes. Locally, however, it is common for new age psychedelic ayahuasca seekers to believe that they have experienced this. See also Daniela Marina Peluso, "*Ese Eja Epona*: Woman's Social Power in Multiple and Hybrid Worlds (PhD diss., Columbia University, 2003), https:// anthropology.columbia.edu/content/ese-eja-epona-womans-social-power.

14. Terence McKenna, "Posthumous Glory" (lecture, AllChemical Arts Conference, Hawaii, September 12–17, 1999), accessed January 28, 2023, http://www .matrixmasters.net/podcasts/TRANSCRIPTS/TMcK-PosthumousGlory.pdf.

15. "Ayahuasca Community Guide for the Awareness of Sexual Abuse," Chacruna .net.

16. "Legal Resources Companion to the Guidelines for the Awareness of Sexual Abuse," Chacruna Institute for Psychedelic Plant Medicines, Sacred Plants, Ayahuasca Community Committee, accessed August 14, 2023, https://chacruna .net/legal-resources-companion-to-the-guidelines-for-the-awareness-of-sexual -abuse/.

17. "Facts and figures: Ending violence against women," UN Women, What We Do, Ending Violence Against Women, updated February 2022, https://www.unwomen .org/en/what-we-do/ending-violence-against-women/facts-and-figures.

LOLA "LA CHATA": THE FIRST IMPORTANT
DRUG TRAFFICKER IN MEXICO CITY (1934–1959)

1. Lamour C. y Lambert, M. (1972). *La Nueva Guerra del Opio*. (Barcelona: Barral), 19.

2. Davenport-Hines, R. (2001). *La búsqueda del olvido. Historia global de las drogas, 1500-2000*, (Madrid: Fondo de Cultura Económica, Turner), 197.

3. Departamento de Salubridad Pública (1920, marzo 15), Disposiciones sobre el comercio de productos que pueden ser utilizados para fomentar vicios que degeneren la raza, y sobre el cultivo de plantas que pueden ser empleadas con el mismo fin, Diario Oficial de la Federación, (México).

4. Secretaría de Gobernación (1929, noviembre 5), Código Penal para el Distrito y Territorios Federales, Diario Oficial de la Federación, (México).

5. Despite the fame of Dolores Estevés there are few studies on the history of drugs that have dealt with this important trafficker. For example, see: Pérez Montfort (1997, 2016); Carey (2009, 2014), Astorga (2015).

6. Archivo Histórico de la Ciudad de México (AHCDMX), fondo Cárceles, Penitenciaría, caja 203, exp. 3820.

7. AHCDMX, fondo Cárceles, Penitenciaría, caja 358, exp. 3496.

8. In relation to the Hospital for Drug Addicts [Hospital del Toxicómanos] see Olguín Alvarado, P. (1995). Aproximación a la Historia del Hospital de Toxicómanos (1931-1949). Cuadernos para la historia de la salud.(México: Secretaría de Salud); Pérez Montfort, R. (2016). Tolerancia y prohibición: aproximaciones a la historia social y cultural de las drogas en México 1840-1940. (México: Colección Debate, Penguin Random House Grupo Editorial); and Bautista Hernández, L. (2016). De la Penitenciaría al Manicomio. El proceso de institucionalización del Hospital Federal de Toxicómanos de la Ciudad de México, 1926-1948. [Tesis de Maestría en Historia Moderna y Contemporánea, Instituto Mora].

9. AHCDMX, fondo Cárceles, Penitenciaría, caja 358, exp. 3496.

10. Pérez Ricart, C. A., & Olvera Hernández, N. A. (2021). Ascenso y declive de la Policía de Narcóticos del Departamento de Salubridad Pública en México (1917-1960). Historia Mexicana, 70 (4), 1661–1714.

11. "Comenzó a declarar el capitán de la Fuente", en Excélsior, Mexico City, April 14, 1938.

12. Ocaña Salazar, M. y Olvera Hernández, M. (2018). El psiquiatra que luchó contra los cuerdos para despenalizar las drogas. Chacruna Latinoamérica. https://chacruna-la.org/el-psiquiatra-que-lucho-contra-los-cuerdos-para-despenalizar-las-drogas/

13. Leopoldo Salazar Viniegra, "Carta abierta a Lola La Chata", El Universal, Mexico City, march 11, 1938.

14. "El capitán Huesca esta en la Penitenciaría", El Universal, Mexico City, April 1, 1938.

15. "Jefe de la Policía de Narcóticos, preso", El Universal, Mexico City, April 1,1938.

16. "Comenzó a declarar el capitán", Excélsior, Mexico City, 14 de abril 1938.

17. "Luis Huesca de la Fuente, abuso de autoridad, falsedad de declaraciones y contra la salud", 1938, AHCDMX, Cárceles, Penitenciaría, caja 402, exp. 1304.

18. Poder Ejecutivo, (1945, mayo 12), Decreto que declara Ley de Emergencia el capitulo 10, titulo 70, libro 20 del Código Penal. Diario Oficial de la Federación, (México).

19. Archivo General de la Nación (AGN), Presidentes, Miguel Ávila Camacho, caja 0818, exp. 549.44/1006.

20. "Dolores Estévez Zulueta, contra la salud", 1947, AHCDMX, Cárceles, Penitenciaría, caja 1014, exp. 1864.

21. "La pobrecita Lola", La Prensa, Mexico City, April 1,1957.

22. "Trata de Hacerse", La Prensa, Mexico City, April , 1957.

23. Los Sabuesos, La Prensa, Mexico City, april 1, 1957.

24. Macías, L. (2017, Julio 19). "Lola la Chata", huésped asidua de Lecumberri". *La Prensa*. https://www.la-prensa.com.mx/archivos-secretos/lola-la-chata-huesped-asidua-de-lecumberri-3538449.html

25. Carey, E. (2009). "Selling is more of a habit than using" Narcotraficante Lola la Chata and her threat to civilization, 1930-1969. *Journal of Women's History*, 21 (2), 62-89.

HOW MUSIC THERAPISTS HELPED BUILD PSYCHEDELIC THERAPY

1. D. B. Blewett, PhD, and N. Chwelos, MD, "Handbook for the Therapeutic Use of Lysergic Acide Diethlyamide-25 Individual and Group Procedures," Chapter 7: Equipment, originally published 1959, digital edition published online 2014, https://maps.org/research-archive/ritesofpassage/lsdhandbook.pdf#page=23.

2. Arthur L. Chandler, MD, and Mortimer A. Hartman, MD, "Lysergic Acid Diethylamide (LSD-25) as a Facilitating Agent in Psychotherapy," *A.M.A Archives of General Psychiatry* vol 2 (1960), 289, https://www.erowid.org/references/texts/show/1843docid1723#page=4

3. N. Chwelos et al., "Use of d-Lysergic Acid Diethylamide in the Treatment of Alcoholism," *Quart. J. Stud. Alcohol* 20 (1959), 580, https://www.erowid.org/references/texts/show/1852docid1733#page=4

4. Betty Grover Eisner, PhD, and Sidney Cohen, MD, "Psychotherapy with Lysergic Acid Diethylamide," *J. Nerv. Ment. Dis.* 127 (1958), 531, https://www.erowid.org/references/texts/show/1733docid1615#page=4.

5. Sidney Cohen, MD, and Betty Grover Eisner, PhD, "Use of Lysergic Acid Diethylamide in a Psychotherapeutic Setting," *A.M.A. Archives of Neurology & Psychiatry* vol 81 (May 1959), 616, https://www.erowid.org/references/texts/show/1767docid6089#page=2

6. Colin M. Smith, MD, FRCP (C), DPM, "Some Reflections on the Possible Therapeutic Effects of the Hallucinogens with Special Reference to Alcoholism," *Quart. J. Stud. Alcohol* 20 (1959), 297, https://www.erowid.org/references/texts/show/1981docid1845#page=6

7. P. O. O'Reilly and Genevieve Reich, "Lysergic Acid and the Alcoholic," *Dis. Nerv. Syst.* 23 (1962), 331, https://www.erowid.org/references/texts/show/2213docid2054.

8. J. Ross MacLean, MD, D. C. MacDonald, MD, Ultan P. Byrne, DPH, and A. M. Hubbard, PhD, "The Use of LSD-25 in the Treatment of Alcoholism and Other Psychiatric Problems," *Quart. J. Stud. Alcohol* 22, (1961), 34–45, https://erowid.org/references/texts/show/1988docid1852.

9. Matt "River Baldwin, MFT, "Introducing Chacruna's Psychedelic Therapy Music Forum," Chacruna.net, Music, October 9, 2018, https://chacruna.net/introducing-chacrunas-psychedelic-therapy-music-forum/.

10. "Hermina Ola Eisele Browne," Find a Grave, accessed August 15, 2023, https://www.findagrave.com/memorial/61229676/hermina-ola-browne

11. Hermina Eisele Brown, "The Use of Music as a Therapy," in *Music Therapy*, edited by Edward Podolsky (New York: Philosophical Library, 1954), 215-30. (page 217 is the specific page I'm referencing here). Current link to that book in the archive: https://hdl.handle.net/10217/184779.

12. Samuel W. Hamilton and Willem van de Wall, "The Use of Music in Hospitals for Mental and Nervous Diseases" (New York: National Music Council, 1944). Current link in the archive: https://hdl.handle.net/10217/184777.

13. Home Missions Council of North America Records, 1903–1951, Presbyterian Historical Society, Philadelphia, PA, https://www.history.pcusa.org/collections/research-tools/guides-archival-collections/ncc-rg-26.

14. Alicia Ann Clair and George N. Heller, "Willem van de Wall: Organizer and Innovator in Music Education and Music Therapy," *Journal of Research in Music Education* vol 37, issue 3 (Fall 1989), https://doi.org/10.2307/3344667.

15. William B. Davis "van de Wall, Willem." *Grove Music Online.* 26 Mar. 2018; Accessed 4 Sep. 2023.

16. Hermina E. Brown, "Psychiatric Treatment with Drug LSD and Music Therapy for Alcoholics," in *Music Therapy 1960: Tenth Book of Proceedings of the National Association for Music Therapy* (Lawrence, Kansas: National Association for Music Therapy, 1961), 154-62. The current link to that book in the archive is https://hdl.handle.net/10217/184945.

17. Charles T. Eagle, "Music and LSD: An Empirical Study," *Journal of Music Therapy* vol 9, issue 1 (Spring 1972), 23–36, https://doi.org/10.1093/jmt/9.1.23.

18. "In Memoriam—Hermine E. Browne June 1902–April 1966," *Journal of Music Therapy*, vol. 3, issue 3 (September 1966), 116, https://doi.org/10.1093/jmt/3.3.116.

19. Eagle, "Music and LSD."

20. E. Thayer Gaston and Charles T. Eagle Jr., "The Function of Music in LSD Therapy for Alcoholic Patients," *Journal of Music Therapy*, vol. 7, issue 1 (Spring 1970), 3–19, https://doi.org/10.1093/jmt/7.1.3.

21. Robert E. Johnson, "E. Thayer Gaston: Leader in Scientific Thought on Music in Therapy and Education," *Journal of Research in Music Education*, vol. 29, issue 4 (Winter 1981), 279–286. https://doi.org/10.2307/3345004.

22. Helen L. Bonny and Walter N. Pahnke, "The Use of Music in Psychedelic (LSD) Psychotherapy," *Journal of Music Therapy* vol 9, no. 2 (Summer 1972), https://www.erowid.org/references/texts/show/2807docid7145.

23. Clare O'Callaghan, AM, PhD, MMus, BMus, BSW, RMT et al., "Experience of Music Used with Psychedelic Therapy: A Rapid Review and Implications," *Journal of Music Therapy* vol. 57, issue 3 (Fall 2020), 282–314, https://doi.org/10.1093/jmt/thaa006.

24. "About Marilyn Clark," Marilyn Clark Integrative Psychotherapist, accessed August 15, 2023, http://www.marilynclarkintegrativepsychotherapist.com/about-marilyn.html.

25. Association for Music & Imagery, accessed August 15, 2023, https://ami-bonnymethod.org/.

WOMEN'S HISTORICAL INFLUENCE ON "SET AND SETTING"

1. Kevin Feeney, PhD, "Beyond Set and Setting: A New Understanding of Psychedelics & Healing," Chacruna.net., Policy, July 3, 2017, https://chacruna.net/beyond-set-and-setting-psychedelic-healing/.

2. Alec Lyons, "Psychiatric Day Hospitals," Ulster Med J. vol 89, issue 1 (January 2020), 34–37, https://www.ncbi.nlm.nih.gov/pmc/articles/PMC7027187/.

3. Joyce Martin, 1964. "L.S.D. Analysis," *The International Journal of Social Psychiatry* 10 (1964), 165–169.

4. Stanislav Grof and Christina Grof, *Holotropic Breathwork: A New Approach to Self-Exploration and Therapy* (Albany, New York: State University of New York Press, 2010).

5. Margot Cutner, "On the Inclusion of Certain 'Body Experiments' in Analysis," *British Journal of Medical Psychology* 26, 3–4 (1953), 262–277.

6. Margot Cutner, "Analytic Work with LSD 25," *Psychiatric Quarterly* 33, issue 4 (1959), 715–757.

7. "Sidney Cohen," Wikipedia, Wikimedia Foundation, Inc., last modified June 19, 2023, 20:27 UTC, accessed August 15, 2023, https://en.wikipedia.org/wiki/Sidney_Cohen.

8. Betty Grover Eisner, 1997. "Set, Setting, and Matrix". *Journal of Psychoactive Drugs* 29(2):21316.

1. Martha Robles, *Mulheres, Mitos E Deusas: O feminine através dos tempos* (São Paulo: Editoria Aleph, 2019).
2. Suzanne G. Cusick, "'Eve . . . Blowing in Our Ears?' Toward a History of Music Scholarship on Women in the Twentieth Century," *Women and Music*, vol. 5 (2001): 125.
3. Laila Rosa, accessed August 16, 2023, http://www.lailarosamusica.com/.
4. Maria Ignez Cruz Mello, "*Iamurikuma*: Música, Mito e Ritual entre os Wauja do Alto Xingu," (PhD diss., Universidade Federal de Santa Catarina, 2005), https://repositorio.ufsc.br/bitstream/handle/123456789/102877/211418.pdf?sequence=1.
5. Cynthia Inés Carrillo Sáenz, "De Mulher a Pajé: Aprendizagem das mulheres pajés Yawanawa como transformação," (master's thesis, Universidade Federal de Minas Gerais, 2017), https://repositorio.ufmg.br/bitstream/1843/32639/1/Disserta%C3%A7%C3%A3o%20Cynthia%20Carrillo%20final.pdf.
6. Camila de Pieri Benedito, ""Maria que me ensina a ser mulher": religião e gênero no Santo Daime," (PhD diss., Universisdade Federal de São Carlos, 2019), https://repositorio.ufscar.br/bitstream/handle/ufscar/11390/Tese_Camila%20de%20Pieri%20Benedito_Corrigida.pdf?sequence=5&isAllowed=y.
7. RezoBrasil (@rezobrasil), "Projeto Rezo Brasil apresenta—FESTIVAL REZA MÃE DIVINA," Instagram video, May 9, 2020, https://www.instagram.com/p/B_-Uf_IJLp_/?utm_source=ig_web_copy_link&igshid=MzRlODBiNWFlZA==.
8. Ana Gretel Echazú Böschemeier and Camila de Pieri Benedito, "Violência Sexual e Políticas de Gênero no Campo Ayahuasqueiro: Uma perspectiva brasileira," Blog, December 14, 2018, https://www.bialabate.net/news/violencia-sexual-e-politicas-de-genero-no-campo-ayahuasqueiro-uma-perspectiva-brasileira.

YAMINAWA WOMEN AND AYAHUASCA: SHAMANISM, GENDER, AND HISTORY IN THE PERUVIAN AMAZON

1. For detailed descriptions and analyses of these songs among the Yaminawa and Sharanahua, see Townsley (1993) and Déléage (2009). The *kuxuiti* songs are different from the songs of ayahuasca (also *rabi*, like the substance itself) and are not directed to the cure. In any case, it is not conceivable to drink ayahuasca without singing.
2. Laura Pérez Gil, "Metamorfoses yaminawa: xamanismo e socialidade na Amazônia peruana," (PhD diss., Universidade Federeal de Sana Catarina, 2006), https://repositorio.ufsc.br/handle/123456789/88415.
3. Faced with the violence of the first contacts, the ancestors of the current Yaminawa retreated to regions of difficult access. This situation of "voluntary isolation" ended in the early 1960s when some young people decided to find ways of having a regular supply of metal tools (Pérez Gil, 2011).

4. See Pérez Gil (2006). For a similar analysis of other Pano groups in the region, see Shepard (2014) and Brabec de Mori (2015).

5. Peter Gow, "River People: Shamanism and History in Western Amazonia," in *Shamanism, History, and the State*, ed. Nicholas Thomas and Caroline Humphrey (Ann Arbor: University of Michigan Press, 1996), 90.

6. Barbara Keifenheim, "*Nixi Pae* as Sensory Participation in the Transforming Principle of Primordial Creation among the Kaxinawa Indians of Eastern Peru," in *O Uso Ritual da Ayahuasca*, ed. Beatriz Caiuby Labate and Wladimyr Sena Araújo (Campinas/São Paulo, Brazil: Editora Mercado de Letra, 2002), https://www.mercado-de-letras.com.br/livro-mway.php?codid=158.

7. Philippe Erikson, "'I,' 'UUU,' 'SHHH': Gritos, Sexos e Metamorfoses Entre Os Matis (Amazônia Brasileria)," *Mana* 6:2 (October 2000), 37–64, http://dx.doi.org/10.1590/S0104-93132000000200002.

8. Carlos Fausto, *Inimigos Fiéis: História, Guerra e Xamanismo na Amazônia* (São Paulo: Editoria da Universidade de São Paulo, 2001).

9. Glenn H. Shepard, "Will the Real Shaman Please Stand Up?" in *Ayahuasca Shamanism in the Amazon and Beyond*, ed. Beatriz Caiuby Labate and Clancy Cavnar (Oxford: Oxford University Press, 2014), 16–39.

10. Jean-Pierre Chaumeil, "Chamanismes à Géométrie Variable en Amazonie," *Diogène*, issue 158 (April 1, 1992), 92.

MADRINHA RITA: BRAZILIAN MATRIARCH OF AYAHUASCA

1. "Madrinha Rita Gregório de Melo," Religião da Floresta, Santo Daime ICEFLU, accessed August 23, 2023, https://www.santodaime.org/site/religiao-da-floresta/madrinha-rita.

2. James A. Brooke, "Manaus Journal; For the Rubber Soldiers of Brazil, Rubber Checks," *New York Times*, World, May 15, 1991, https://www.nytimes.com/1991/05/15/world/manaus-journal-for-the-rubber-soldiers-of-brazil-rubber-checks.html.

3. Lucio Mortimer, *Bença, Padrinho!* A História do Expansor da Religião do Santo Daime (São Paulo: Editora Reviver, 2019).

4. Ibid.

5. Albina Luiza Autran de Mendonça Pinto, *Costurando os retalhos: Crônicas do Céu do Mapiá* (São Paulo: Editora Reviver, 2021).

6. Ibid.

7. Ibid.

8. Ibid.

9. Lígia Platero and Klarissa Platero, "Uma experiência de casamento homossexual no Santo Daime," Chacruna Latinoamérica, Cultura Português, December 30, 2020. https://chacruna-la.org/uma-experiencia-de-casamento-homossexual-no-santo-daime/.

THE RELIGIOUS USES OF LICIT AND ILLICIT PSYCHOACTIVE SUBSTANCES IN A BRANCH OF THE SANTO DAIME RELIGION

1. Jessica Rochester, "How Our Santo Daime Church Received Religious Exemption to Use Ayahuasca in Canada," Chacruna.net, Policy, July 17, 2017, https://chacruna.net/how-ayahuasca-church-received-religious-exemption-canada/.

A BRIDGE BETWEEN TWO WORLDS: AYAHUASCA AND INTERCULTURAL MEDICINE—AN INTERVIEW WITH ANJA LOIZAGA-VELDER

1. "Psychointegrative" is a concept coined by Michael Winkelman to propose that, as they are analogues of serotonin, classic psychedelics (tryptamines) modulate not only a specific brain process, but various activities of other neurotransmitters, thus integrating the thalamus, which regulates the flow of information between the nervous system and the cortex, which then interprets this information.

PSYCHEDELICS AND DEATH: TRANSITIONING FROM THIS WORLD WITH CONSCIOUSNESS

1. Thomas C. Swift et al., "Caner at the Dinner Table: Experiences of Psilocybin-Assisted Psychotherapy for the Treatment of Cancer-Related Distress," *Journal of Humanistic Psychology* 57, issue 5 (September 2017), 439–564, https://doi.org/10.1177/0022167817715966.
2. BACII, accessed August 23, 2023, bacii.co.
3. Jasmine Virdi, "Psychedelics and the Default Mode Network," *Psychedelics Today*, Research, February 4, 2020, https://psychedelicstoday.com/2020/02/04/psychedelics-and-the-default-mode-network/.
4. Roland R. Griffiths et al., "Psilocybin produces substantial and sustained decreases in depression and anxiety in patients with life-threatening cancer: A randomized double-blind trial," *Journal of Psychopharmacology* 30, issue 12 (December 2016), 1181–1197, https://doi.org/10.1177%2F0269881116675513.
5. Timothy Leary, Ralph Metzner, and Richard Alpert, *The Psychedelic Experience: A Manual Based on the Tibetan Book of the Dead* (1964; repr. New York City: Kensington Publishing Corp., 1992).
6. Andrea Ens, MA, "'Please Write Up Your Work!': Laura Archera Huxley as a Psychedelic Pioneer," Chacruna.net, Women, December 2, 2020, https://chacruna.net/laura-archera-huxley-as-a-psychedelic-pioneer/.
7. Laura Huxley, *This Timeless Moment: A Personal View of Aldous Huxley* (New York City: Farrar, Straus and Giroux,1968).
8. Francis Gerard, "Pain, Death and LSD: A Retrospective of the Work of Dr. Eric Kast," *Psychedelic Monographs and Essays* 5 (Autumn/Winter 1990), 114–121, https://bibliography.maps.org/bibliography/default/resource/7851.

9. Eric C. Kast, "A Concept of Death," in *Psychedelics: The Uses and Implications of Hallucinogenic Drugs*, ed. Bernard Aaronson and Humphry Osmond (Cambridge, Massachusetts: Schenkman Publishing Company, 1971), https://www.samorini.it/doc1/alt_aut/ek/kast-a-concept-of-death.pdf.

10. Charles S. Grob, MD, Anthony P. Bossis, PhD, and Roland R. Griffiths, PhD, "Use of the Classic Hallucinogen Psilocybin for Treatment of Existential Distress Associated with Cancer," in *Psychological Aspects of Cancer: A Guide to Emotional and Psychological Consequences of Cancer, Their Causes and Their Management*, ed. Brian I. Carr and Jennifer Steel (New York City: Springer, 2013), 291–308, https://link.springer.com/chapter/10.1007/978-1-4614-4866-2_17.

11. Elyse Bais, "Terminally Ill Patients Sue DEA for Psilocybin Treatment Under Right to Try Act," Chacruna.net, Indigenous Voices, Policy, June 8, 2021, https://chacruna.net/terminally_ill_sue_dea_psilocybin/?.

12. *Advanced Integrative Medical Science Institute, PLLC v. U.S. Drug Enforcement Agency*, No. 21-70544 (9th Cir. 2021).

13. JoNel Aleccia, "New Legal Push Aims to Speed Magic Mushrooms to Dying Patients," KKFF Health News, November 24, 2020, https://kffhealthnews.org/news/new-legal-push-aims-to-speed-magic-mushrooms-to-dying-patients/.

14. Trickett Wendler, Frank Mongiello, Jordan McLinn, and Matthew Bellina Right to Try Act of 2017, Pub. L. No. 115-176, 132 Stat. 1372 (2018).

15. Troy Farah, "After Permitting Psilocybin for Terminal Patients, Canada Could Open the Door to Psychedelics," *DoubleBlind*, originally published August 5, 2020, updated May 26, 2021, https://doubleblindmag.com/canada-psilocybin-for-terminally-ill-patients-therapsil-bruce-tobin/.

AYAHUASCA AND CHILDBIRTH IN THE SANTO DAIME TRADITION: SOLIDARITY AMONG WOMEN AND PSYCHEDELIC CULTURAL RESISTANCE

1. Jacqueline Alves Rodigues and Glauber Loures de Assis, PhD, "Madrinha Rita: Matriarca brasileira da ayahuasca," Chacruna.net, Women, January 31, 2022, https://chacruna.net/madrinha-rita-brazilian-matriarch-ayahuasca/.

2. Edward MacRae, PhD, "The Religious Uses of Licit and Illicit Psychoactive Substances in a Branch of the Santo Daime Religion," Chacruna.net, Women, February 15, 2022, https://chacruna.net/the-religious-uses-of-licit-and-illicit-psychoactive-substances-in-a-branch-of-the-santo-daime-religion/.

3. Beatriz Caiuby Labate, PhD, "Consumption of Ayahuasca by Children and Pregnant Women: Medical Controversies and Religious Perspectives," *Journal of Psychoactive Drugs*, 43: 1 (2011), 27–35, http://dx.doi.org/10.1080/02791072.2011.566498.

4. CONAD (2010). Resolução n.01. Disponível em: www.bialabate.net/wpcontent/uploads/2008/08/Resolução-Conad-_1_25_01_2010.pdf

5. Vera Fróes, *History of the People of Juramidam: The Santo Daime Culture* (Manaus: Suframa, 1986).

6. Marlo Eakes Meyer and Matthew D. S. Meyer, "Los Niños de la Reina, Ayahuasca y Embarazo: Um Informe Preliminar," in *Ayahuasca y salud*, ed. Beatriz Caiuby Labate and José C. Bouso (Barcelona: La Liebre de Marzo, 2013).
7. Vera Fróes Fernandes, "O uso do Santo Daime no parto," Chacruna Latinoamérica, Política Português, November 14, 2017, https://chacruna-la .org/o-uso-do-santo-daime-no-parto/.
8. Adelise Noal, "Os Psicodélicos no Universo Feminino do Partejar," Chacruna Latinoamérica , Saúde Português, October 21, 2021, https://chacruna-la.org /psicodelicos-no-partejar.
9. Froes, Relato #04.

ABORTION, PLANTS, AND WHISPERED NETWORKS OF BOTANICAL KNOWLEDGE

1. Sean McAllister, Esq., "Myths and Realities About the Decriminalization of Psychedelics in the US," Chacruna.net, Policy, March 18, 2020, https://chacruna.net/ myths-and-realities-about-the-decriminalization-of-psychedelics-in-the-us/.

PSYCHEDELIC MOTHERHOOD: THE ALTERED STATES OF BIRTH

1. Rebecca Kronman, LCSW, "Children and Psychedelics: Using Indigenous Wisdom to Examine Western Paradigms," Chacruna.net, Integration, June 5, 2020, https://chacruna.net/children-and-psychedelics-using-indigenous-wisdom-to-examine-western-paradigms/.
2. Stacy B. Schaefer, PhD, "Beautiful Flowers: Women and Peyote in Indigenous Traditions," *MAPS Bulletin* 29, no. 1 (Spring 2019), 8–13, https://maps.org/news/bulletin/ beautiful-flowers-women-and-peyote-in-indigenous-traditions-spring-2019/.
3. Beatriz Caiuby Labate, PhD, "Consumption of Ayahuasca by Children and Pregnant Women: Medical Controversies and Religious Perspectives," *Journal of Psychoactive Drugs*, 43: 1 (2011), 27–35, http://dx.doi.org/10.1080/02791072.2011.566498.

Index

abortion, 267–268
activism, 13, 70, 184, 189
Aggarwal, Sunil, 257
Alberts, Leni, 19, 21–23
Alpert, Richard, 38, 43, 151, 255
Alvarado, C. S., 105
amazon, 47, 163, 215, 219, 221, 225, 231, 236, 260, 270, 296
amphetamines, 14, 65, 131
Anderson, Warwick, 142
Anslinger, Harry, 179
Anthropocene, 149
anthropology, 8, 12, 139, 296, 298, 300
Arizona, 36, 281–282, 285, 292
assimilation, 285
ayahuasca, 7, 10, 139, 145–146, 169, 174, 207, 211, 213, 215, 221, 227, 241, 259, 264
ayahuasqueros, 52
Ayni, 291
Aztec, 53, 115, 179

Baba, Prem (Janderson Fernandes), 145
Barquinha, 145, 210
Barton, Camille, 183
Baul (religion), 210
Bayer, 175
Beatles, The, 131, 135
Beauvoir, Simone de, 13
Bencioli, María, 55
Bender, Lauretta, 63–65, 67
Benedito, Camila de Pieri, 209

Betsy Gordon Psychoactive Substances Research Collection, 128
Beyonce, 279
Big Brother and the Holding Company, 133
Bina, Dona, 226
Black Panther Party, 135, 154
Black Sabbath, 135
Blewett, Duncan, 106, 295
Bolsonaro, Jair, 146, 148
Bolton, Frances, 105
Bonny, Helen L., 196, 198–199
Bosque Redondo, 284–285
Botanical Dimensions, 122–123
breathwork, 126
Bresler, Johannes, 20–21
Brotherhood of Eternal Love, 75
Brown, Hermina E., 195–196
Bufo alvarius, 240
Burning Man, 190, 246
Burroughs, William, 179

Camacho, Ávila, 178
Cameron, Ewen, 91
Campos, Wilma Mahua, 47
Canada, 25, 69, 77, 81, 91, 299, 303
cancer, 31, 36
cannabis, 43, 74, 189, 225, 232, 265
Cardenas, Amada, 25–26
Carey, Martin, 43
Carhart–Harris, Robin, 21, 190
ceremony, 49, 109, 115, 157, 159–160, 260, 294
Cerqueda, Osiris García, 120

Chacruna guidelines, 169
Chaumeil, Jean–Pierre, 7, 12
Church of the Eagle and Condor, 290
Civil Rights Movement, 250
Civil War, 284
Cleaver, Elridge, 155
Cleaver, Kathleen, 154–155
Clinical Theology, 94–96
clown, 289
cocaine, 175, 177, 296
Cohen, Sidney, 63, 201, 204
colonialism, 97, 123, 187–188
Coltrane, John, 130–131
Columbus, Christopher, 284
cosmopolitics, 8, 218
cosmovision, 211
Cubero, María de Lourdes Baez, 55
Cultivator of Beloved Community,
    243, 246, 248–249
Culture of Belonging, 247–248
curandeirismo, 11
curandera, 109
curandero, 139–140, 290
Cusick, Suzanne, 207
Cutner, Margot, 201, 203, 205

dance, 183, 185–186, 212
Dancing Wisdom (book), 186
Dass, Ram, 38, 57, 255
Davis, Miles, 135
Davis, Wade, 143
death, 179, 253–255
decolonization, 183
decriminalization, 188–189
decriminalize nature, 291
DEI, 246–247
DeMille, Cecil B., 105
Denison, Virginia, 151, 153
Dent, Rosanna, 142
depression, 13, 16, 19, 21, 204, 238,
    255, 278
diet, 32, 208–209, 217

dieting, 49
Diné people, 285
DMT, 127, 131, 229
Dobkin de Ríos, Marlene, 55, 128, 139,
    142–143
Doctrine of Discovery, The, 283
domestic violence, 72, 282
Doors, The, 31, 33, 38, 66, 101, 106
dying, 5, 110, 251, 253
Dylan, Bob, 130–131

E. Merck, 20
Eagle, Charles T., 197
Eisner, Betty, 57–61, 63, 201, 204–205
electroconvulsive therapy (ECT), 94
embodiment, 183–185, 243
entheogen, 19, 187, 189, 190–191, 229,
    241
entheogens, 187, 190–191, 229
ergot, 4, 268–270
Eriacho, Belinda, 281–282
Erikson, Philippe, 219
Estrada, Álvaro, 117–118
Estrada, Yarelix, 192
ethnobotany, 123, 142–143
ethnography, 9, 142, 163, 208
extra–sensory perception (ESP),
    104

Fagetti, Antonella, 55
Fausto, Carlos, 219
FBI, 75–76, 287
feminism, 89, 137, 213, 271, 298
Fireside Project, 243, 246, 248–249
Fort Sumner284–285
Fróes, Vera, 262–263, 265

Garrett, Eileen, 85, 103–106, 108
Garza, Mercedes de la, 53, 55
Gaskin, Ina May, 273, 275
Gaskin, Stephen, 273
Gaston, E. Thayer, 197–198

Gathering of the Elders Conference, 35, 126, 128
Gaye, Marvin, 131
gender 20, 34, 42, 44, 145, 148, 207, 215, 298
gender roles, 92, 147, 158, 174
Gindler, Elsa, 203
González, Lilián, 55
Gordon, Betsy, 125, 128, 301
Gow, Peter, 218
Graboi, Nina, 41, 44–45
Grateful Dead, 41, 121, 133, 135
Greenfield, Robert, 77
Gregório de Melo, Rita, 221
Grof, Stanislav, 95, 126–128

Hagin, Rosa, 64
hallucinogen, 23, 139–141, 232
harm, 189–190, 192–193, 231, 244, 249, 274, 295
harm reduction, 192, 295
Harrison, Kathleen, 121
Have a Good Trip (documentary), 192
healing, 11, 28, 38, 49, 100, 199
healing practices, 139, 141, 87, 245, 93
Heffter, Arthur, 20
Hendrix, Jimi, 129
herbs, 215, 262, 268, 283
heroin, 17, 19, 57, 175, 178
Hildebrando de Rios, Yando, 141
Hoffer, Abram, 91, 101, 106, 196, 295
Hoffman, Abbie, 131–132
Hofmann, Albert, 3–4, 110, 268
Hollywood Hospital, 195
homophobia, 157, 161, 213
Hubbard, Al, 83, 91, 107, 201
Hubbard, Rita, 83
Huichol, 159, 274, 301
Huni Kuin, 160, 219
Huxley, Aldous, 31, 45, 83, 101–102, 106, 255–257, 303–304
Huxley, Ellen, 83

Huxley, Julian, 85
Huxley, Laura, 151, 255–257
Huxley, Maria Nys, 31–32, 34
Huxley, Matthew, 83

Ibogaine, 134
icaros, 48, 58
Indigenous, 7–12, 16, 29, 52–55, 106, 115, 117, 119–120, 122, 139, 142, 145, 160, 186, 213, 290
Indigenous Peyote Conservation Initiative, 29
integration, 192, 240–241, 244, 247, 278
intergenerational trauma, 184, 281–283, 285–286
Irineu Raimundo, Serra (Mestre), 223, 229–230, 260
Isherwood, Christopher, 33, 151
Island (Huxley), 38, 42, 69, 83, 178
Izumi, Amy, 83
Izumi, Kiyoshi, 83

Jackson, Andrew, 284
Janiger, Oscar, 151
Jarawara, 163–167, 298
Johnson, Lyndon B., 153

Kaalogii, 281
Kanner, Leo, 64
Kast, Eric, 256
Keifenheim, Barbara, 219
Kesey, Ken, 45
Ketamine, 58–59, 297
Kiev, Ari, 140
Kopenawa, Davi, 166
Krippner, Stanley, 66
Krishnamurti, Jiddu, 33, 38

Lake, Frank, 94–96, 151, 64
Langdon, Esther Jean, 7
Le Guin, Ursula K., 60

League of Spiritual Discovery, 42

Leary, Rosemary Woodruff, 69–71, 75, 78–79

Leary, Timothy, 38, 41–43, 57, 63, 69, 71–72, 79, 151, 173

liberation psychology, 193

Liberation Training, 192

Liddy, G. Gordon, 73

lightning medicine, 281, 288

Ling, Thomas, 201

Loizaga-Velder, Anja, 235–236, 241

Lola "La Chata" (María Dolores Estévez Zulueta), 175–176

Long Walk, The, 85–86, 284

LSD, 3–4, 6, 41–43, 66, 94

LSD–25, 4, 23, 37

lupus, 281, 288, 294

manic–depressive psychosis, 100

marijuana, 44, 55, 131, 175–178, 232, 283

marijuana, 44, 55, 131, 175–178, 232, 283

Martin, Joyce, 201–202, 205

Maya, 53, 54, 56, 115

Mazatec, 110, 115–118, 120, 123

McClary, Susan, 207

McCririck, Pauline, 203

McDonald, Kathy, 133

McKenna, Dennis, 128

McKenna, Terence, 121–122, 173

MDMA, 127, 186–187, 294, 297

Medical Apartheid (book), 188

Mehrabian, Albert Dr, 185

Mello, Maria Ignez Cruz, 208

mental illness, 65, 91, 93, 95, 100–102

mescaline, 13, 16, 19, 20, 22, 140

mestizo, 139, 210, 219, 230, 240

methamphetamine, 131

Metzner, Ralph, 255

midwifery, 253–254, 260–263, 273–275

Millbrook, 69, 73, 74, 77

Miller, Steve, 133

Monteiro de Souza, Raimundo, 146

Morgan, Francis P. , 19

morphine, 84, 175, 176, 297

Morrison, Van, 133, 135

Mota de Melo, Sebastião Padrinho, 158, 222

music, 14, 35, 43, 58, 73, 121, 126, 130, 196, 200, 207

 psychedelic, 195-198

touch, 199

mysticism, 106, 236

Nahua, 54, 56

Native American Church (NAC), 25, 27, 292, 301

Navajo, 26, 281–282, 284–285, 293–294

Navajo Nation, 281–282

Negrín, Yvonne, 129, 133–134, 299

neoshamanism, 240

NeuroTribes (book), 188

New Age religions, 146, 207

Nichols, David, 127–128

Nichols, Florence, 91–94, 97

Nin, Anaïs, 151

Nixon, Richard, 135

Noal, Adelise, 265

Ongaro, Alberto, 118

oppression, 77, 183–185, 193, 212, 244, 249

Orozco, Soledad (de Ávila), 178

Osmond, Humphry, 31, 33, 36, 81–82, 84, 86, 91, 101, 106, 196, 295, 303–304

Osmond, Jane, 81

Pahnke, Walter N., 199

paranormal, 104, 106

parapsychology, 103–107, 238

Parapsychology Foundation, 105
Parley, Kay, 99–100
Pedalino, Suzana, 210
Peregrina, Madrinha, 260
peyote (*Lophophora williamsii*), 25
peyoteros, 25–26
PHEI, 243
Phillips, David E., 70
Powick Hospital, 94, 203
pregnancy, 259, 261, 263, 268, 270, 274–275, 278
Prentiss, D. W., 19
psilocybin, 55, 66, 96, 106, 109–110, 120, 238, 244
Psychedelic Health Equity Initiative (PHEI), 243
Psychedelic Liberty Summit, 293
psychedelic movement, the, 42, 44, 108, 112, 123, 190, 249–250
psychedelic renaissance, 56, 110, 112, 120, 123, 187, 200, 292
psychedelic–assisted therapy, 184, 192, 303
psychiatry, 23, 60, 65, 85, 92, 99, 303
psychoanalysis, 93–95
psychosis, 16–17, 23, 100, 202
psychotomimetic, 202
Putumayo, 8

racism, 148, 183–185, 189, 213, 249
Radin, Joanna, 142
Ramstein, Susi, 3–6
Rank, Otto, 95
rape, 170, 191, 208, 287
Raulino, Madrinha Cristina, 262
Red Dress Project, 287
reiki, 244
Rhine, J. B., 105
Richards, Bill, 128
Riddle, John, 268
Ríos, María Gabriela Garrett, 55
Ríos, Oscar, 140

Rosa, Laila, 207
Rothlin, Ernest, 5
Rutherford, Alexandra, 60

Sabina, María, 110, 115–120
Sáenz, Cynthia Inés Carrillo, 208
Salazar Viniegra, Leopoldo, 177
San Pedro, 227
Sandison, Ronald, 94, 201, 203
Sandoz (lab), 4
Santo Daime, 145, 157–161, 209–210, 221–223, 227, 229, 233, 259, 260
Saraswati, Jagadananda, 210
Sartre, Jean–Paul, 13
Schizophrenia, 64–66, 82, 86, 101
Schultes, Richard Evans, 143
Sebastião, Padrinho, 157, 159, 161, 222, 225–226, 264
Seguín, Carlos Alberto, 140
Sengvanhpheng, Mangda, 254
set and setting, 18, 58, 95, 107, 126, 132, 181, 201–202
sexism, 183, 213
sexual abuse, 145, 169, 174
Shamanism, 7–8, 215
Sheprd, Glenn, 219
Shipibo, 47, 49
Shire, Warsan, 276, 279
Shorter, Edward, 269
Shulgin, Alexander "Sasha", 134
Siona, 8–9
Smythies, John, 82
snuff, 163–168
somatic practices, 184
Späth, Ernst, 21
speed, 15, 133, 135
spiritualism, 104
spirituality, 42–44, 92, 117, 145, 266, 292
Stoll, Arthur, 5
STP, 131, 133
suicide, 104, 204, 286–287

Tafur, Joe, 290
TallBear, Kim, 142
Tejanos, 26, 29
telepathy, 104, 107
therapy, 37, 58, 66, 91, 195, 200
This Week (magazine), 120
tobacco, 28, 51, 55, 154, 165–168,
    215–218, 232
Tomorrow (magazine), 105
transgender, 161
transphobia, 185, 213
trauma, 94–95, 183–184, 188,
    198–199, 240, 244, 273, 281, 285
Txitonawa, 219

Ucayali, 47, 216, 219
Unger, Sanford, 38, 128
União do Vegetal, 145, 210, 231

Vietnam War, 135

War on Drugs, 71, 79, 135, 189, 192,
    261, 266, 271

Washington, Hanifa Nayo,
    243–244
Wasson, R. Gordon, 109–110
Wasson, Valentina Pavlovna, 120
Watts, Alan, 151
Wauja, 208
Weather Underground, 75
Wells, Mary, 131
white privilege, 249
white supremacy, 129, 187, 249
Wilson, Bill, 83
Window Rock, 281–282
Wixárika, 135, 274, 298–299

yajé, 8–9, 11
Yaminawa, 215–216, 218–221
Yanomami, 166
Yawanawa, 208–209
Yippies, 132

Zappa, Frank, 131
Zulueta, María Dolores Estévez,
    175–176